Union Renegades

To Ron Formisano

This book wouldn't have happened
without your guidance & support.
Thanks for being a great advisor.

Best,

Dan Myin

THE WORKING CLASS IN AMERICAN HISTORY

Editorial Advisors
James R. Barrett, Julie Greene, William P. Jones, Alice Kessler-Harris, and
Nelson Lichtenstein

A list of books in the series appears at the end of this book.

Union Renegades

Miners, Capitalism, and Organizing in the Gilded Age

DANA M. CALDEMEYER

UNIVERSITY OF ILLINOIS PRESS
Urbana, Chicago, and Springfield

Library of Congress Cataloging-in-Publication Data
Names: Caldemeyer, Dana M., 1986– author.
Title: Union renegades : miners, capitalism, and organizing in the
    Gilded Age / Dana M. Caldemeyer.
Description: Urbana : University of Illinois Press, [2021] | Series:
    The working class in American history | Includes bibliographical
    references and index.
Identifiers: LCCN 2020022805 (print) | LCCN 2020022806 (ebook) |
    ISBN 9780252043505 (cloth) | ISBN 9780252085406 (paperback) |
    ISBN 9780252052385 (ebook)
Subjects: LCSH: Coal miners—Labor unions—Middle West—History—
    19th century. | Coal miners—Middle West—History—19th century.
    | Labor movement—Middle West—History—19th century.
Classification: LCC HD6515.M615 C45 2021 (print) | LCC HD6515.M615
    (ebook) | DDC 331.88/122334097709034—dc23
LC record available at https://lccn.loc.gov/2020022805
LC ebook record available at https://lccn.loc.gov/2020022806

Contents

Acknowledgments

I hardly know where to begin acknowledging everyone who helped and guided me on this project. It's been a long road, and so many people have aided me as I worked on the various stages of this book. This section doesn't do justice to how much they have helped me, but I'll do my best here.

James Engelhardt and the staff at the University of Illinois Press patiently worked with me through manuscript revisions. Deborah Oliver did a masterful job copyediting this book. The reviewers for this book likewise gave thoughtful and much-needed advice. Their excellent questions caused me to dig even more deeply into the subject, and their insights were crucial in shaping this book.

I am grateful to the organizations and institutions that invested in *Union Renegades*. University of Kentucky's Bryan Fellowship and the Colonial Dames Fellowship gave me the travel funding for research. The Kentucky Historical Society provided a great environment to learn about publishing while giving me the opportunity to work on this book. As I was finishing the manuscript, South Georgia State College provided additional travel funds for conferences and to nearby archives.

I am indebted to many individuals for giving me their time and feedback at various points of this project. Many years ago, Burton Kirkwood helped me start on this topic and provided the much-needed guidance to begin researching. Ken Fones-Wolf and Ron Formisano helped me develop the themes and ideas that eventually appeared in these pages. Along the way, countless archivists, librarians, and special collections staff across the country went out of their way to locate sources. Andrew Arnold, Edward Blum, Cindy Hahamovitch, Matt Hild, Michael Kazin, Bruce Laurie, Joanne Melish, Keri Leigh Merritt, Chad Montrie, Robert Murray, Scott Nelson, Jarod Roll, Mark Summers, Amy Taylor, and Ashley Sorrell all offered valuable comments on portions of the manuscript or the entire work. Their feedback made this book much stronger than it otherwise would have been.

Anyone who knows me knows that my family has always been more important than anything else. No matter how many miles apart or how long it's been since we've seen each other face to face, I can always count on them for a laugh and lots of encouragement. My parents, Chuck and Joan Caldemeyer, likely did not know where this project would lead when it began, but they encouraged me to pursue it anyway. My grandparents, David and Helen Caldemeyer, were always excited to hear of the progress, and I wish my grandfather were here to see it finally in print. Deanne and Scott Jones, Jill and Dustin Hagman, and Beth and Nathan Forshey were always delightful distractions throughout this process. My nieces and nephews, Ethan, Jacob, Hallie, Mason, Landon, and Rosalie, do not care about one word of this book, but spending time with them (or staring at the latest photos) always presented a welcome diversion from working on revisions. Jimmy and Denise King have become my second parents. They welcomed me as one of their own and excitedly cheered me on as I finalized this book.

Finally, Brantley King, my sounding board, cheerleader, proofreader, husband, and best friend, deserves the biggest thanks of all. He patiently waited as I spent weekends and evenings working on this book, sat with me as I researched in the archives, proofread countless pages, and never stopped reminding me that one day this would all be worth it. I love and appreciate him more than I know how to say.

Union Renegades

Introduction

Jimmy Wilson was nineteen years old when he died. Although he normally worked on his father's farm, in 1888 both he and his father decided to make extra money working in a local coal mine while their fields sat idle for the Kansas winter. Wilson had only limited mining experience, and while he was hired to drive mules, by November 1888 he was digging coal for the Frontenac No. 2 mine. The pay for miners was higher than for mule drivers and even though Wilson's father wanted him to help with the last harvest of the season and go to school, the young farmer-turned-miner decided to continue earning extra money in the mine.[1] Unfortunately, Wilson's ambition exceeded his mining skill. On November 14, during the evening blast to loosen the coal, Wilson packed his "shot" improperly. His blast backfired, ignited the coal dust in the dry mine, and shot fire down the corridors. The explosion tore through the earth, creating rifts in the soil above. It blew out the fan house, moving it two feet from its foundation. It shattered the hoist and shot out blazing timbers, which lay smoldering around the shaft. It incinerated dozens of men and boys laboring inside, including Wilson.[2]

Rescuers, many of whom were miners or worked in the mines intermittently, rushed from nearby towns and mines to search for survivors. They knew the dangers of the mining industry, and many had firsthand experience with companies who, in their minds, all too casually disregarded miners' lives and well-being for the sake of profit. When word spread, then, that the Cherokee and Pittsburg Coal and Mining Company had purposefully misidentified some of the bodies burned in the explosion, the rescuers grew irate. According to the rumor, company officials did not bother to verify anyone's identity but instead assigned names to the unidentified bodies and "requested" that a handful of miners in their employ claim the names were correct.

As the story spread, miners gathered to discuss the situation. The crowd's "angry murmur swelled into a roar" as word circulated that the company refused to let Jean Baptiste Labecq's wife and son view the miner's remains. It mounted higher still when several miners claimed that they knew for a fact that the body the company identified as Joe Keller was not actually his. "The body should not be interred as Keller," one miner declared. Others heartily agreed, for they could not "allow the public and his parents to be deceived" by burying a body as Keller when he actually remained among the missing. The crowd fumed at the "injustice" of a company who looked at the laborers so callously that they were interchangeable in both life and in death.[3]

Such disregard for the Frontenac miners touched a nerve among workers throughout the nation. Frontenac was but the latest result of company disregard for miners' lives, Ohio Federation of Miners and Mine Laborers officers declared. "Surely such occurrences demonstrate neglect, carelessness or incompetency on part of the mine managers, and if not punished it is because of the laxity of laws passed apparently to protect the health and lives of the miners," they insisted. The "mercenary policy," seemed criminal, yet explosions and accidents constantly killed and crippled miners throughout the country. By the turn of the century, coal mine deaths in the United States were nearly triple the mining deaths in Western Europe.[4]

The miners who gathered at the Frontenac mine felt this frustration on a level even more personal. Most of the miners in the crowd did not work for the Cherokee and Pittsburg Coal Company, but their mines were all owned by the Atchison, Topeka, and Santa Fe Railroad, a parent company to nearly every coal mining company in Kansas. The railroad expected cheap coal from all of its mines, and the Cherokee and Pittsburg miners were simply the latest casualties in the quest to cut production costs. As they searched for bodies, the miners understood that the next time a mine exploded, they themselves could be the ones trapped below, and as they discussed the misidentification of the recovered bodies, they understood that one day their own bodies might be identified incorrectly.

The angst caused by the explosion and subsequent rumor, then, arose from a personal and intimate understanding of the disregard mining companies had for their workforce. These miners did not need a labor leader or a labor organization to bind them together on this point, and on the night they gathered at Frontenac, the mostly nonunion miners did not form or join a union. Instead, they decided to write their grievances for Kansas governor John Martin to protect themselves from what they considered the fruits of corporate greed.[5]

The miners' decision to collectively appeal to Governor Martin indicated that they were aware of the problems associated with their craft and believed that collective action could successfully remedy their problems. Yet most of these miners were not union members and most did not join the union in the years following the explosion.[6] Perhaps more interestingly, the actions at Frontenac were not isolated. Historian Melvyn Dubofsky notes that 39 percent of the strikes staged by workers in the 1880s were *not* initiated by unions.[7] For some reason, a substantial portion of workers clearly valued collective action but were not always willing to fully commit to a union.

These are the workers *Union Renegades* examines. Focusing primarily on laborers connected to the coal industry in Indiana, Kentucky, Illinois, Iowa, Missouri, and Kansas, it looks closely at the lives of those who, in eking out a living, decided not to fully commit to a union. It tells a story of how some of the laborers' biggest problems stemmed from capitalism at both the corporate and individual levels. As a system that prioritizes economic competition and individual profit over cooperation and the collective good, capitalism is often associated with business owners undercutting competition and slashing production costs to turn a higher profit. In this book, corporate capitalism caused companies to fight unions, disregard safety procedures, decrease workers' wages, and hire inexperienced miners like Jimmy Wilson. But, as this book argues, these same capitalist incentives also applied to the workers themselves. At the individual level, farmer/laborers like Wilson were determined to do whatever they could to increase their own profits regardless of whether it benefited the collective good. Wilson stood to gain from the company's lax safety policies because the company provided him a steady income. In other cases, accepting lower wages and breaking strikes allowed laborers to secure more work while undercutting fellow miners who refused to work for so little. In these instances, like corporations guided by capitalism, workers put their individual interests ahead of collective concerns, even when these decisions put others physically or economically at risk. Although labor organizers condemned these actions as nonunion, this book argues that individuals like Wilson who at times acted against union orders were neither "union" nor fully "nonunion." They were instead laborers whose actions and affiliations changed according to what benefited them and their families in the moment.

"Mine Run" Men

For many workers, decisions to turn for or against the union were neither easy nor permanent. As historian Theresa Case observes in her examination of the Southwest Railroad strike, many of the workers on either side of the conflict were largely ambivalent about the strike, choosing instead a "middle ground" that would allow them the best chances for success with the lowest risk. Many of these workers held a definition of "free labor" different from the definitions that labor activists maintained. Some strikebreakers, Case noted, insisted that "free labor" meant that a worker had the ability to choose when and where they worked, including workplaces on strike.[8]

This idea of having the freedom to pursue whatever labor one desired was crucial to many workers' mindsets in the late nineteenth century. An 1879 poem from *Punch* titled "Non-unionist Miner Loquitur" expresses these ideals to explain why a worker would not follow union orders during a coal strike in Britain. During a period when the "Market's bad, so wage is low," workers abandoned unions in order to sustain their families. The situation caused the miner in the poem to proclaim that he was

> "A blackleg!"—well, I know it—
>   And a blackleg still I'll be:
> Tyrant man or tyrant Union,—
>   Neither makes a slave of *me*.[9]

Such sentiments indicated that some workers believed that unions were not always trustworthy when it came to caring for workers' interests and that a laborer could be just as enslaved to an unfair union as they could an unfair employer. For some workers, the ability to work without being beholden to any entity became the surest way to look after their own interests.

Capitalism, then, became a crucial factor in determining whether a worker supported a union or acted against a union order. Scholars have noted how such pursuits of individual gain influenced workers' decisions to turn against the union, particularly through strikebreaking. Historian Jarod Roll observes that this pursuit of economic advancement dramatically informed workers' worldviews, sometimes causing them to look at life as though it were a gamble. This prompted workers to believe that great risk brought great payout and sometimes encouraged them to become career strikebreakers with open hostility toward unions. Such an understanding caused entire strikebreaking businesses to form and operate throughout the nineteenth and early twentieth centuries. Laborers turned to strikebreaking, Timothy Minchin and other scholars argue, because they provided stable employment and a chance at upward mobility. The promise of profit and payout became just as motivating for workers as it was for their employers.[10]

Union Renegades looks closely at how these sentiments informed workers' relationships with the world around them. It includes "practical miners," or skilled miners who dug coal year-round and comprised the majority of the mining force, and seasonal workers like Jimmy Wilson who only intended to mine temporarily. Many, accustomed to cobbling together their livelihoods through multiple trades and economic endeavors, had what might be considered a practical outlook toward unions, seeing them as tools for personal gain rather than achieving a societal goal. According to United Mine Workers (UMW) vice president Phil Penna, these miners were like "run of mine" or "mine run" coal, a pressurized mix of slate, clay, and silt, that remained fused with coal as it was weighed. They were mine run men, the organizer explained, because, like the coal they extracted, their various identities were mixed together, leading them to seemingly contradictory actions that simultaneously helped and hurt organized labor.[11] This book examines how these seemingly competing identities affected worker relationships with each other and at times pitted them against unions and union leaders.

Rural workers' decisions regarding union membership were rooted in an independence that often made unions unnecessary in many workers' minds. Whereas workplaces like factories could control workers' actions, industries difficult to regulate, like late nineteenth-century mining, were more relaxed. Workers were accustomed to operating with little managerial oversight and made independent decisions in the workplace daily. Local terms of work, then, were almost continuously under negotiation. Miners appointed pit committees, or committees of miners, to present a workplace concern to their employer. They also hired checkweighmen to ensure the weight of coal mined was correctly attributed to each miner. Miners usually selected the committees and checkweighmen themselves and paid the checkweighman's salary out of their own earnings. These individuals were not necessarily union leaders but rather experienced miners respected in the mining community. Union involvement, then, was already a secondary factor in negotiations between miners and boss. This autonomy, political theorist Timothy Mitchell argues, at times promoted workers' concepts of independence. Mitchell found that workers' independence contributed to workers' sense of democracy and resulted in greater union militancy in the coal and oil fields.[12]

This independence also influenced workers' decisions regarding union membership. Laborers who frequently moved between occupations for economic opportunity often behaved similarly when deciding to join or remain in a union. Rather than give the unwavering loyalty union leaders expected from the rank and file, workers more frequently saw unions as a means to achieve an immediate goal. When union membership was beneficial, workers joined. When opportunities appeared elsewhere, however, workers chased those benefits as well.

Most typically, miners saw union membership as a useful tool for negotiating pay rates for the next year. Each May marked the beginning of a new "contract" for the workers in the coal mining industry, and it was often the time employers would announce a coming wage reduction to workers. Unionization was one way miners could fight wage depreciation, which caused union membership to swell when workers wished to fight for better terms. Instead of creating a consistently strong union, it created a pattern that, according to one Illinois miner, pulled miners into the union between January and April 30, and caused them to "disappear" from May until January. It was "not good union principle," he wrote, but miners practiced it just the same.[13] While such lack of faithfulness baffled union officers, workers' understandings of unionism often caused them to continually decide whether union membership was advantageous. The workers the Illinois miner described saw merit in unionism, but not during the months when they believed they paid dues for no gain. In short, workers who turned away from labor organizations were not always opposed to unionism, but the circumstances they faced at times caused them to act against unions to secure the surest opportunity for personal success.

In many cases, then, multiple understandings of "unionism" existed in the late nineteenth-century workplace, at times making terms like *union* and *nonunion* misleading. Although Gilded Age workers and leaders used the term *union* freely, their understandings of unionism differed from the unionism that grew in the twentieth century. As Robert Weir and other scholars have shown, groups like the Knights of Labor and Patrons of Husbandry fused moral understandings with their understandings of how society should function, allowing these orders to be as much fraternal and social clubs as they were laborer organizations. In addition to committing to overarching goals like abolishing the wage system and establishing cooperatives, Knights were expected to abstain from alcohol and to quote biblical scripture in meetings. In the workplace, they observed "honest principles" of not stealing or undercutting fellow workers, and working together for the collective good. Such moral components carried over into other farmer and laborer organizations as well. The National Federation of Miners and Mine Laborers, the National Progressive Union of Miners and Mine Laborers, and the Farmers' Alliances all professed moral and at times even religious conviction to their tenets. Consequently, a moral obligation undergirded union affiliation so that to organizers and dedicated rank-and-file members, a true "union man" was not only a member of a labor organization but also one who lived and labored with moral conviction. The reverse was true when organizers identified someone as nonunion. Their claim implied that the worker rejected union membership and its principles. To go against the union, then, was to act immorally.[14]

Such a clear-cut understanding of unionism became more muddled when put into practice. Although most workers recognized a shared understanding of what was "fair," they did not always follow these convictions.[15] Part-time union members, as well as those who refused to join the union entirely, rejected the notion that the only "good men" were those who resided in union ranks. They were quick to point out that, despite leaders' claims, union membership did not denote "honest" labor. Rather, plenty of union members disregarded the "honest principles" they professed or rejected leader orders. Likewise, some "good men" upheld "honest labor principles" without ever joining union ranks. One Illinois miner insisted that most of the nonunion miners in his town "are with the members of the assembly in their undertaking, with the exception of joining the organization and paying their little mine monthly."[16] Such an understanding prompted many local organizers to insist that hundreds of workers had the "spirit of unionism" even if they did not carry its card.[17]

Profit-Seeking Unionists

This wavering faithfulness among workers often pulled unions into an ongoing tug-of-war with corporations battling for worker loyalty. Unions formed to protect workers from companies that exploited their labor, often giving workers' organizations an adversarial relationship with employers. Although union leaders frequently believed this ideology and antagonism extended to the workers' relationships with their employers, this was not always the case. When employers offered hope for immediate advancement, profit, or economic stability, they traded on the capitalist desires that lay at the heart of what many workers wanted and needed. As they did so, corporations pulled workers away from fully supporting the unions. Consequently, unions had to find a way to mediate the problems that alienated workers from union ranks while wrestling with the hostile employers and unsympathetic state and federal governments that weakened union strength. Labor organizers soon found themselves in the middle of this conflict, trying to sell an idea of cooperation to workers who often found the capitalist mindset of their employers more appealing.

Often more committed to the agenda of unionism than the rank and file, many labor organizers grew exasperated by what, to them, appeared to be widespread rejection of unionism. "There is no reason in God's World why Illinois mine workers should have less than 10,000 members in a union," organizer Patrick Donnelly wrote of the thirty thousand miners who labored in his home state in 1893.[18] His frustration was emblematic of a problem in nearly every industrial workplace in the nation. Workers were sympathetic to union goals, but membership remained low. Organizers had consistently tried to unionize Illinois since the 1880s, but instead of ten thousand members, Illinois had fewer than three thousand.[19]

Many organizers claimed workers' reluctance to join or decisions to abandon unions were because they were "indifferent to their own interests."[20] Organization, UMW organizer William Bauchop Wilson wrote, was the laborer's only hope to confront the economic conditions that plagued him. Even if "circumstances" and hardship made membership difficult and success unpromising, good workers remained true to the order.[21] Organizer Richard L. Davis shared similar views. "I cannot see the sense of such a move," he wrote when he learned that an Ohio local planned to leave the UMW to form a rival miners' union. Such acts were not to the workers' benefit, Davis argued, and were akin to "suicide."[22] His arguments and others like them suggested that abandoning the national union meant the workers had abandoned hope for a better future.

These problems are mirrored in histories of the recent past, when modern conservatism began to rise in the late twentieth century. Scholars have given careful attention to the growth of corporate power in modern politics and the seemingly increasing sway employers have in carrying the allegiance of their workforce. With support from state and federal governments, companies utilized concerns about communism, instituted widespread collective bargaining, and offered workers shares in company stock to win worker loyalty and diminish union influence.[23] Scholars have also given close attention to the power of evangelical Christianity in connecting faith in God to free enterprise in the late twentieth century.[24] Such a trend, historian Steve Fraser notes, has caused present-day workers to look at major corporations with a "populist romance" that seemingly allows them to tolerate corporate exploitation more than those of the Gilded Age.[25]

This book argues that worker admiration for corporate capitalism existed long before the postwar period and that this affinity for profit making informed workers' identities and their relationship with unions. Gilded Age organizers may have claimed that workers' reluctance to join or be faithful to the union was a product of indifference, but many laborers, both outside and in organization ranks, held a more complicated and pragmatic view of unionism. They were laborers, but in an effort to provide for their families they also became farmers, investors, business owners, and bosses. Like Jimmy Wilson, many labored in multiple occupations to make ends meet. As a result, while unions may have looked after some interests of workers, membership in a national union did not always meet their most pressing needs.

Workers' multiple occupations allowed many workers to see common grounds in their troubles so that even if they did not fully organize, they at least recognized major problems they shared with their neighbors. Scholars have long called attention to the aspects of rural life that brought farmer and laborer together and shaped rural politics and society. Many rural laborers and farmers saw themselves as "producers" whose labor produced the commodities that society needed like farm products, raw materials, and manufactured goods. Though essential, they believed, their labor was largely unappreciated and stood in stark contrast to what many producers called the "parasites" of society. Such a term seemed fitting for the bankers, stock market traders, government officials, and other businessmen who made fortunes off producers' labor. As historian Chester Destler notes, this desire to revive the positions of the common farmer and laborer created a kind of radicalism that "lacked any philosophical basis other than a desire to restore the working prosperity of a small entrepreneur, rural economy." According to Destler, urban and rural groups influenced each other to create a kind of culture determined to promote economic opportunity for the common man. Historian Leon Fink notes in his examination of Kansas farmer and labor movements that these common sentiments at times allowed farmer and laborer movements to feed off each other.[26]

Many of the connections between laborers and farmers, however, remain invisible in current histories. Often, studies that examine common folk focus specifically on workers or organizations in one specific industry. For instance, studies that concern agrarian work seldom discuss agricultural connections to rural industries like coal or railroading in detail. The dozens of studies that focus on the coal industry rarely discuss workers' connections to railroads or farms. Only in political examinations do farmers and laborers overlap, but even then these groups remain more politically and ideologically linked rather than physically connected in common workplaces. Historian Matthew Hild notes that this creates a kind of false dichotomy between farmers, laborers, and their organizing efforts.[27] Connections between occupations are therefore hidden, skewing our understanding of how rank-and-file workers interacted with each other and the organizations that claimed to represent their interests. For the thousands of farmers like Jimmy Wilson who worked in the mines during the winter months, these cross-occupational intersections were a critical part of life, even though they seldom called themselves "miners" and rarely joined the miners' organizations year-round.

The common experiences rural farmers and labors shared helped forge the desire for economic justice that served as the foundation for many of the farmer and labor movements of the 1890s.[28] This desire, however, influenced more than political persuasions—it also provided a foundation to push for greater personal profit. Historian Charles Postel argues that while farmers envisioned a more egalitarian society, they also maintained a business-oriented mindset that shaped their agendas just as much as their identities as producers. According to Postel, this duality made Populists both traditional and modern and caused them to try "to fashion an alternative modernity suitable to their own interests." Often, these interests were geared toward fighting big business while carving out a piece of the capitalist market for themselves. "When farmers in Kansas or Texas spoke of uniting in a trust," he writes, "that was precisely what they meant. Farming was a business, and large-scale cooperation was a business enterprise writ large."[29] In desiring to see economic justice for the common man, many farmers and laborers envisioned themselves as being or becoming small businessmen and women.

Similar trends emerged within labor organizations like the Knights of Labor. That laborers claimed to be "wage slaves," according to Tobias Higbie, "was both an echo of agrarian republicanism and a sign of dissatisfaction with modern labor relations." As Leon Fink observes, the Knights' ideology was in part rooted in nostalgia for a day when a producer's labor was still valued. At the same time, it also drew from what Fink calls a "transcendent vision of a cooperative industrial future." Knights looked to the capitalists of society hoping to emulate their enterprise and success but wished to apply them to a new social structure that would allow workers to own their own businesses and become their own employers. Historian Steve Leikin argues that, even though organizations like the Knights maintained a "utopian" vision for equality, they approached the goal with a "practical" mindset, aiming to achieve it within the standing capitalist system. But, such a vision was difficult to implement. According to Leikin, the Knights' cooperative agenda fell short because the cooperatives could not adhere to a workable policy that promoted cooperation while still allowing co-operatives to compete with mainstream capitalist enterprises.[30] To survive, the cooperatives had to price their products competitively, which meant engaging in the same practices their collective formed to prevent. Although many workers understood that these cost-cutting tactics caused them to be exploited by their employers, they still pursued business ventures seeking their own capitalist gain.

No "Solid Phalanx"

Organizers seeking to establish unions often had a hard time seeing how one could be a good unionist while embracing the capitalist tactics that led to exploitation. Many believed that unions were the only way for workers to unite and effectively protect the interests and wages of the workforce. To them, corporations exploiting workers were the opposition rather than entities worth emulating. This disconnect spelled trouble for many aspiring national unions. If unions wanted to create a society where laborers were treated fairly, they needed the collective power generated by a unified workforce that could force companies—and the governments sympathetic to them—to listen to their demands.

But, as many union leaders noted, the circumstances unions faced often made it "impossible to unite . . . in one solid phalanx for any given object of reform."[31] State and federal governments often sided with companies in strike situations, state governors sent in militias to put down strikes, and courts busted up unions. Companies battled to keep unions out of their workplaces, using racial, ethnic, and skill differences to create fractures within the workforce. Workers known for being staunch unionists were targeted and blacklisted, preventing them from earning a living. In addition, many rural industrial trades were susceptible to boom-and-bust markets that tended to drive material prices—and workers' wages—down.[32] Organizations seeking to improve the workers' lives, then, would not only have to fight the employers, the simplification of skilled trades, ethnic divides, and government hostility, but also the entire economic system. These factors contributed to a kind of skepticism that at times ran through workers' ranks. Even if workers *wanted* unions to succeed, success was unlikely. This awareness of obstacles preventing union success created what sociologist Kim Voss calls a "cognitive encumbrance" that caused workers to lose faith in labor organizing.[33]

All of these factors made it difficult for unions to exert much power in the Gilded Age. As a result, Gilded Age unions tended to be more abstract and feeble than the ideologies they claimed to embody. When their leaders spoke, workers did not always believe them. Whether union leaders promised certain victory or, at times, assured defeat, workers looked at their situations and made their own assessments independent from union leaders. Consequently, while leaders claimed authority over the rank-and-file masses, their words often reflected more organizational ambition than actual strength.[34]

Unions were not the only groups struggling for control in the Gilded Age. The boom-and-bust economy that made it increasingly difficult for workers to make a living also pressed railroads and other corporations. Richard White's examination of the railroad industry shows the fragility of the seemingly indominable railroad "octopus" that reached into nearly every industry. This fragility, Andrew Arnold argues, was matched by coal company operators who, crippled by declining prices in the coal industry, were learning how to market their coal nationally. As railroaders and operators wrestled for control over the coal industry, unions also developed in a way that allowed them to insert worker concerns in workplace negotiations. This approach, Arnold claims, helped shape negotiations and relationships that laid the foundation for modern-day business and labor dealings. Most notably, it drove unions to become increasingly centralized to navigate these negotiations.[35]

Worker, employer, and union, then, all faced harsh realities that contributed to a kind of hard-scrabble mindset of the Gilded Age. As companies and unions fought for control of the market, workers sought to carve out a place for themselves. Just as many workers cobbled together their livelihoods through laboring in multiple occupations, many took ideologies from both their employers and unions, fusing them together to create better economic security for themselves and their families.

Such an independent mindset was a crucial factor in union development. If unions wanted to be successful, they needed to be both strong enough to fight corporations over control of the national market and flexible enough to accommodate the desires of the rank and file. This lesson, however, proved difficult for many union leaders to learn. Throughout much of the Gilded Age, the differing concepts of unionism created rifts between union leadership and their rank and file.

Midwestern Coal

The Midwest is an ideal place to study the conflicts and changing relationships between worker, employer, and union. Although the Midwest was deeply tied both to the national competitive coal market and the railroad industry, few studies consider the region's mining history. As Tobias Higbie observes, the rural industrializing countryside, especially in the Midwest, became a place where laborers traveled in search of work. Often laboring seasonally in various occupations throughout the year, many farmhands and industrial workers traveled from town to town. As they did so, they built up common understandings of the world around them that affected not only rural culture but also workers' expectations for their unions.[36] In this region, mining often took place beside—or under—farm fields, allowing labor organizing to coincide with the farm organization efforts that swept portions of the Midwest in the 1890s.

Coal mining was one of the most widespread occupations in the rural Midwest. Although it was extremely dangerous work and often demanded precision and care, it was largely semiskilled labor learned on the job without prior experience. Coal mining therefore better reflected the 1880s and 1890s workforce that grew increasingly unskilled rather than the skilled workers typically examined in labor studies. The semiskilled labor aspect limited the union-busting tactics mining companies could use. Employers or operators ran their mines with the goal of selling the most coal, which often required underpricing their competition. In this race to have the cheapest coal, operators did not pay workers according to their ethnicity or skill. Although employers frequently exploited racial differences to bust unions, this favoritism did not typically come in the form of stratifying workloads or paying some miners a better rate than others. All miners working in the mine worked according to the same wage contract. This caused workers across ethnic lines to share concerns about low wages, safety, and market competition, rather than dividing them, as in other industries.[37]

In addition to these problems, miners' wages continuously fell. While a host of industries in the late nineteenth century saw wages decline, coal was often at the head of this decline, forcing down prices and wages in other industries. This situation was ideal for industrialists desiring cheap steel and for consumers wanting affordable products, but it caused rural workers to compete for jobs at lower wages, especially in the coal mining industry. By 1896, coal miners made roughly 68 percent of what the average manufactory worker earned.[38]

Those who dug midwestern coal readily understood this concept. The coalfields extended far beyond the frequently studied Appalachian region and were essential to national expansion. The development of railroads and cities intensified the demand for cheap coal and brought the competitive coal market to a national scale. Miners in Illinois, Indiana, and western Kentucky competed against Appalachian miners for coal sales, driving down prices more quickly than ever before. Meanwhile, miners in Iowa, Missouri, Kansas, and Indian Territory were more concerned about railroads driving down prices than they were about market competition, creating an east–west divide that became more pronounced in unionizing efforts. As organizers focused on creating a national pay scale in the competitive districts, miners west of the Mississippi balked, unable to see how such efforts met their immediate needs.

Miners in Indiana's block coalfield voiced similar cries of neglect. Block coal was more valuable than typical bituminous coal mined elsewhere in the Midwest, which caused block coal miners' wages and concerns to differ from those in the rest of the competitive district. Despite its differences, however, the block field was part of the Indiana bituminous district and, as in Missouri and Kansas, miners there were often forced to accept UMW terms that applied more to bituminous mines in the competitive fields than to the western mines or the block mines of Clay County, Indiana. As a result, the declining national coal market dictated nearly every aspect of the mining industry even if a region's coal did not enter the competitive market.

These grievances against national forces and corporations like railroads dovetailed with the complaints many contemporary farmers expressed in this same region. Richard Jensen and others argue that the proximity of minable coal to these rural regions only furthered the drive for organized labor. This allowed labor organizing to coincide with the farm organization efforts like the Farmers' Alliances or the Farmers' Mutual Benefit Association that swept across portions of the midwestern countryside in the 1890s. In Illinois, Jensen observes, half of the dozen precincts that voted Populist in 1894 were coal towns.[39]

The strong history of labor organizing in the coalfields also makes this industry a useful focal point. Miners' efforts to form a national trade union began in the 1860s with the American Miners' Association in Belleville, Illinois. The order had died by 1870, but other movements followed. Leaders like John Siney, Dan McLaughlin, and Richard Trevellick became household names at the vanguard not only of miners' organizations but of organized labor in general. By the 1880s, miners already had a long history of organizing attempts and successes. Although the number of miners laboring in the Midwest were fewer than those laboring in the Appalachian coalfields and other regions, the Midwest had the highest percentage of unionized miners. If any industry and region had the ability to organize thoroughly, the midwestern coal mines were among the likeliest of candidates. However, even in Indiana, one of the most thoroughly unionized coal regions, unionization among the miners by 1896 had never exceeded 33 percent. Members who paid dues regularly numbered even fewer.[40]

These numbers were so low partly due to corporate and governmental hostility to unions that, as discussed previously, contributed to worker disillusion with unions. Historians have given excellent attention to how corporate hegemony, state and federal laws, governmental leaders, and courts systematically crippled Gilded Age unions and affected workers' attitudes toward unionism. Less is known about the problems that also injured unions from within and how potential rank-and-file members reacted to union decisions. This study aims to dig deeper into the rank and file's understanding of union roles, and how union actions could, at times, alienate the workers they sought to organize.

The concerns midwestern workers faced were likely similar to those faced by rural laborers in other regions of the nation. Unlike other regions, however, the presence of unions in the Midwest made workers' organizations more visible and accessible to workers than in regions where unions had little or no presence. In the Midwest, trade journals like the *National Labor Tribune* and the *United Mine Workers' Journal* had higher circulation, workers were more likely to discuss union issues with each other, and they were also more likely to have their grievances against the union documented by union officials or trade newspapers. Midwestern workers' letters to trade journals, then, provide valuable insight into the problems they identified in labor organizations.

The connections trade newspapers created did not guarantee union membership, but they were crucial to developing national conversations that extended beyond the workplace. Individuals not actively working in the mines could participate in newspaper discussions related to the trade while seasonal laborers could remain apprised of situations in the local mines.

Trade papers also afforded workers' wives a way to join in on union discussions by writing letters. In doing so, they demonstrated the power of connections to the mining trade that existed outside the union hall.[41] Elsa Barkley Brown and others find that newly enfranchised black working-class families decided together how to spend money and which way to cast the husband's vote in elections.[42] For rural wives, these decisions extended beyond the home and into the union hall. Farmwives often joined and participated in organizations like the Grange and the Alliances.[43] Julie Roy Jeffrey observes that farmwives regularly voiced their opinions in newspapers like the *Progressive Farmer*.[44]

These trends also extended into the mining industry. Miners' wives were not eligible for union membership, yet their involvement with balancing the family budget often allowed women to identify themselves as miners without touching a pick. When wives wrote letters to the papers discussing union matters, mining men considered, debated, and disagreed with wives' opinions as they did the opinions presented by miners themselves. The female leaders of the Gilded Age like Mary Lease and Mother Jones (Mary G. Harris Jones), then, were part of a much larger informal trend that allowed women to participate in organizations and decisions typically associated with men, even though these informal connections did not always result in actual union membership.

The letters and reports printed in trade journals are the main sources for this examination. As early as the 1870s, workers who were upset with officers or wished to see change in union structure frequently wrote to these same newspapers to discuss how to resolve organizational problems as well as those in the workplace. Miners' organizations forming and faltering presented a potential problem for the UMW when it established its journal in 1891. This official organ of the UMW was edited by the union's national officers, primarily the

British-born miner and UMW executive officer John Kane of Indiana.[45] The problem was that miners had already developed a mistrust of labor leadership. Many believed the *United Mine Workers' Journal* (*UMWJ*) would be merely a mouthpiece for UMW executives and therefore less reliable than competing labor papers like the *National Labor Tribune*, which claimed to be for the workers rather than any particular organization.[46] If UMW officers wished to sell subscriptions and build the trust of the union's rank and file, they needed to present a newspaper that truly reflected rank-and-file views, not propaganda for an order that thousands of miners already questioned. As a result, during the *UMWJ*'s first three years, editors promised to publish all letters submitted, regardless of how critical they were of the miners' organization.[47] Designed to build the miners' trust for the organization in its early years, this effort afforded members and nonmembers a place to voice their frustrations with the UMW, its leaders, and its policies in a place where leaders, the rank and file, and nonmembers could interact. Consequently, the letters printed in the *UMWJ* during its first years offer a unique window into workers' lives and are crucial to understanding how and why rank and file support for workers' organizations like the UMW ebbed and flowed in the Gilded Age.

Using personal accounts from those associated with the mining trades, *Union Renegades* puts forward four main arguments regarding the most pressing challenges labor organizations faced concerning rank-and-file loyalty to the union. First and foremost, it argues that rural workers were associated with several different trades and that their simultaneous identities as farmers, laborers, and investors directly shaped their relationship with unions. Like mine run coal, these identities were muddled together and directly shaped family life, incomes, and work. Second, this book demonstrates that workers understood the economic forces that dictated work conditions and wages as well as what successful collective action could potentially achieve. Third, it maintains that these first two factors dictated whether workers followed or rejected unions. Workers and wives formed their own objectives and concepts of unionism. Their views were not always compatible with union agendas and sometimes allowed them to affiliate with two seemingly different unions simultaneously. Consequently, the divisions emphasized between organizations like the Knights of Labor and the American Federation of Labor (AFL) were more important to union leadership than to the rank and file. Workers' decisions to reject unions, then, did not always denote a dislike for unions in principle. Finally, this book argues that workers did not necessarily reject unions because they were apathetic about their conditions or disillusioned with unionism. Instead, many workers left because they believed that the labor organizations did not adequately address their most pressing needs and desires.

To demonstrate these key points and to exemplify some of the major concerns that hindered union membership, I examine six instances when workers acted against union officers' orders. Workers rejecting union mergers, expelling leaders from the union, forming rival unions, breaking strikes, and staging strikes against union orders are but a few of the situations that illustrate the complexities of worker nonunionism in the late nineteenth century. Workers' actions in these situations caused many union leaders to write these individuals off as nonunion. When looking at these instances from a worker's perspective, however, these decisions to turn toward or away from the union reflect the pragmatism inherent in workers' actions throughout the Gilded Age.

Chapter 1 examines how farmer and laborer grievances against what they perceived as the greed and deceptive practices of Gilded Age business, politics, and society informed their suspicions of agricultural and labor organizations. Fearing that the same corruption that populated the burgeoning world of corporate investing also plagued their organizations, many workers looked at the centralizing labor organizations with suspicion. Mistrust ran rampant, causing many to wonder whether these orders truly looked after rank-and-file interests or if these new national organizations were another example of Gilded Age farce.

The second chapter looks more closely at the rural workers' world. Although they criticized the greed of "the money power" and those who exploited the lower classes, many of these producers committed the very acts they condemned. Examining the overlap between farmers, laborers, and speculative investing, this chapter demonstrates not only that laborers appreciated business concepts of profit but that looking out for one's own interest was infectious. This drive for self-preservation extended to the miners' union. To prevent what organizers were certain would be a loss, they ordered a group of Illinois miners to accept a wage reduction. As nonunion workers went on strike for an "honest wage," organized miners—under union orders—broke the strike. The instance demonstrated that even unions did not uphold what were considered union principles. Distinctions between "union" and "nonunion," then, were not as clear as organizers claimed.

Chapter 3 continues with this theme of worker dissatisfaction with a close examination of the effects of a canceled UMW national strike. Historians often attribute union membership decline to worker disillusion with union capabilities after a strike failure. This chapter challenges this notion, showing that membership initially increased after the failed strike until workers, dissatisfied with UMW leadership, abandoned the national organization and formed their own unions that rivaled the UMW. Workers' decisions to form new unions indicated that their problems with the UMW were not rooted in disillusion with unions but in mistrust for national union leadership.

While chapter 3 examines individuals who turned their back on major labor organizations, chapter 4 focuses on the workers who claimed national unions turned their backs on them. Black, nonnative-English-speaking miners, farmers who worked in the mines, and miners' wives who did not work in the mines were associated with the miners' unions in ways different from the white males that trade unions typically organized. This chapter shows that inclusion in the UMW often fell along ethnic lines rather than those of occupation or skill. Stereotypes that white English speakers associated with black and nonnative-English-speaking workers, such as immorality, criminality, carelessness, and lack of skill, kept minority groups from full inclusion in UMW ranks. Consequently, although union officers insisted that the UMW welcomed all miners regardless of race, ethnicity, or religion, the organization did little to address the workplace problems unique to these groups. Instead, the UMW more readily welcomed English-speaking white women, who were not miners, and white inexperienced farmer-miners than people of color or non-English-speakers who were experts in the trade.

Chapter 5 looks closely at the disjunction between organizational leadership and the rank and file, showing that workers' differing expectations for unions often placed worker and organizer at odds with each other over the function of the organization. In 1894, producers in several trades challenged the social, political, and economic systems of the United States. Although organizations like the American Railway Union and the United Mine Workers organized strike efforts, those who joined were not always willing to accept the centralized union structures or recognize the authority the union leaders tried to exercise. While differing concepts of unionism frequently created tenuous relationships within labor organizations, in 1894 these conflicting concepts unleashed widespread backlashes against union decisions that crippled union efforts and threatened to kill the orders from within.

The final chapter reexamines the union infighting that historians claim contributed to union weakness in the Gilded Age. These fights, however, extended much further than the upper echelons of labor unions. The frequent fights, coups, and changes in union leadership in the mid-1890s were not isolated events but were part of a larger disorganized impulse to "purify" producer organizations of corrupt and complacent leadership. The ongoing tumult turned unions against each other and tore unions apart. "Organized labor," then, was no unified force, but a fragmented and weakened conglomeration of producers who saw less and less value in maintaining a union affiliation. Their doubts coincided with the Populist push in 1896, when rural workers and farmers, disillusioned with the structures that claimed to help them, looked at the national election with ambivalence, unable to agree on the best candidate to suit their needs.

In the end, worker rejection of unions or union leadership was neither a sign of unwillingness to care for "their interests" nor unique to the Gilded Age. Rather, it was the result of workers looking after their own self-interest, a trend that can be found in many industries and in all time periods, including the present day. What follows are stories of those like Jimmy Wilson, who spent his short life pursuing greater opportunity, even if it meant ignoring safety protocols. But these are also stories of hope and despair, of community and division, and of union and nonunion that are mixed and fused together in ways that cannot be easily separated.

CHAPTER ONE

Deceived

Producers in a Dishonest World

Of the dozens of buildings in Ottumwa, Iowa, one in particular stood out, and it was both a source and a symbol of the city's pride. The enormous two-story "coal palace" was over 325 feet tall and gilded with polished Iowa coal, an ornamented castle that stood in contrast to the otherwise drab Iowa countryside. Inside the palace were dozens of displays exhibiting the region's farm surplus and manufactured products. It was "marvelously attractive," President Benjamin Harrison declared to a crowd of forty thousand at the palace's opening, not only because it found beauty in common materials but also because it symbolized the wealth in Ottumwa. "You are favored here in having not only a surface soil that yields richly to the labor of the farmer, but in also having hidden beneath that surface rich mines of coal which are to be converted into power to propel the mills that will supply the wants of your people," he proclaimed.[1] The Coal Palace was more than an example of the lavish architecture of the period, it was a demonstration of a region's ease of access to the raw material that fueled the Gilded Age.

Like many raw materials, the value of coal relied on the fact that it had little monetary worth. "Cheap coal" made cheap steel that allowed the railroads to stretch farther and more affordably than it had on iron rails.[2] It connected local markets to larger, more competitive ones via railways and steamship lines that stretched across the nation and world.[3] Ornamental coal, then, like hundreds of other raw materials arranged and presented as art became a way to flaunt wealth and modernity, to boast of abundance so great it could be displayed rather than consumed. "Sioux City [Iowa] will have a corn palace at the World's fair; Yankton, Dak., a cement palace; Hutchinson [Kansas] a salt palace, and Newton [Kansas] when she gets her four sorghum mills to running will doubtless build one of molasses candy," the *Topeka (KS) State Journal* quipped, prompting newspapers throughout eastern Kansas to joke that their cities would also build a palace of coal. Such a claim was only partially in jest. In addition to Ottumwa, Streator (IL), East St. Louis (IL), and Brazil (IN) erected their own palaces celebrating the abundant "black diamonds" that came from their soil.[4]

The cheapness of coal was not a reflection of its quality, but rather a devaluation of production costs. As a result, the phrase "cheap coal" had an entirely different meaning to those who mined it. To them, it meant devaluation of their life and labor. No one knew this more than the miner who dug a five-ton lump of coal to be displayed in the Pittsburg Hotel in Pittsburg, Kansas. Due to his mine's conditions and the size of the piece, no machine could be used to mine the coal, so the miner extracted it by hand. Such a technique had remained unchanged for decades, but the wages the miner received for the work continually declined. The miner had agreed to extract the block in exchange for eleven dollars, which he would split with his assistant, and a keg of beer to be given to the extra men needed to hoist the massive block to the surface intact. But after the miner spent days carefully extracting the piece, he received only five dollars for his toil. Keeping his word when his employer did not, the miner split the five dollars with his assistant and purchased the promised beer out of his own earnings.[5]

The company and town could afford to proudly display the coal instead of burning it, but they would not pay the miner his promised wage. Such disregard for producers ran rampant in the Gilded Age when employers sought to keep profits high and production costs low. The frequency of such instances of employer dishonesty prompted the *Christian Advocate* to call for "Christianizing the upper masses" rather than focus solely on converting the lower classes to Christianity. "If religion is a good thing to make a servant submissive, why is it not a good thing to make an employer human?" the editors asked. They pressed: "if the Christian religion will . . . prevent miners from deeds of violence, why will it not also cause mine owners to treat their men as men?"[6]

But it was difficult to treat "men as men" when coal was sold competitively. If producers wanted work, they needed to perform the labor for less and less. "Cheap coal" needed to become cheaper, and with that came the shared understanding among many producers that farmers and laborers were expected to produce the wealth, but they could never hold onto it. Producers "plant all the water melons and live on the rind," miner "A Thinker" declared. They "build all the mine mansions" but were "sheltered in the desert." The "Thinker" was not alone in these sentiments. "Where would the late J. Gould have got his sixty millions had it not been for the miner," one Illinois miner wife asked. The nation depended on the miners "and yet," she grumbled, "the miner today is thought very little above the brute."[7] As market competition drove down crop and coal prices, producers and their families saw and understood that their own value to society was tied to this decrease.

Producer devaluation, then, became the moral grounds that mobilized many producers in the Gilded Age. Employers and much of upper- and middle-class society regarded the poorer classes as immoral and untrustworthy, but producers saw themselves as honorable and upright. Historians have been careful to highlight the common moral rhetoric that mobilized producers and earned sympathy and support from middle-class constituents.[8] But to the workers, this problem was more than rhetorical. The dishonesty workers experienced, such as not being paid as agreed upon for extracting a five-ton lump of coal, demonstrated not only the devaluation such producers endured in the late nineteenth century, but also how this deception influenced workers' understanding of the world around them. To them, the exploitive relationship between those who produced the nation's wealth and those who benefited from it was morally wrong. They couched their grievances in moral and political terms that continually reaffirmed their identities as moral citizens and human beings entitled to kindness and fair treatment.

In many producers' minds, employers and the rest of society were truly heartless beings who gambled, lied, and stole. Their desires for profit created the working conditions that endangered industrial laborers' lives. Farmers looked in dismay at the increasingly popular futures market that seemed to steal their profits before they could even harvest them. To many producers, it seemed that the only ones who looked closely at the laborer did so to make money off them.

In fact, when the families of the miners killed in the 1888 Frontenac, Kansas, explosion sued the Cherokee and Pittsburg Mining Company several years later, the case ended with the families' lawyer settling with the company without the families' consent. Instead of giving them the settlement money, however, the lawyer ran off with the cash, leaving the victims' families in more debt than when they began the lawsuit. Even the lawyers on the producers' side, it seemed, only deceived.[9]

This mistrust extended to the miners' own organizations. Workers frequently debated whether labor organizations truly worked on the producers' behalf. Indeed, as the miners in Frontenac worked to identify bodies incinerated in the

1888 explosion, the Knights of Labor and the National Federation of Miners and Mine Laborers (NFM) were locked in a battle to be the sole miners' union. To the rank and file, the competition indicated that leaders cared for their union's prominence over the workers' interests. Consequently, when leaders of the two organizations finally decided to merge the following year, thousands of union miners refused to acknowledge the merger. Although many held memberships in both orders, they believed it was a ploy to grant union leadership power and profit at the rank and file's expense. This false start did not come from workers' apathy toward unionism. Rather, it came from workers' fears that, like deceitful businessmen, corrupt politicians, and selfish employers, labor leaders benefitted from Gilded Age fraud and acknowledged the nation's producers only in order to exploit them.

Deceptive Markets

To many rural producers, deceit and immorality were integral to Gilded Age business and were epitomized by men like Charles J. Devlin. Born around 1853 to Irish immigrants in northern Illinois, Devlin grew up in poverty. His mother, Bridget, worked as a washerwoman and raised her son and his younger sister alone. Devlin was arrested for larceny as a teenager and spent the early years of adulthood in the Illinois State Penitentiary. On his release, he began working as a clerk for a coal company.[10] He climbed the ladder to manager, and, in 1884, with the financial support of his father-in-law, Devlin founded the Spring Valley Coal Company, the start to a vast coal-powered empire that eventually made him millions of dollars.[11]

But Devlin's rise from criminal to coal baron was not due solely to hard work or savvy investing. Rather, it came from the railroads, eastern businessmen, and government financiers who needed a manager to look after their companies and investments in rural and western lands. His success reflected a broader trend within Gilded Age business in which false fronts, false markets, and false products generated millions of real dollars. In addition to his father-in-law's funds, Devlin received subsidies from local businessmen and railroad operators seeking to develop Spring Valley. Journalist Henry Demarest Lloyd claimed that several local railroads worked with Devlin's Spring Valley Coal Company to control the city's development and ensure their businesses received the greatest profits. This growth, Lloyd asserted, only came with hushed agreements for "special freight rates needed to enable the 'enterprise' to steal the business of its competitors."[12]

More importantly, although he was one of its founders, Devlin was not the primary shareholder of the Spring Valley Coal Company. He managed the mines but answered to eastern stockholders such as Democratic Pennsylvania Congressman William L. Scott, who was more than an investor and politician. His interests tied him to multiple regions and industries, making him a shipping magnate, New York Stock Exchange operator, railroader, and bank president. To miners, however, Scott was a "coal king," with mines in Pennsylvania, West Virginia, and Illinois, including the Spring Valley Coal Company.[13] Devlin served as Scott's manager and continued this relationship with other investors, pushing westward with the railroad. By 1894, Devlin had amassed a fortune running the Devlin Coal Company, the Marquette Third Vein Coal Company, and other companies used to manage the holdings for the Atchison Topeka and Santa Fe Railroad (ATSF).[14]

Managers like Devlin were integral to Gilded Age investment and often served as the first line of defense against corporate financial ruin. In cases like the mines Devlin managed for Scott and the ATSF, individual mines or mining companies were small parts of a larger whole that often teetered on the edge of bankruptcy.[15] Usually, they were small companies used to shuffle property back and forth to avoid expenses and bankruptcies.[16] When bankruptcies occurred, which frequently happened in the Gilded Age, managers like Devlin were left holding the bag.[17] This happened to Devlin in 1905, leaving him responsible for several indebted companies, nearly $4 million of missing government and corporate money, and at least four bank closings in three states. After filing for bankruptcy, Devlin was placed under investigation and died of a stroke before his case was settled.[18] Despite his close relationship with the railroad, the ATSF was not implicated and seldom even mentioned in the news stories regarding the scandal. Even by 1907, two years after Devlin's death, the investigation had not untangled Devlin's web of business connections. A 1910 article in *Fuel* remembered Devlin as a coal magnate who singlehandedly developed the western coalfields, not as a high-level railroad employee whose coal interests depended on corporations like the ATSF.[19]

The market instability that brought Devlin both fortune and failure was common in the Gilded Age coal industry. On one hand, the opportunity for success was promising for those who kept their costs low enough, but the low cost of production also made the market open to cutthroat competition. Unlike other industries where a handful of corporations dominated the trade, many rural industries remained largely decentralized in the late nineteenth century. Coal mining, logging, and turpentining required little industrial equipment and low up-front cost. For coal mining, this meant that landowners with the means to reach the coal and hoist it out could produce coal as cheaply as the largest mine enterprises. The low overhead cost prevented major corporations from dominating the industry.[20] As railroads stretched into the countryside, these mines began shipping their coal to urban markets, causing Indiana and Illinois mines to compete with those in Ohio and western Pennsylvania. The sheer number of mine owners and operators made it impossible for the nation's coal operators to organize like other industries that could control prices. Even if William Scott and other big coal barons had attempted to set a high coal price, other companies underbid them, rendering any operator organization unable to raise profits.[21]

Still, if they could not corner the coal market, large operators could undersell it. By underpricing coal, companies landed more contracts with urban coal dealers and consumers so that the increased volume of sales absorbed the cut in profit.[22] In doing so, they forced other mine owners to lower their costs as well. The result created a competitive and overstocked national coal market as companies battled for the lowest prices.[23]

Making a fortune off financial decline, however, was not limited to the coal industry. Historian Steve Fraser observes that Gilded Age corporations often took advantage of depressions to buy up bankrupt companies. "Rockefeller's oil combine, Armour's meatpacking supremacy, Carnegie's steel dominion, Frick's coke and coal mine empire, among others," he writes, "all emerged first out of the ruins of the catastrophic depression that lasted through the heart of the 1870s." During that period, the Mellon family "swallowed up liquidated businesses auctioned off at sheriff sales and evictions," using the profits to extend their investments into other industries such as natural gas and plate glass.[24] Profit declines, then, at times helped major corporations most of all.

Although farm labor is seldom classified with industrial operations, midwestern farmers faced a similar problem. Like coal, the crops they produced were sold in nationwide markets that were flooded by the 1880s. Enormous farms consisting of hundreds of thousands of acres, such as the bonanza farms in the Dakotas, turned farming into a corporatized industry. These farms, often owned by landowners who lived in the East, were divided and subdivided into tracts worked by hundreds of farm laborers who earned daily wages and were managed by foremen. Like miners in company towns, these workers lived in company-owned boardinghouses and some shopped at company stores. The scale of production enabled bonanza wheat farms to sell their grain at a substantially lower price than smaller farmers, affecting grain prices throughout the nation. The Missouri State Board of Agriculture found that these farms were one of the primary factors in declining grain prices. Wheat, which averaged

$1.14 in Chicago in 1882, fell to $0.85 in 1889. Corn and oat prices during the same period were cut in half. But production only increased. By 1892, the US Secretary of Agriculture reported that wheat production in the Dakotas alone surpassed the entire national output just fifty years earlier.[25]

By the 1880s, the United States exported about a third of its wheat crop each year, primarily to European countries. Market competition intensified as wheat farmers in India, Argentina, and Egypt dramatically increased their production in the 1880s and sold their crops at lower prices than US farmers could afford. Between 1868 and 1887, India increased its wheat production from 558,852 bushels to 41,558,765 bushels. This escalation was mirrored in wheat-producing nations throughout the world, all competing to sell their grain to Europe. In an 1887 study of global wheat cultivation, the statistician to the US Department of Agriculture reasoned that European immigration to South America would only intensify the "wheat culture" in Argentina and Chile. The growth of this industry would dramatically increase competition. Wheat prices, which were governed by the global market, would steadily decline.[26]

But such a decline was not as visible at the New York Produce Exchange, the Chicago Board of Trade, and the dozens of other trading centers throughout the United States and Europe. Despite the growing agricultural crisis in the fields, traders a world away bought and sold wheat and other crops before they were harvested. The new kind of trading, known as "futures" markets, was a kind of market speculation and trade that gambled on the expected value of future crops without any products physically changing hands.[27] Like coal companies that formed contracts with businesses promising to supply coal, dealers in agricultural products like wheat, cotton, hemp, and livestock arranged contracts, settling prices for goods yet to be produced. This allowed merchants who purchased crops from farmers or farmers' agents to sell their future products while prices were high rather than for the market price when the crops were ripe. Doing so involved investing with money borrowed from banks with interest.[28] If the merchant sold at the right time, their profit absorbed the interest and their investment proved worthwhile. If they sold at the wrong time their gains would be substantially less, even leaving them in debt.[29]

The risks involved with futures investing and the uncertainties that came from selling products not yet grown, however, gave many farmers and merchants pause. By the late 1880s, futures trading had become a major form of trade, but to many the entire system seemed dishonest and immoral. "This gambling—I call it gambling—the most shrewd, subtle system that ever emanated from the brain of man and the most hard to get at the bottom of. They will bamboozle you out of your senses," former grain dealer William Howard argued

to a congressional committee investigating futures trading. A farm agent for
Iowa, Nebraska, Missouri, and Minnesota farmers, Howard argued that futures
trading involved more than merchants hedging their purchases. It only protected
merchants when the price of crops went down and therefore encouraged merchants to manipulate crop prices in order to increase investment returns. "How
is it? How is it that the hog product of the United States has not paid the cost for
the last ten years, and yet these [merchants] have grown to be millionaires. How
did they do it?" In the constant fluctuation of prices, Howard claimed, futures
stock opened the door for corruption and wild speculations disproportionate
to crop supply. "I say it is the greatest evil that ever struck the United States of
America," he insisted. "I tried it far enough to see that an honest man could not
make a living at it and I got out."[30]

The notion of evil lurking within the burgeoning economic system indicated
a growing conflict within society between capitalist profit and morality. Because
of the potential for high returns, futures markets reached as far as the global
wheat and cotton trade, from England to India to Chile to Kansas. But farmers
like C. Wood Davis of Kansas believed it injured farmers' profits and gave businessmen more control over crop prices than the farmers. To Wood, the physical
supply of wheat did not matter as much as the amount traders anticipated on
the exchange floor when they traded "enormous quantities of fiat or fictitious
products." Everything emanating from the futures sale seemed fabricated by
businessmen who turned a profit without physically owning anything.[31] Historian Ann Fabian contends these claims of dishonesty and immorality stemmed
from citizens trying to reconcile not only how hard work was not rewarded, but
also how previously unacceptable practices such as gambling became the norm.
To the average rural producer, these dealings were part of a new and dishonest
world where invisible empires rose out of nothing, profits came from pushing
prices lower, and success seemed to defy morality and logic. The government's
willingness to allow these practices seemed to indicate that business mattered
more than producers' livelihoods. Dishonest dealings, it seemed, were perfectly
acceptable for everyone but the producer.[32]

Inhuman

The business practices inherent in the market system stood at odds with how
many rural producers believed the nation should function. Moral acts such as
respecting one's neighbor, not stealing, not lying, working hard, and pursuing
honesty over corruption, they believed, were the keys to a successful life.[33] Yet,
the new fast-paced market system offered a new alternative for success. Instead

of rewarding labor, it seemed the national market rewarded greed, corruption, and gambling while slighting those who toiled. Efforts to gain higher profits forced debts onto producing classes, created high interest rates on mortgages, contributed to falling earnings in mining and agriculture, and cut corners in workplace safety while demanding more work for less pay.[34]

In many workers' minds, this cultural shift was degrading to those who toiled. Although workers saw themselves as moral and upright people who performed honest work, they also believed that much of late nineteenth-century society did not agree. Falling crop prices, combined with shipping costs, taxes, interest, and mortgage all chipped away at a farmer's earnings so that, as one Kansas farmer put it, farming "don't pay worth a—."[35] Farmers like Richard Wilson and his son Jimmy of Frontenac looked to the mines to supplement their incomes. Others, along with thousands of unneeded farm hands, entirely abandoned their farms for the mines, iron works, railroads, and factories. Because moving from farm to industrial work was often temporary, it is difficult to discern exactly how many farmers supplemented their incomes. However, the fact that counties frequently reported that "a great many of the operators and miners of this county farm through the summer and mine coal through the winter," indicates this was not uncommon.[36]

Few industries demonstrated disregard for workers' well-being more than the coal industry. Like other rural industries, fighting for higher pay involved challenging more than the employer. In an industry governed by market competition, pushing for higher wages meant potentially losing coal contracts that provided steady work to neighboring mines that produced coal more cheaply. One Indiana miner claimed that these conditions prevented miners from dealing with their employers "between man and man" and forced them to accept any terms their employers offered. Missouri miner "A K. of L." agreed, claiming that "the operators here hardly realized that the miners were human beings. The company has ruled with an iron rod so long that they thought when a man went to work for them he had no voice in anything." Instead of being equals in society, they asserted, miners were less than men and cowered to their boss's demands.[37]

The process of degrading from "man" to "thing" intensified as industrialization transformed the way Americans worked. By the late nineteenth century, machines had made their way into dozens of industries but were less useful in outdoor rural workplaces, where hills, forests, and the underground made for unstable working conditions.[38] In brickyards, dust from the clay extraction damaged engines and made boilers prone to fire, causing operators to select the simplest equipment over the more sophisticated machines.[39] Tunnels with level, dry ground and wide openings, and big coal seams allowed machines to fly at unprecedented rates. In ideal conditions, they moved as fast as human hands. On uneven and flooded spaces, hard rock and in small coal seams and narrow passages, however, human labor remained most efficient. Human-made holes were smooth, their blows comparatively dustless, and when they mined coal, workers could discern between rock types to extract the coal efficiently.[40]

The limitations of mining technology prevented machines from making hand labor obsolete.[41] For miners, then, their conflict with mechanization was less a fight for their jobs than a fight against employers' tendency to reduce them to a machine. Northern Illinois miner "Pro Bono Publico" claimed that the hand miners were "driven from pillar to post to get a living" due to the competition with machine mines. Because machines required the most ideal conditions to be cost effective, mining was easier in machine mines than in the mines with conditions that demanded hand miners who, mining narrower veins, worked harder to extract less coal. Regardless, the coal was valued the same. Machines did not work in northern Illinois, Pro Bono Publico explained, "while in southern Illinois the conditions are reversed." The mines in the southernmost part of the state were ideal for machines, allowing them to turn out more coal faster and cheaper so that they could sell their coal in the Chicago market for lower prices than the northern hand mines. "We are asked to come down [in wages] and compete with machinery that is producing coal in an 8 foot vein, while we have the human machine and 2½ to 3 feet, except in one or two places," the miner continued. "Now it is unjust and unreasonable to ask the miners of northern Illinois to compete. They cannot do it."[42]

Pro Bono Publico worked like a machine for a machine miner's wages even though he worked by hand in his mine, but the devaluation of workers did not end with wage decline. Most mines required miners to perform extra jobs, such as laying railroad track, pumping water out of mines, or propping up the roof. Commonly known as "dead work," these tasks took a miner's time and energy but did not add to his coal production or pay.[43] In one Kentucky mine, dead work included prying up rail tracks from old parts of the mine and re-laying them in a new room. Otherwise, the miners had to push their loaded coal cars across the mine floor from their rooms to the roadway. "A man should have iron track," miner "Justice" grumbled, but the company would not furnish it. "Illiterate" and "A Would-Be Knight" described similar conditions. Their mines saved on mule purchases by having the miners "tram their own coal instead of mules pulling it." Still, Illiterate commented bitterly, "even if they had long ears, [the miners] could not favorably compare with mules," because unlike miners, mules "kick when overloaded."[44] Miner "Jumbo" complained that his mine cared more for its mules than its miners. When the safety catch broke on one of its two hoisting cages, the company did not fix it, even though the malfunction would kill its riders if the cage fell. "The north cage is the best," the miner noted, "and they use it for hoisting and lowering the mules, and the men have to go on the broken cage."[45] The decision to protect mules over miners reflected how the competitive market shifted the ways companies valued their workers. A miner could be replaced at no cost, whereas replacing a dead mule required additional funds.

In other cases, mines disregarded safety protocol because upkeep was too expensive. Ignoring regulations on timber spacing, gas monitoring, "sprinkling" dry mines to keep coal dust down, and proper powder storage saved the company money but increased the risk of mishaps and injuries. Having clear airways was essential to proper mine ventilation and offered the surest means of escape in the event of an accident. Still, mines often neglected their upkeep. One western Kentucky miner reported that the only way to escape his mine in the event of an accident was for all the miners to climb "a very narrow winding stairway up which you must crawl on hands and knees for over 200 feet in the dark with water pouring down like rain upon you." The distance made it unlikely that all men would escape, yet, to have a new airway, the miners had to dig it without pay.[46]

Such a precaution would have been valuable to the miners in the Diamond Mine in Braidwood, Illinois. After the mine flooded, the company refused to dig a new shaft to drain the water and aid in the rescue. Rescuers instead waded through the water, taking days longer to search for miners. They pulled out twenty-eight bodies, most either drowned or suffocated, but miner Adam Stewart reported that the last six recovered "neither drowned nor choked," but starved awaiting rescue. Saying that the miners remaining in the mine must have suffered the same fate, the company declared the missing miners dead, abandoned the search, and sealed the mine. For Stewart, who lost two sons in the mine, this was unthinkable. "I believe it possible that there may be live men in the mine yet," he wrote, noting that miners in other disasters found their way out of mines weeks after rescuers abandoned the search. The grieving father asserted that "no country that claims to be civilized would have done the same as was done at the Diamond mine." But many mines did. Unless a mine was in good enough condition to resume production, companies saw little point in repairing the mine or locating miners who were likely dead. It was more economical, and expedient, to entomb the miners and sink a new shaft elsewhere.[47]

Mine inspectors, then, also played a role in the devaluation of miners. Missouri mine engineer William Porter argued that at least two mine inspectors were needed to visit the "many important mining operations scattered over so large a territory as in this State." Even in his plan, smaller mines, such as the hundreds of Missouri mines that employed fewer than ten workers, would not be inspected at all.[48] Throughout the nation, miners complained that state mine inspectors failed to do inspections, were unfamiliar with the mining process, or gave their mines safety approvals despite eminent and visible dangers.[49] "I am under the impression that the mine inspector laws are lived up to on one side, but not the other," Illinois miner William Gardner claimed. "The salary side is lived up to, but the duty side is deficient." His words came in response to the latest death in a local mine. "He was a Polander that was killed, but a Polander is not supposed to be human, so I did not hear of any investigation as to how the accident occurred." Gardner's bitter words, which indicated the ethnic inequalities that ran through the mines and government, also revealed the inspectors' power of discretion. Some accidents were more worthy of investigation than others. Some deaths were not worth reporting at all.[50]

These trends were echoed in other rural industries. Turpentine, brickyards, and logging work, like other industries that used convicts as a workforce, claimed thousands each year by accidents or overwork. Historian Steve Fraser notes that railroad repair shops and roundhouses claimed over 150,000 lives between 1890 and 1917. On the Illinois Central alone, one of every twenty trainmen and one in seven brakemen were killed or maimed between 1874 and 1884. The industrial progress of the Gilded Age came at a price that workers paid with their lives and limbs.[51]

The hardship that rural workers suffered, from the indifference to their labor to the disregard for their deaths, all indicated to laborers that their employers and government officials viewed the mine workers as less than human. Indiana miner "Cambrian" claimed miners were defenseless "prey to every vicious human being." Miner "Justice" agreed, writing that miners struggled between being "men or mice."[52] As coal prices declined, miners became timid "mice" who labored hard in harsh conditions, entering the mine each day wondering if they would emerge unharmed.

Unpaid

Company and governmental effort to protect earnings at employee expense extended beyond the rural workplace and into nearly every aspect of laborers' and their families' lives. Although some historians claim that workers like miners had the power to move to the best paying mine to avoid exploitation, the complexity of the payment system made this exceedingly difficult.[53] As with other rural industries like logging or turpentining that paid by the piece, a simple wage comparison did not account for the extra labor, quality of the material, and the conditions surrounding the workplace, which tended to vary much more than indoor workplaces. In mining, a "cent per ton" wage could only be understood when also considering the amount of dead work, supply costs, and weighing method. While miners settled on a payment rate for winter and summer mining each year, the cent-per-ton agreement was subject to the deductions as well as dead work that chipped away at a miner's earnings. In addition to these factors, companies frequently switched between a variety of weighing techniques and payment methods, further eroding miners' paychecks while maintaining that they paid a high cent-per-ton wage.[54]

Because there was no uniform weighing method, it was simple for companies to lower wages even if the cents paid per ton remained the same. When the coal was extracted, the "slack"—clay, stone, and silt mixed in with the coal—had to be filtered out before the coal was sold. To do this, the coal was placed over large screens with bars spaced apart to allow the slack to fall through. Coal chunks remained above, eventually tumbling into a new car separate from the slack. "Run of the mine" coal, which was weighed before it was filtered, was heavier due to the slack, making it worth less than screened coal, which was filtered before it was weighed. In some cases, mine run coal earned fewer cents per ton than screened coal; in other instances, operators paid screen-coal wages for run-of-the-mine coal but deducted a percentage of the overall weight to account for the slack, at times deducting as much as 50 percent of the weight.[55]

Screened coal was more common in late nineteenth-century mines, but the screening process was uneven. Mines often changed the "bars" on the screen to increase the amount of slack that fell through the gaps. In changing the bars' shape or spacing or using corroded bars and broken screens, companies could increase the amount of slack, which lightened the load that was weighed to determine the miners' pay. Illinois organizer William Scaife quipped that the spaces between bars in one Illinois mine were so large that "the operator's pug dog went down the screen and fell through into the nut car."[56]

By increasing the gaps, the company not only increased the amount of slack filtered away. Small pieces of coal called nut coal also fell through the screens with the slack and into a separate car designated for nut coal. This coal was not credited to the miner's coal weight, meaning he dug it for free, even though the company sold this coal.[57] Kentucky miner "Snake Eye Saul" claimed that, at his mine, the company charged the miners fifty cents a load to burn nut coal in their homes. "We consider this very unjust as we get [paid] nothing for mining and sending out nut coal," he complained. The action, in his mind, was akin to theft.[58]

Any means of denying or delaying workers' pay saved the company money. For companies with small budgets or large railroad mines like those owned by the ATSF that relied more on investments and speculation than cash, avoiding laborers' payroll was crucial to keeping the company afloat. Even when miners were paid, companies seldom paid miners their full amount due. An 1891 Missouri Bureau of Labor Statistics study, for example, reported that even the largest coal corporations withheld five to twenty days' worth of wages in each pay.[59] Many employers paid in "checks" that could not be cashed immediately. In an extensive study on rural wage payment, Missouri Labor Commissioner Lee Meriwether found that the checks frequently required workers to wait anywhere from one to ten years before redeeming the check for its full cash amount.[60]

In addition to mines, railroads, sawmills, and even larger plantation or bonanza-style farms not only paid irregularly but often avoided paying their workers in cash. Such methods were useful for more than balancing company budgets. They also ensured the workforce would remain dependent on their employer. According to Meriwether, the check system frequently worked in conjunction with commissary stores that the company owned. Known by the miners as the truck or pluck-me store because they "plucked" wages from the miners, these stores frequently charged high prices for goods that could be purchased without cash. For thousands of miners facing unreliable and irregular payment periods, these stores were often the only place that extended credit. Similarly, although the checks were seldom good anywhere else, workers waiting for their checks to mature could spend the full amount in the pluck-me before the cash-in date. Any amount not spent when the check had matured could be redeemed for cash, but the checks often could only be cashed at a bank, which was often several miles from the coal camp. In other cases, companies issued vouchers known as coupons or scrip instead of legal tender.[61]

Whether the company used checks or scrip, the outcome was the same. Workers wanting cash immediately typically received only seventy-five to eighty cents for each dollar earned.[62] Meriwether believed the companies implemented this system to force miners to shop at the company store. The tactic worked. Less than two years after Meriwether's initial report, the Missouri Bureau of Labor Statistics reported that most miners in the state received all their wages in food and merchandise purchased on credit *prior* to pay day.[63]

The incentives for shopping in the company store often compelled mining families to accept the system rather than challenge its procedures. "J.D." claimed that his Iowa mine did not pay their miners in scrip and did not force them to purchase their items at the commissary through debt. Rather, the company used the prospect of punishment to guarantee patronage, telling the miners, "the more you spend in our store the harder you may work; the more you spend in our store the better place [in the mine] we will give you." Conversely, those who did not shop at the store found that their wages were less. "I notice when I do not buy there that some thing is the matter with my coal," one miner reported to Meriwether. "It has more sulphur in it or more slack, or I get a room where it is harder to mine coal. My wages invariably decrease, and I have found the only way to get a better room and fairer wages is to deal at the company store."[64]

Not all rural laborers were compelled to shop at the store, but those that were had no control over the store's selection. They also had no means to fight how much they cost. One Missouri lumber worker's wife claimed that she had no wash tub and that her husband was shoeless because the commissary had neither item in stock. Because no other stores accepted the company's tender, she "was compelled to wait two months until the Holladay store had obtained its new supply."[65] These conditions enraged miners, who claimed the pluck-me stores deprived them of their freedom. "It is a system that plucks me of my civil rights," Missouri miner S. C. Pierce complained to Meriwether. It took "one of the dearest privileges of my life, that of having the dollar that I have earned by the sweat of my brow, to go with it to the place I like, to trade it for food to put on the table and for clothes to put on my children's backs."[66]

It was not fair, Iowa miner J.D. railed: "They rob us while producing their wealth. They rob our wives while they are compelled to trade in their store. Is this all? No. They rob our children of the intellect that God has given them."[67] Even in his frustration, J.D. knew that few government officials cared to end this kind of robbery by creating useful laws. Since most "anti-truck" laws (after "truck" stores) focused on either abolishing scrip or overturning the requirement, the miners had no way to fight the stores.[68] Worse, as Meriwether discovered, operators regularly defied standing laws with impunity. "The law requires corporations to redeem all checks or tokens of indebtedness issued to their employees within thirty days after the date of delivery," Meriwether explained. "This law is laid down so plainly and explicitly that I hesitated to believe any company in Missouri made a practice to issue checks to their employees and refuse to redeem such checks in cash until the expiration of ten years."[69] Yet several companies in Missouri and elsewhere violated this law and others regarding pay, weighing techniques, and mine safety.[70] "We seemingly have no means of protection," J.D. concluded.[71] Miners and farmers desperate for work had no choice but to accept the terms offered or try to find work elsewhere.

Honest Work

For thousands of rural workers, the system that allowed businessmen like Devlin to grow wealthy while treating workers as less than human seemed blatantly immoral. Observing the greed within the coal industry, "A Well Wisher" called attention to the irony of businessmen "claiming to be civilized, and some of them Christianized" while treating their laborers harshly. They forced their employees "to work down in the dark and dangerous mines more than eight hours per day, while they themselves are enjoying all the sunlight and the pure fresh air and riding about to all the places of amusement . . . and then claim to be human."[72]

Although late nineteenth-century workers seldom affiliated with a specific denomination, many still upheld general Christian beliefs and, like Well Wisher, at times used moral arguments to condemn those who claimed to look after the miners' interests.[73] This religious thought offered a way for rural producers to present their hardships as clear moral, economic, and political wrongs against them and their families. Although reformers played into such religious sentiments, these understandings transcended union rhetoric and came out of genuine spiritual conviction often independent of the religious values middle-class society professed.[74]

This moral outrage came in many forms. In the case of the Frontenac explosion, moral outrage against the company stemmed from the mere suggestion that the company had denied miners a proper burial. Regardless of whether the Cherokee and Pittsburg had refused to ascertain the miners' correct identities or let their families properly mourn their deaths, the miners' anger was rooted in the fact that such instances *had* happened in the past. These understandings were reaffirmed each time mules were treated with more respect than workers and when workers' bodies—whether living or dead—were sealed in the mines.

Such understandings reached into daily life and informed not only worker understandings of how he or she should be treated by their employer, but also how workers interacted with each other. "Honest labor," as thousands of workers called it, involved working hard, helping those in need, not stealing, and not showing favoritism.[75] Those who abided by these principles and performed their jobs honestly and well, then, became informal leaders in working communities. They served as members of "pit committees" that determined what work was fair and negotiated with employers on the miners' behalf.[76] Consequently, these ideas of moral and honest work also served as the foundation for workers' organizations, with the local respected leaders enforcing the ideals in the workplace. "There is Christianity in these principles," one Ohio laborer wrote, noting that the union embodied the ideals that workers wished to honor. "God is not a respector of persons," yet "the rich are crushing the poor" while claiming to be Christian. "Is it becoming necessary for one kind of theology for the poor and another for the rich? Not in God's view." For this reason, the laborer urged, workers needed to organize, not only to make a better life for themselves, but to stamp out "prejudices" and "corruptness that is in existence." Christianity, then, gave many workers a framework to understand the injustice they received, but the union helped workers put this framework into action.[77]

But if moral arguments could be made against employers, they could also be made against unions or leaders the workers suspected of not abiding by these values. Local leaders climbed local union ranks because the workers they represented personally witnessed the leaders' integrity on a regular basis. This trust was harder to establish in state and national unions where leaders came from outside the local community and often no longer worked the jobs they were supposed to represent. Although they frequently used the same religious and moral language as the workers, the Knights of Labor, the NFM, and other workers' organizations often found it difficult to earn worker allegiance. Neither organization swayed a majority of the nation's coal miners into their ranks. Even those who joined one or both organizations did not always follow their leaders' orders. Just as Christian convictions did not correlate with worker church attendance, workers' desire to reform the system that injured them did not always lead to union faithfulness.

Part of the lack of faith in labor organizing came from the enormity of the system that hurt rural producers. Worker mistreatment stretched across the nation and connected disparate industries in complex ways. For the coal industry, resolving miners' grievances required a powerful national union capable of addressing questions of crop prices and farm debts so that the farmers and their farm hands could return to the fields. It meant engaging the steel and railroad industries that demanded cheaper coal and were crucial to coal mining and transport. It required government support to pass new safety laws and enforce those already in place. Most importantly, it meant finding a way to fight the entire coal market that forced companies to constantly undercut prices by cutting costs in their mines.

Although workers understood the enormity of this undertaking and many believed organization was important to confronting these concerns, they stopped short of agreeing how such an organization would function. Some, like miners in Indiana, formed an alliance with their bosses to help regulate local coal prices. Leaders of this group included Philip Penna, T. F. Bolser, Joseph Dunkerly, and John Duddy, who were also affiliated with either the Knights or the NFM. Their partnership indicated that at least some workers were willing to work with their employers to increase coal profits to both companies and workers.[78]

While some workers saw local alliances with operators as one way to fight the coal market, the Knights and NFM each offered other options to confront these issues. The Knights' cooperation and education plans were long-term endeavors that many producers believed were essential to restoring economic independence.[79] More importantly, its structure of "mixed locals" allowed farmers, miners, and other trades to all attend the same union meetings, creating and fortifying connections across trade lines. The NFM, which was founded in 1885, was more adept at looking after specific trade concerns. Its dedication to the mining industry allowed it to focus on regulating companies' cutthroat competition by negotiating a nationwide pay scale with coal operators each year from 1886 forward. Often, leadership in the two orders stood at odds with each other. Many of the founding members of the NFM began as Knights and, like hundreds of workers in other industries, left the order to organize along trade lines.[80]

By 1886, neither group was strong enough to secure the changes they promised. The NFM established a national pay scale but could not enforce it in all states. Companies in weakly unionized areas took advantage of the agreement and undersold mines that honored the scale, intensifying competition rather than diminishing it.[81] Similarly, the Knights' rapid growth in the mid-1880s did not translate into successful mining reform. The mixed occupational leadership within assemblies made it difficult for the union to address problems specific to the mining industry. In many cases, Knights decisions regarding the coal industry were made not by miners but by workers in other industries whose unfamiliarity with the coal industry was a liability.[82] Because of this, the Knights formed National Trades Assembly 135 (NTA 135) in 1886. Like the NFM, NTA 135 was specifically for miners, essentially a trade union under the Knights' umbrella. This structure allowed miners to remain as Knights while producing leaders who were well acquainted with the mining trade.[83]

In many ways, the formation of NTA 135 upset an already shaky balance between the two orders. NFM leaders viewed it as an open attack on their trade union structure, with the Knights working to undermine NFM authority in mining reform. NTA 135 officers were outraged at NFM leadership's unwillingness to cooperate, particularly at its resolution forbidding NFM officers from holding an office in any other labor organization.[84]

The following two years were plagued with bitter disputes between organization leaderships. Unable to win support from all miners, the NFM could not enforce pay scales or safety laws. Although the Knights of Labor declined in the urban centers that once formed the organization's stronghold, rural workers often remained in the order and NTA 135 remained as strong as its rival organization.[85] The two orders' leadership therefore remained locked in a battle to destroy their rival in the name of protecting miners.

Many miners sympathetic to the union disagreed. They believed the two organizations were complementary and held membership in both unions. "Perhaps what could not be achieved in one [organization] might in the other," Thomas Faulds of Indiana suggested. G. W. Dinsmoor of Missouri agreed with this thought, noting that the miners in his region held memberships in both orders without conflict, declaring "This method is far the best I have ever seen tried yet."[86]

Consequently, most rank-and-file miners saw little benefit in the ongoing division between NFM and NTA 135 leadership. Like competition between coal companies, competition between unions only seemed to hurt the laborer. Many questioned whether the leaders' actions, like those of ministers, government officials, and employers, were guided more by personal ambition than by care for the rank and file. "We feel that there can be no peace or comfort until that rule or ruin policy is abandoned and the order of the K. of L. brought back to first principles again," NFM organizer Patrick H. Donnelly wrote. If the Knights truly cared about the miners, he insisted, it would "do away with the so-called National District Trades assemblies of different callings" and stick to its original goal of eradicating the wage system. While it is unclear how common dual loyalty was among laborers, Donnelly was not the only representative to express these sentiments. Officers of both the NFM and NTA 135 collaborated on wage scales and produced joint circulars in 1887, even though the two orders were firmly divided. T. J. Roberts argued that NTA 135's formation brought unnecessary strife to miners already struggling in their workplaces. "I myself respect the K. of L. as much as any man living, having been connected with it for a number of years, but I don't like to hear men trying to break down the best trades union my craft has ever had, simply to further the ends of a few men who really have not the interest of my craft at heart." Roberts did not love the Knights of Labor any less, he insisted, rather, "I love the Federation more."[87]

Despite the dual loyalty, there was no denying that the union divide came at the miners' expense. "We are the ones who have to suffer," miner and organizer John Duddey explained. Because of the division, the miners were "taxed and levied on by both organizations." Indiana organizer Samuel Anderson described similar conditions, noting that miners in his district paid dues to both organizations but could barely earn a living. If the miners of both organizations could cooperate with each other, surely their organizations could as well, he wrote.[88]

In December 1888, union leaders heeded the miners' demands. Meeting in Columbus, Ohio, leaders in both organizations agreed to sever ties to their old orders, killing both NTA 135 and the NFM along with the autonomous state unions within the NFM. In its place, they established the National Progressive Union of Miners and Mine Laborers (NPU), a unified labor organization that would represent all miners.[89]

This was what miners had demanded for years, but hundreds of NTA 135 members balked at the idea of abandoning the Knights. The NPU was little more than a renaming of the NFM, they complained. It did not offer any structure resembling what the Knights offered, so miners who enjoyed the benefits of both orders saw no reason to desert NTA 135, even if its leadership did. Kansas organizer Robert Linn wrote he was not pleased with NTA 135's structure and function, but he could not justify leaving the order. "I am, and have been for the past ten years, a Knight of Labor," he declared. "I never have had a thought or expressed a wish to abandon N. T. A. 135 or the Order of the Knights of Labor." His words reflected many miners' sentiments on the amalgamation debate. As a result, while some refused to join the NPU altogether, many miners opted to retain their dual memberships in both orders. In fact, union miners in Spring Valley, Illinois, kept their minutes for their Knights of Labor local assembly and their NPU lodge in the same bound volumes.[90]

Instead of unity, the formation of the NPU drew an even larger divide between organizations and increased frustration among the rank and file.[91] Indiana miner "Coffee," one of the thousands who refused to abandon NTA 135 and retained memberships in both orders, claimed that the division between the organizations created a cloud "as dark as a coal operator's conscience" that hovered over the miners. Coffee's description equated the union fighting with operators' callous actions in the mines that endangered miners' lives. "Now I would like for some one of either side to show me where there is anything gained by being continually at 'outs,'" he demanded.[92] Dual member Aaron Littin agreed, charging that "this [fighting] originated and is advocated principally by disappointed office seekers." Such men, like employers and government officials, only looked to the miners as a means for personal gain, Littin believed. "A man that will join an organization to get an office is not worthy of recognition by any honest laboring man," he insisted, "and when [honest men] find one of that caliber [they should] at once brand him as an imposter, and when they succeed in getting the heads of all such demagogues chopped off then they will find peace and success will crown their every effort."[93]

Coffee's and Littin's descriptions of organization leadership as selfish impostors tapped into the suspicions rural producers already had against national leaders. To many, the union leaders became another foe to many miners. "A man can be a hypocrite in a labor movement just as easily as in a church," Indiana miner "X" wrote.[94] In a world of deception that seemed to continually take advantage of the laborer, claims of honesty and goodwill meant little even if it came from organized labor's ranks.

The NPU's inability to unite the miners or earn their trust was part of a larger culture of suspicion and fraud in the Gilded Age. Corporations' reach into multiple industries, government ties, and backroom deals that pulled up profits while driving down prices contributed to a sense that corruption lurked everywhere, from businesses to their own trade organizations.

Although union leadership also claimed that producers were exploited, rhetoric alone did not sway miners to the union cause. When unions focused more on defeating each other than promoting safety and fair treatment, miners believed their claims were less than genuine. In these cases, even the thousands who joined the labor movement stopped short of supporting leadership objectives. Consequently, although thousands of organized miners called for a peaceful merger of the unions, they refused to obey a new organization that demanded they abandon their labor union ties. The officers who orchestrated the failed merger, they believed, acted out of their own self-preserving interests and seemed equally as fraudulent as their employers or government officials who often claimed to have the miners' best interests at heart.

Still, miners and farmers found it difficult to hold fast to their sense of moral right in a competitive market. A network larger than community bonds had changed the rural producers' world. As earnings continued to decline, the competition between mines and farms, union and nonunion seeped into the ground itself. Producers' need to provide for their families facilitated a new kind of competition on the local level, turning neighbor against neighbor and complicating the divisions between miner, farmer, and businesspeople more than ever before.

CHAPTER TWO

Undermined

Winter Diggers, Union Strikebreakers

One hundred feet below the frozen Illinois topsoil, a handful of farmers turned up the earth not by the plow, but by the pick. Rather than work their fields, they spent February 1888 in the Enterprise Mine, digging coal destined for the Chicago market. Their mine was in the southernmost region of the state, commonly known as Egypt, whose coal industry was among the fastest growing in the country. Nearly four thousand Egypt miners turned out over 2.6 million tons of coal in 1888 alone, almost one-quarter of the state's total output.[1] Laborers came from all over the world to dig Egypt coal, but in February 1888, only farmers went down to work in the Enterprise Mine.

No one but farmers dared descend the Enterprise shaft because it was one of several Egypt mines on strike. The miners were already working below scale rates when Egypt coal operators ordered another wage reduction that would bring their wages nearly 25 percent lower than competing mines. "The men thought it unjust," miner Robert Smith explained, because it not only cut wages deeper than market competition required but would also trigger wage reductions in mines throughout Illinois, Indiana, Ohio, and Pennsylvania as they lowered costs to compete with Egypt for the Chicago market. "We therefore resolved to resist the cut, and not give the operators surrounding us the excuse to cut their miners, as it seems southern Illinois is always below our fellow craftsmen."[2]

Not all Egypt residents shared this conviction. Smith's emphasis on the miners' desire to not go further "below" their craftsmen stood at odds with the local farmers who broke the strike. Since it was run as a joint stock company, anyone who wished to purchase stock in the Enterprise Mine could do so at twenty cents a share. It is unclear how many took advantage of the sale, but local miners reported that several local farmers had seized the investment opportunity and purchased as many shares as they could afford in hopes of generating extra income for minimal effort.[3] The February strike jeopardized their investment. Unwilling to let the mine shut down and risk losing their money, the farmers entered the mines to dig the coal themselves. As the miners remained above ground fighting a reduction that would lower wages throughout the region, the farmers protected their financial assets by literally going under the miners to extract the coal. The farmers' ideological actions mirrored their physical labor. By going into the mines, the farmers went "below" their neighbors, undercutting the wage scale, taking their jobs, and challenging the cooperation that bound community members together.

The Egypt farmers who became miners because they owned a stake in the mines reflected how competitive markets fundamentally altered daily life in the Gilded Age. As farm profits decreased, farmers and farmhands alike looked to mines and other rural industries to cover expenses. Some, like the Egypt farmers, approached these industries as small-scale investors. Others entered the mines as hired hands employed by the miners themselves. Such occupational confusion allowed workers to be owner, employer, and employee simultaneously and allowed these tangled relationships to stretch into multiple industries. This meant that rural laborers like farmers, miners, and railroad workers worked in a host of industries from farms to mines to lumber camps, cobbling together various incomes to eke out a living. Rural folks had used these connections between industries for decades, but as the agricultural crisis intensified, coal profits declined, and the number of industrial laborers looking for work swelled, the overlap between industries became more hazard than help. As budgets tightened, rural folks like the Egypt farmers and countless others moved to protect their own interests, even when their actions were similar to the large-scale employers they often condemned. They "cheated" their coworkers by accepting favoritism in the mines, discarded mine rules to earn extra pay, and broke strikes to preserve investments or simply earn a wage. Laborers who once worked together now competed, at times turning communities against each other.

In many ways, historians have noted this change, demonstrating how the economic forces that pushed thousands of producers into poverty also pressed them against each other, even as they held fast to the community bonds and cooperation that undergirded rural society. Throughout the nation, ordinary farmers and laborers struggled with the contradiction between ideas of republican equality and reciprocity and their need to earn a profit or a living wage.[4] But these shifts did more than drive wedges in local communities. They reconfigured relationships between owner, laborer, and neighbor, tangling them in new ways within the national market system. The term *neighbor* took on new meaning as states grew connected through trade, competing against each other for the first time. Consequently, the "honest principles" that miners prized, such as honoring contractual agreements, not undercutting wages, rejecting favoritism in the mines, and not "stealing" another worker's livelihood, grew harder to maintain. Local and individual need tugged against the grain of national competition and growing national unions, blurring rural producers' understandings of how to live a moral life.[5]

In such cases, union laborers did not always act according to the values they professed. Thousands of union miners broke each other's strikes and filled each other's coal contracts. They insisted their actions were justified due to their economic need, but condemned miners in other regions performing these same acts, calling them dishonest and immoral "blacklegs."[6] In the process, honest labor in the mines and community was often determined more by occupational background and geographic lines than by any clear definition of moral behavior. This trend was exemplified in 1889 Illinois, when union concepts of what it meant to be "honest" and what it meant to be a "blackleg" were turned on their heads. During that year, nonunion miners went on strike for higher wages while union coal miners followed union orders to *break* the strike. In this strange turn, the nonunion miners typically regarded by union leaders as "immoral" became the ones claiming to fight for "honest labor" while the union miners became the "blacklegs" trying to stop them. The circumstances prompting farmers not to farm and union miners not to strike indicated the complicated ways the market system turned rural workers against each other and prompted them to put personal need before public good. Their justification of their decisions to abandon their neighbors and principles, however, signaled to many miners not only the futility of local strikes in a national market, but also the moral bankruptcy that seemed to run through the miners' unions and Gilded Age business alike.

Assorted Incomes

Peter Shirkey was already an experienced coal miner when he arrived in the United States from the British Isles at age fifteen in 1850. On his arrival, he quickly set out for the coalfields, traveling from mine to mine for higher wages. In 1870, he worked in a mine outside Wadsworth, Ohio, boarding with miner

Henry Mendinhall's family and several other miners before heading west. He later settled in southern Indiana, where he married Lydia Minnis in 1891.[7] By then, however, Shirkey was more than a migrant coal miner. Even though he still identified himself as a miner on the 1900 census schedule, Shirkey also owned his own farm, mortgage free. He and his wife shared their home with seventeen-year-old Isum Stout, who worked with Shirkey in the field and the mines.[8]

Shirkey's life demonstrated how multiple incomes and cooperation jointly shaped rural life in the Gilded Age. As Robert Weise has shown, average farmers and laborers regularly made small-scale investments to earn extra cash. They borrowed money to purchase more land in efforts to increase crop yields, bought and sold items on credit, and sold their lumber for cash. Jonathan Levy found this same trend among farmers who participated in futures market speculation and pursued western farm mortgages, believing such investments would generate larger income or at least protect their economic stability.[9] It kept Shirkey traveling from mine to mine in search of better pay, ultimately enabling him to purchase a farm.

It is difficult to discern exactly how many workers cobbled together their earnings in this way. Often, workers reported only one job to census takers even if they held two jobs. Incomes that homemaker wives earned were often not reported at all. Transient workers, those who performed seasonal labor, and those who worked informal odd jobs were also unlikely to leave complete records of their employment histories. Still, US Census schedules from 1880 and 1900 show that Shirkey was not alone in this endeavor. Salesmen, hotel owners, and a host of laborers in various industries owned or rented houses surrounded by farms, rented parcels of farmland, or, like Shirkey, owned their own farms despite not describing themselves as a farmer on the census. The fact that they claimed one occupation on the census but clearly owned or rented farmland indicates they also farmed. Edward Davis and Pete Buss, for example, were black miners who both rented houses outside of Earlington, Kentucky, surrounded by farms owned or rented by white families. Thomas Davis and Lincoln Guthrie were salesmen in Coffee County, Georgia, in 1900, but they also owned or rented farmland. In Crawford County, Kansas, Adair Orin and John Tressel were carpenters, Eugene Wear was a switchman, Barney Gluglione and Jacob Klaus were teamsters, Wiley Johnson was a blacksmith, and John Slater, Julius Heckscher, and John Robertson were coal miners, but they all also claimed to own or rent nearby farms. These trends were echoed all over the country, demonstrating that laborers seldom worked in a single occupation. Instead, they were both farmers and laborers who worked in multiple occupations to increase their incomes.[10]

"Leveling ground," n.p., n.d. Courtesy of the Evansville Museum of Arts, History, and Science Collection, University of Southern Indiana Special Collections.

Not all workers experienced Peter Shirkey's success, instead engaging in multiple occupations in order to make ends meet. Shirkey's neighbors Daniel and Martha Hornback understood this point well. Although they were the same age as the Shirkeys, were white, and farmed in the same community, the Hornbacks did not own their land. Instead, they shared their rented farm with their disabled son and sixteen-year-old grandson, Shirley, who worked in a local coal mine.[11] Unlike Shirkey, who saved funds and used his dual occupation to maintain a steady income, the Hornbacks faced a steady decline in farm profits combined with the added expense of caring for a disabled relative. For the Hornbacks, mining was a way to make ends meet. By 1910, the Shirkeys and Stout still lived on their farm, while the Hornbacks had relocated. Shirley Hornback continued to work as a coal miner but lived in a rented home with his wife, Lillie, and his widowed grandfather. In the following years, the Hornbacks regularly uprooted and moved throughout the coalfields looking for work.[12]

Although their situations differed, Shirkey and Hornback both relied on multiple occupations and incomes to survive. For Hornback, it was a way to balance the family budget while Shirkey cobbled together these occupations to get ahead. Not all who worked in the mines also worked in the fields (or vice versa), but their efforts were examples of larger cooperative networks engrained in rural society that allowed multiple hands and multiple revenues to contribute to a single family's income.

Workers like the Hornbacks chose their occupations and sometimes even their residence based on which industries paid the highest. During the late nineteenth century when farm laborers' daily wages without board averaged $0.92 nationally, this shift was particularly clear. The US Department of Agriculture reported in 1892 that Georgia and Florida farmers frequently complained that their farm laborers preferred working turpentine farms or sawmills over farm fields. The furnaces, mines, and mills attracted rural laborers in Alabama, whereas circumstances in West Virginia, Pennsylvania, and Kansas were similar to those in Georgia and Florida. Conversely, in states like Tennessee, Kentucky, Ohio, Indiana, and Missouri, where wages were more competitive with other rural industries, the supply of farm labor remained much more consistent.[13]

In most cases, these occupational shifts were not permanent; workers moved back and forth between industries, depending on pay rates that varied based on the seasonal rhythms inherent in both farming and other rural trades. Small-scale brickyard workers, especially in northern states, seldom worked in the winter when the ground was frozen.[14] Like farmers, turpentine workers performed specific tasks at different points of the year, with some seasons demanding more laborers than others. Tasks like preparing the trees to "dip" could be performed in the winter months when the sap was not flowing. These jobs paid less than harvesting the sap, causing some workers who relied on the turpentine industry in the summer to find other work in the winter. It also allowed farmers to participate in turpentining while tending to their fields. As with the coal industry, children and wives of turpentine workers also worked to contribute to the family income by raking pine straw and dried grass away from the pine trunks and performing other tasks in ways that mirrored the antebellum rice-growing culture of the region. This pattern also appeared in the lumbering and sawmilling aspects of the timber industry, which saw a decreased supply of labor during harvest time when timber workers took jobs as farm laborers. Such a rotation allowed some rural farmers and laborers to move between farms, forests, railyards, coal mines, and a host of other rural occupations, creating a continuous crossflow of rural semiskilled industrial workers throughout the year according to seasonal demand.[15]

Flow between occupations, then, was not limited to the coal and farming industries. However, because coal mining and agriculture were practiced in an area far more widespread than many other rural industries, the flow between coal mining and farming was particularly common. During the winter months when farms lay dormant, more mines were open. In Illinois alone, the number of miners working in the mines increased from 16,771 in the 1887 summer to over 23,648 the following winter.[16]

Many farmers took advantage of this seasonal work and labored in the mines before returning to the farm in the spring. "We farm in summer and dig coal in winter," one Kansas farmer and small mine operator explained to the Kansas Bureau of Labor Statistics. In the summer months, a mine that he shared with other local farmers closed and only resumed work after harvest when coal demand increased.[17] No state records exist stating exactly how many workers shared these experiences, and certainly not all rural residents took advantage of these opportunities. However, the frequency with which such stories appear in state surveys of individual manufacturers indicates that dual occupations among workers was common. Likewise, miners often found work as farmhands in the summer months when mines shut down or reduced operations because of reduced demand.[18]

These trends rippled through families, connecting sons to the same rhythms their fathers followed. Like farmers who used their sons in the fields, miners used their sons to help load coal in the mines, in some cases sending them to school at night so they could work in the mines year-round.[19] Companies granted father-son mining teams extra cars to transport coal, increasing the overall amount credited to the miner while allowing the son to learn the mining trade. Men without sons, like Shirkey, hired contract miners to help. Such hired loaders were often young men like Isum Stout or farmers like Shirley Hornback who needed the additional income while tending the farm. As with sons, companies granted miners with loaders extra cars, but, because most were the miners' employees, most loaders did not receive their pay from the company. When a loader placed coal on a coal car, the company counted it as coal belonging to the miner. On payday, the miner then paid his loader a flat daily wage out of his own earnings, or at times, paid a portion of the wage in cash in addition to providing room and board.[20]

In many cases, this shared labor made the difference between rural workers earning a living wage and going into debt. For farmers, it provided an income that supplemented crop profits. It dramatically increased a miner's coal output, well-worth the money spent to hire a hand. In an 1893 study of coal mining families, the Missouri Bureau of Labor Statistics and Inspection found that miners' yearly wages ranged from $200 to $560. Those who worked alone typically earned a little over $200 each year and never earned more than $300. Miners with a loader reported earning $400 to $560 each year. The Missouri report did not note how much money these miners paid loaders, but reports from elsewhere indicated that, depending on whether room and board was part of their payment, loaders received 5 to 30 percent of what miners earned. Even considering the wages they paid to their hands, then, miners stood to earn more when they shared their labor.[21]

It is unclear how Missouri miners' shared wages compared to miners elsewhere, as most assessments examined real wages and did not discern whether miners shared their work. In addition, market competition, mining method, coal quality, and the number of days the mine was running all affected an individual miner's net earnings. Still, miners hired loaders in mines across the nation, indicating that they saw a similar benefit in dividing their work. At the time, the US Commissioner of Labor estimated that the average yearly expenditures for a US working-class family ranged from $400 to $700, meaning that using a loader or, in the very least, relying on other family members for income, was crucial to balancing a mining family's budget.[22]

Relying on multiple income streams, however, was not limited to those affiliated with the mining industry. Wage laborers and farmers throughout the country relied on wives, sons, and daughters to make ends meet. Historian Steve Fraser notes that children in Pennsylvania contributed up to 40 percent of family earnings. By the turn of the century, one-fifth of the nation's children aged fifteen or under labored for wages, and, he noted, "this doesn't count the millions who worked on farms."[23]

Wives' contributions were likewise crucial to the family economy. Historian Sally Zanjani found that wives of western prospectors were far from passive helpmeets. Instead, women like Ellie Nay labored passionately in the prospecting field. They "saw themselves as full partners" in their husband's, father's, and brother's prospecting enterprises and "demanded the financial rewards due them as such."[24] In the process, wives were crucial in balancing family budgets, not only helping to decide how money would be spent but also discerning the proper time to strike.

Although Henry Mendinhall owned the house that boarded young bachelor Peter Shirkey in 1870, Barbra Mendinhall cared for him. In paying board, Shirkey and the other miners hired her to cook their meals and wash their clothes. Other wives used these same roles differently. Unlike Mendinhall's housemates, who were boarders, the Shirkeys declared their housemate was an employee. The room and meals Isum Stout received were a portion of his payment, making Lydia and Peter Shirkey joint employers. In other cases, wives were even more enterprising. Missouri Labor Commissioner Lee Meriwether noted that farmer wives with cash purchased mine scrip and company checks from local miners' wives for roughly 80 percent of their value. These arrangements enabled mining families to have cash without forfeiting wages to the company, freeing them to shop for cheaper goods elsewhere or even move away if desired. Meanwhile, farmwives saved the scrip and checks for purchases when company store goods were cheap, maximizing the return on their investment.[25] Such actions as employees, employers, and investors made wives not only crucial in sustaining family finances, but also placed them in the center of rural market networks.

The multiple incomes and occupations provided by rural men and women in industrializing rural society, then, were built upon long-standing cooperative networks that relied upon friends and family aiding each other. A miner hiring a neighboring farmer to load coal in the winter helped both men increase their incomes just as a farmwife purchasing mine scrip from a neighboring miner wife allowed both women to better provide for their families. Such traditions opened the door for neighbors to join each other in forming cooperatives with the expectation and understanding that all would benefit from jointly owning and investing in a store or mine.[26] Industrialization did not separate farmers from laborers at all; it pulled them together as they cobbled together their incomes side by side.

Turns

If common experiences and community ties could pull workers in various occupations together, it could also push them apart. For many, the wedge between miners and farmers who worked in the mines began with "the turn." In the mines, the turn referred to the length of the miners' wait for a car to transport their coal to be weighed. In most mines, the number of available cars was limited or the weighing process was backlogged so that a miner might receive only four cars a day, which limited the amount of coal they produced. When mines became overcrowded, such as when companies recruited miners from elsewhere or when farmers entered the mines, the number of miners "claiming a turn" increased. This lengthened each miner's wait, making the turn "slow" and decreasing each miner's total output.[27] Because a miner's wage depended on the amount of coal they produced, even miners working at high-paying mines found it difficult to make ends meet. Iowa miner "Rambler" complained that miners came from all over the country to take advantage of the high wages paid at his mine, but in the process overcrowded the mine and slowed the turn. "The shafts here would need to run night and day to hoist all the coal the men here could send out, and still they come," he continued bitterly. Despite the company's high wages per ton of coal, the slow turn meant that the average miner in Rambler's mine still received only $1.50 for a day's labor.[28]

But crowded mines did not come solely from traveling workers. Mines also became overcrowded as farm profits decreased and farmers grew more dependent on the mines to sustain their families. Farmers like Shirley Hornback who began working in the mines as miners' employees working for a flat daily wage soon learned they could earn more by mining and loading their own coal during the winter months or abandoning their farms entirely.[29] Their decisions to work as miners further glutted the labor market, slowing the turn so that all miners earned less. "The farmers have crowded us out," Indiana miner John Neal complained. The "coal butchers from the farm" needed only a supplemental income rather than a living wage. They accepted increased dead work and lower wages to gain a spot in the mine, forcing "practical miners," or those who mined as their primary occupation, to accept the same terms.[30] Miner "Bald Head" replied to Neal's grievance, claiming that the practical miners had only themselves to blame. In their quest to increase their pay, the "practical coal miners that are so selfish" had trained the farmers how to mine. "They go to work and give the Hay John [farmer] fifty or seventy-five cents per day, and about three or four weeks afterward they get to ask the boss for a room to themselves, and the boss gives them one," he explained bitterly. "That's the way winter diggers have got such a foothold," he continued. "You don't count the risk you are taking when you hire such men as they."[31] But little could be done. The need that drove farmers to the mine was the same that prompted miners to hire farmers to help load coal.

Systems like the turn, then, ultimately caused rural workers like coal miners to be more competitive in their labors than in other industries. Urban trades that produced furniture, clothing, or other finished goods required building space and machinery that limited the number of employees. Increasing production in these industries therefore meant constantly encouraging workers to speed up production. As David Montgomery found, these pushes to increase production often placed workers at odds with management, creating a comradery that at times encouraged workers to "slow down" their production to keep production quotas low.[32] This trend was reversed in the mines, where the workplace could accommodate more workers. Operators packed the workplace and, by forcing miners to wait turns, they maximized mine production while slowing individual output. The more crowded the mine, the slower the turn, the lower the individual earnings, even though the mine's earnings remained high.

As the turn slowed, mining and farming families turned their own value systems to accommodate their need. Producer understandings of what was right and fair became twisted and molded into new notions of honor and respectability, even as they condemned employers for the same behavior. In the coal mines, labor deemed "dishonest" came in several forms. Some miners took advantage of the mines' constant accessibility, which allowed them to loosen or load coal on Sundays or late nights when the mines were closed. Because the cars used to load the coal were often in short supply, loading cars when the mine was closed enabled a worker to load his coal without waiting for a car. In the process, it took cars away from "honest" miners working during operating hours. Miner "Working Slack" noted that fathers claimed turns for their sons, but the sons did not actually help their fathers load coal. Instead, fathers loaded extra coal on the cars designated for their sons while the sons earned daily wages as mule drivers.[33] Other miners complained of coworkers accepting wage reductions, extra dead work, or larger spaces between screen bars to gain a better spot in the mine or secure steady work. In doing so, miners allowed employers to charge less for their coal, sell more coal, and keep the mines open longer. Still, the dead work and large screens, combined with miners accepting wage reductions, ultimately forced other miners and mine operators to accept the same terms or else face shutdowns in their own mines.[34] Illinois miner "K.R." insisted no honest man of union principle would engage in such cutthroat actions, yet many workers accepted the terms. "The result," he claimed, "is that good men have been made a target of by the operators" and thus were forced to accept lower wages or lose their jobs entirely.[35]

Few components of the mining industry revealed this moral compromise more than the free click. Much like the pluck-me, the free click or free turn was a system companies enforced in mines throughout the nation. Most mines required entries, or long corridors that extended from the shaft to the face of the mine. Miners worked in "rooms" situated along these corridors, but a handful of miners were needed to drive entry, or dig the coal from the face to extend the corridor for more rooms.[36] The faster the entry men cleared, the faster production increased. Companies therefore lost money when entry men waited for cars to transport their coal. To solve this, many operators implemented the free click, which permitted entry men to skip the line and take an empty car whenever they needed it instead of having to wait with the room men.

The practice helped keep the mine functioning, but it had the added benefit of dramatically increasing the entry men's pay at the expense of the room men, who continued to wait for access to coal cars. In most instances, companies used entry driving positions to reward miners for good behavior, such as taking on extra dead work, shopping at the company store, or accepting a wage reduction without complaint. Such favoritism used the miners' economic need to keep the workforce divided.[37] Although some miners and companies managed to create a system that allowed all miners a turn at the entry to keep wages even, this grew more difficult to uphold as wages declined. "We had a mass meeting and a resolution was passed for the entry men to get six cars ahead and then to stop until the room men can catch up to them," Kentucky miner "Penrod" reported. "This worked all right until they had to stop [after their six cars] and then they kicked against it and now it is the same old tune—free click."[38] Mine workers may have remained opposed the idea of favoritism in the mines, but such an opportunity to earn more proved too valuable for workers who benefited from the system.

"Too Enterprising"

The moral turns that working families faced demonstrated how economic circumstances transformed social and cultural norms, undermining resident's values even as they tried to hold onto them. But not all dishonest labor came because of economic desperation. Hoping to grow wealthy, some producers invested in businesses like cooperative stores or coal mines while others took advantage of workplace favoritism and strikes to gain higher wages. Like the employers and merchants with whom they dealt, many producers adopted cutthroat practices not to scrape by, but to improve their economic position.

Hundreds of farmers operated what many knew as a one-horse rig, or a small operation on their land that used a single horse to extract resources from their land. Some farmers used their land to extract clay for small-scale brickmaking ventures while others dug small pits to mine coal. Their wives, children, and hired hands often aided in the labor, allowing them to produce a meager amount of coal cheaply. Because these mines were informal arrangements rather than an actual mining company, one-horse rigs did not always pay their miners a per-ton wage but instead gave their miners a percentage of the profit earned on the coal, further reducing production costs compared to miners paid by the ton. One-horse mines often operated only in winter months and seldom produced enough to compete for coal contracts. Still, their production supplied local markets so that, collectively, these low-cost enterprises cut into demand enough to force larger companies to lower their own production costs. More importantly to miners, when miners struck against coal companies, one-horse rigs often remained in operation, benefiting from the high coal demand.[39]

Landowners with private mines were not the only small-scale operations to turn their back on miners' perceptions of honest principles. Small mine owners, like the farmers who owned stock in Egypt's Enterprise Mine, also disregarded their neighbors' and employees' interests when their investments were at risk. This dynamic that caused farmers to become both stockholders and strikebreakers runs against how these groups have been typically presented in the literature. Scholars seldom consider the connections between cooperative investment and strikebreaking. As a result, those who took part in cooperatives appear to have little in common with those who broke strikes.[40] Historian Charles Postel saw cooperative efforts as evidence of business-minded farmers and farm laborers capable and willing to participate in the modern market yet cast their efforts as an alternative vision to mainstream market ventures.[41] Scholars of strikebreaking have maintained a similar dichotomy. They have highlighted social, economic, and cultural reasons for strikebreaking and noted common ground between strikers and strikebreakers, but in most instances, these examinations cast strikebreakers as the antithesis of cooperative participants and union workers.[42]

In practice, however, union-associated entities like cooperatives and actions like strikebreaking overlapped. For thousands of workers, the nation's leading capitalists were not the only investors privy to risk management tactics like joint-stock ownership or cooperative investment. Instead, they involved average workers looking to earn extra income for their families. Such opportunities had more in common with strikebreaking than historians have typically understood. Cooperative mines could seldom price their coal competitively without cutting into shareholder profits. When prices fell, they were frequently the first mines to sit idle and the last to resume work. For the duration of its closure, investors gained nothing. Larger businesses absorbed the loss, but small investors, like farmers and miners, lost their wages in addition to their investment. As was the case with the Enterprise mine in Egypt, the prospect of losing such an investment was enough for stockholding farmers to become strikebreakers.[43]

The Egypt farmers' willingness to break a strike demonstrated the surest way for an individual or cooperative to survive in the competitive market. The comparatively few cooperative mines that succeeded often did so by implementing the same cutthroat tactics as other firms. A Knights of Labor cooperative in Avery, Iowa, not only cut coal prices but offered a free car of nut coal for each ten cars of coal purchased. The tactic stole contracts from their biggest competitor, the Avery Coal Company, allowing the cooperative to dominate the local coal trade.[44] Regardless of the Knights' ideals of fair labor, the cooperative's survival depended on its ability to compete in the market.[45]

Consequently, although they were founded on the premise of allowing average workers ownership, cooperatives and joint-stock initiatives often helped the owners at their employees' expense. The Knights of Labor executive board, for example, owned the Mutual Mine near Cannelburg, Indiana. It had operated as a cooperative since 1884, but only a few of its owners worked in the mine. Instead, most were Knights from Ohio, including the mine superintendent and NTA 135 master workman William T. Lewis. By 1892, the Knights could not afford to run the mine and leased it to the Watkins, Lunch and Company, a coal company based in Peoria, Illinois. Technically, the mine remained a cooperative. Its owners continued to receive a twelve cent per ton royalty on all coal mined, but, like hundreds of other mine owners, the Knights were absentee proprietors who left most decisions to local managers. In these instances, already low profits fell further for cooperative owners who split their dividends with third-party companies while those working in the mines received little or no benefit from the cooperative at all.[46]

The Cannelburg mine was "in Reality a stock Co. sailing under the Head of Cooperative," UMW Indiana District president George Purcell complained to labor leader William B. Wilson. Technically, the mine remained a Knights cooperative and was still attached to the Knights local assembly, yet when Purcell and others protested, they were fired from the Cannelburg mine and blacklisted from other area mines. With the blessing of the Knights, the cooperative opposed the local assembly's rule to force farmers and other nonpractical miners to pay a higher premium. Instead, they left the local assembly, joined the General Assembly, and accepted the farmers "and some noted Blacklegs that had been black Balled by the old LA." Such "Dirty tricks," Purcell wrote, were a hallmark of how the "so Called Knights of Labor Co" treated its workers. Their capitalist endeavors happened on a smaller scale, but cooperative owners still practiced absentee landownership, hired and exploited employees, and endeavored to bust union solidarity among their workers, even as they retained union affiliation.[47]

These conflicts were not limited to cooperative mines. They cropped up in cooperative endeavors in every industry. Historian Philip Foner notes that teamsters in a Knights cooperative bus company in Toronto went on strike for higher wages, forcing the company to shut down. A cooper cooperative in Minneapolis replaced many of its workers with the latest machinery needed to compete in the industry. The expense of the machinery eventually caused the cooperative to close, but not before it implemented child labor to minimize production costs. Instances like these prompted historian Steve Leikin to note that, while the abstract idea of cooperation "was a powerful grantor of liberty and challenge to capital," when put into practice, "it distanced itself from the shop floor issues that resonated with the rank and file." In short, when operating cooperatives, unions could look after their profits or they could look after the workers, but they could not do both.[48]

Similarly, joint-stock companies like the Enterprise mine in Egypt were forced to comply with the wage reductions or shut down entirely.[49] Indiana miner and union organizer J. C. Heenan's joint-stock mine in southern Illinois faced a similar problem. Unable to compete while paying the union-sanctioned scale, Heenan and his business partners cut their miners' wages to price their coal under the largest Egypt mines. While mining coal and organizing local unions in the Indiana coalfields, Heenan simultaneously drove down wages under union scale rates as a mine owner in a neighboring state.[50]

Such instances blurred divisions between owner and employee as well as between union and nonunion. Heenan was all four at once. While he pushed for higher wages, market competition made it impossible for him to pay what he and other miners deemed fair. Other labor leaders, such as UMW leader Phil Penna and UMW Indiana District president Joseph Dunkerly, also partly owned and/or managed mining companies while holding official office in the miners' union. In another instance, the vice president of the Illinois District of the UMW also served as the president of a Bloomington, Illinois, mine that refused to pay what miners in the district deemed was a fair wage.[51] In Petersburg, Illinois, miners who were stockholders in the mine forced their coworkers to shop at their company store and gave themselves first access to mine cars so that their coworkers "only get what cars they [the stockholders] can't fill and that is few." When the miners complained, the stockholding miners fired their employees and continued mining coal on their own.[52]

Companies with more capital used similar incentives to their advantage, offering miners mine stock to soothe wage grievances. In doing so, companies decreased the likelihood of miners' strikes because it sliced into miners' gains as shareholders. In at least one case, these tactics were so injurious to miners that one committee of Illinois miners wrote to the *National Labor Tribune* to end the practice. "We earnestly implore of you fellow men not to increase the force of the shyster stockholders whose acts always tend to keep the iron heel of oppression down heavily on us." Claiming these actions were "a dodge from men's duty," the committee wanted the stockholding miners to "be branded as traitors to their fellow men and the people's cause."[53]

The committee's distinction between duty to the community's well-being and personal investment opportunities tied into a larger moral conflict that ran throughout nineteenth-century society. Historian Ann Fabian notes that as the market economy shifted to one fueled by immediate profits and enormous gains, it changed the entire nation's attitude toward investment, risk, and gambling, not just those of big investors.[54] Farmers may have decried the speculators that seemed to manipulate crop prices in New York and Chicago, but by the late

1880s, futures trading was as accessible to ordinary people hoping to turn a dime into a dollar as it was big investors. Unofficial trading venues commonly known as bucket shops brought the exciting new world of futures speculation and stock trading into rural communities throughout the nation.[55] Because they were unincorporated venues, they were classified as illegal gambling dens in most states by the mid-1890s.[56] Regardless of their legality, however, bucket shops functioned on the same principles as future traders in urban market exchanges. They gambled on future prices by selling "fictitious" or "fiat" products without physically owning or exchanging merchandise.[57] Such cases blurred the lines between businessman and gambler. The hope for easy profit drove big businessmen and ordinary people alike into the world of shareholding and futures investing.

Few aspects captured this conflation of business, gambling, and dishonesty better than the term *blackleg*. Labor historians have often dismissed it as a word interchangeable with *strikebreaker*. While the term was used to denote strikebreakers in England by the 1870s, *blackleg* also had other meanings that most laborers and farmers understood well. To farmers and ranchers, it was a name for the gangrene that killed cattle, literally eating away the investments they worked so hard to raise. Throughout the nineteenth century, the same term described gamblers and degenerates, not unlike bucket shop patrons, who gambled illegally with the futures market. By the end of the century, it applied to any dishonest "cheat" or "swindler" who unfairly took another person's rightful gain.[58]

All of these meanings likely ran through rural workers' minds when they heard and used the word *blackleg*. Those who used it meant it as an insult that not only described a dishonorable action, but dishonorable intent. Far from simply describing a person who broke a strike, a blackleg took without caring whom they injured. Blacklegs were malicious beings whose behaviors seemed to spread like disease, ravaging the earnings of honest laborers, creating a moral, mental, and physical threat. In the mining industry, "blackleg labor" implied any kind of dishonest mining practice that injured one's coworkers for the sake of personal profit. While this often applied to strikebreaking, it also included men who labored below scale rates, accepted free clicks, claimed another man's coal, loosened coal on a Sunday, and engaged in any practice that miners deemed dishonest.[59] To "D.N.P." and hundreds of others, such miners were hypocrites. D.N.P. insisted: "I would ask your readers how these men can sit on their seats, in the sight of Almighty God and the men they are sitting and working beside, whom they know that they have taken, as it were, the bread out of their wives and children's mouths to satisfy self."[60]

But the distinction between dishonest and upright was not always as clear as D.N.P. envisioned.[61] Thousands of miners acknowledged that they labored unscrupulously but denied being blacklegs. Rather, they claimed they were forced to accept dishonest labor to protect their own interests. Consequently, although the *National Labor Tribune* charged that such miners were "a little too enterprising" and looked after themselves while betraying other workers, the promise of living comfortably tempted union miners just as it did nonunion.[62] Although both Knights and miners' unions condemned the free click, union miners continued to participate in the system. "I am sorry to say the majority of the entry men are Knights of Labor," western Kentucky miner "Penrod" claimed of his local mine. Such men, he insisted, were Knights "in name only, not the principle, if I am not mistaken, or they would not accept of a free click if they want to act right towards their fellow man, as they get all [the work] they can do and the room men in some parts of the mine not making a livelihood." Penrod's coworkers were not the only organized men who disregarded honest principles. Indiana miner "T.B.T." noted that his local's president "and most of the committee" regularly took free clicks, causing him and at least a few of his fellow miners to conclude that "we ought not to ask others to join [the Miners' Federation] if we violate the rules ourselves." Union affiliation meant little when it came to the workers' starving, one Missouri miner later reflected. "The dollar makes the man out here regardless of principle or anything else," he wrote. For union and nonunion alike, "business is business" and it was "better to be without friends out here than without dollars." As a result, "moral worth has disappeared."[63]

The fruits of the moral decline the Missouri miner described were visible throughout the industry. William Houston of Indiana noted that the Knights at one local mine accepted a ten-cent-per-ton reduction that would force all mines in the region to "go down" in wages. "There is only one name for this and that is blacklegging," he argued. But the effects of blacklegging did more than allow blacklegs an advantage to earn more at their neighbors' expense.[64] Like a contagion, it spread as miners injured by those they condemned as blacklegs had no choice but to labor dishonestly themselves. Illinois miners faced a similar situation when operators initiated an immediate ten-cent-per-ton reduction in wages that would increase to twenty cents if the miners resisted. NPU organizer Patrick H. Donnelly advised the miners to "keep cool" and accept the terms. "All who can get work at something else should do it," he asserted, continuing that "those who can't get work should adapt themselves to the conditions and make themselves as useful to the cause as possible."[65] Such orders were a far cry from the rallies that typically associated unionism with solidarity and strength.

Rather, Donnelly's words reflected a language of compromise that developed from the realization that market prices for coal had dropped too low for unions to enforce the agreements made with employers. "We are getting more demoralized every week in Clay City," Houston concluded in his letter, acknowledging the guilt many union miners felt when they accepted their wage reduction. The mining Knights were over twelve hundred strong, he observed, but they could not honor their own principles.[66]

Concessions

Miners' belief in honest principles, then, did not guide them when they faced hardship. When Iowa miners in NTA 135 fell on hard times, they had little choice but to undercut their neighbors. Rather than face scorn in their own communities, several miners traveled to Grape Creek, Illinois, an NFM stronghold during an ongoing strike. Carrying union cards, the Iowa Knights insisted they were honorable men forced to break the strike and meant no harm. "My God, what way would they help us?" Illinois NFM officers asked. "My neighbor to starve my family and then ask that I consider him a good and true neighbor!"[67]

The officers' description of the strikebreaking union miners as "neighbors" reflected the difficult position miners occupied in the Gilded Age. Although the Iowa mines were over a hundred miles from Grape Creek, rail lines placed miners, and their coal, side by side. Regardless of distance, they were neighbors. At the same time, "neighbor" pulled on miners' sense of working-class community. More than ever before, miners across the nation were connected and their actions had an impact on each other. Such an image called for miners to "love thy neighbor as thyself" and to look after each other's needs rather than tear them down.[68]

Still, a miner's duties to his neighbors remained secondary to his personal duties. Regional boundaries and union divides therefore became means for otherwise "honest" men to justify "dishonest" behavior. Notions of honor that caused a miner to think twice before blacklegging at home held less sway when he did not personally know the miners he injured. As a result, the Iowa Knights were not alone in their behavior. Missouri miners broke Kansas strikes, Indiana miners broke strikes in southern Illinois, and western Kentucky miners broke strikes in southern Indiana.[69]

But in the growing competitive market, miners did not need to travel to break a strike. Because the goal of the strike was to deplete the coal supply, miners who accepted the low-paying coal contracts that propelled neighboring mines to strike technically blacklegged by ensuring the supply of cheap coal remained unchanged. Business boomed in Danville, Illinois, when nearby Springfield miners went on strike. But, as one Danville miner noted, it would not be long before Springfield's strike would end with a defeat that forced Danville to take a reduction. Danville would go on strike, the miner continued, and while it was out, Springfield would fill its contracts until the Danville strike failed. Workers in both towns technically broke each other's strikes and claimed the competition was blacklegging, but neither side viewed its own strikebreaking actions as blacklegging. Rather, each community justified its willingness to fill strikers' contracts by claiming that it was only taking back what the "blacklegs" had taken from it in the last strike. "That is the way Springfield and Danville men have been fighting for twenty years," he concluded.[70]

This dynamic grew more complicated as the national market web expanded, pulling more mines into the same competitive network. Springfield and Danville competed not only against each other but against the entire region from Pennsylvania to southern Illinois. By 1889, miners in Ohio could fill Illinois contracts or Pennsylvania miners could compete against Indiana without leaving their home state.[71] Although the NPU had formed less than five months earlier, the organization failed to unite the miners and could not stop the steady fall of wages across the coalfields. Pennsylvania and Ohio mines reduced their wages by 5 cents per ton, forcing Indiana and Illinois mines to lower their wages to compete for the Chicago market. In Indiana, bituminous wages fell from 75 to 55 cents per ton and block coal from 90 to 70.[72] Mine owner William L. Scott, "coal king of Pennsylvania," imposed even harder terms. He instructed his mine manager, Charles Devlin, to reduce the Spring Valley, Illinois, miners' wages from 90 cents per ton to 72½ cents per ton, double the dead work, and crowd the mines by adding a third miner to each two-man room.[73]

Most Indiana miners managed to negotiate a settlement for a five-cent-per-ton reduction comparable to a reduction Pennsylvania and Ohio miners accepted.[74] Some Illinois operators offered similar terms if the miners agreed to sign an iron-clad agreement rejecting the union.[75] NPU leader Dan McLaughlin advised the miners to accept all terms except the iron-clad agreement. The operators had stockpiled coal and would not need to reopen their mines for at least six months, "so that when the markets require our labor we would, through hunger and other causes, be ready to accept their terms." Accepting the reduction immediately, he and other union leaders insisted, "is the very best we can do and should do."[76]

By ordering the union to *not* strike, McLaughlin initiated a wave of reactions that ran against the typical understandings of how union and nonunion workers were expected to behave. The overwhelmingly nonunion northern Illinois miners were among the most furious with McLaughlin's orders. When they heard the new wage terms, they called a mass meeting in English, Polish, and German to discuss the terms along with McLcaughlin's orders. Labor leaders like McLaughlin may have claimed that the union upheld "honest" labor terms, but the northern Illinois miners disagreed. Declaring that the new terms were dishonest and unjust, the nonunion Illinois miners, along with the Indiana block field, decided to strike for honest principles and fair pay even when the unions would not.[77]

As the miners walked out, however, their actions were met with disdain from union leaders. If the miners wished for higher wages, McLaughlin contended, they needed to be thoroughly organized across state lines. Southern and central Illinois needed to honor the pay scale, or their coal would flood the Chicago market. The only way a strike could be successful was if all underpaid miners in all states struck simultaneously. Considering this, McLaughlin condemned the northern Illinois strike, calling the striking miners "knaves" for believing that a regional strike would solve a national problem. They were willing to ruin the progress the national organization had made for the sake of a local pay increase, "though some of them [claim to] be followers of the meek and lowly Savior," he wrote. Such a claim indicated that the nonunion strike for higher wages was not only ill-conceived but morally wrong and dishonorable. "They will have plenty of time to do penance in sackcloth and ashes for the ruin they have brought on our people," he intoned. The native English-speaking miners in particular should have known better, McLaughlin insisted, adding that he felt "sorry" that they had rejected union orders. "They are men who would like to do what was right, but they have listened to the wily tongue of the deceiver and not to their friends." With that, McLaughlin and other NPU and NTA 135 leaders ordered all organized men to sign the contract and return to the mines.[78]

The labor leader's words demonstrated how quickly union ideals could twist in times of desperation. Although union leaders often used religious and moral rhetoric to bolster a united fight for workers across ethnic lines, in this instance McLaughlin used religious rhetoric to condemn the miners' decisions to fight for "honest work" and drew moral distinctions between ethnic groups. The native-English-speaking, German, and Polish miners' willingness to stand together in this fight was not praised by McLaughlin. Instead, the nonnative-English-speaking miners played the role of the "deceiver," pulling the native-English-speaking miners away from their "friends." If the English-speaking miners wanted to be true followers of "the meek and lowly Savior," they had to turn from the deception that the nonnative-English speakers had accepted, and if they wanted to be good and moral workers, they had to become strikebreakers.[79]

As union workers began breaking the strike, the balance of strikers grew more outraged. They believed that McLaughlin's orders were "a cowardly stab at manhood's rights."[80] Such a phrase implied that McLaughlin's actions to preserve the union over miners' wages made him no better than employers who treated their workers poorly. "Old Dan [McLaughlin]" had no right to order the miners living "under enforced slavery" to further "sign away their manhood," miner and local organizer T. J. Llewellyn argued.[81] To his mind, organizers like McLaughlin were as guilty as the employers who refused to treat them fairly. "As to Dan meeting tyranny and oppression," miner "Pro Bono Publico" asserted, "it is an easy matter to meet it in the way he has advised for eight years. We have been advised to accept reduction after reduction until the thing has grown monotonous and irksome." Union officers like McLaughlin were seen to be so far removed from the miners' daily struggle that they had lost sight of honest principles. Instead, they grew complicit to the cutthroat practices that drove wages down. "Keep quiet, 'Dan,'" Pro Bono Publico ordered. "Don't censure any man or men for doing something you never dared do."[82]

To Pro Bono Publico and his supporters, McLaughlin and those who followed his orders and accepted the depreciated terms were bowing to company demands. Missouri miner George Palfreyman, like many northern Illinois miners at the time, insisted that such workers were not humans but "things in the shape of men." Illinois organizer William Scaife agreed, writing that the "hordes" of union men who broke the strike were worse than mice who timidly accepted company terms. Rather, they were "rats" that "did not possess a spark of manhood." Accepting the terms did more than make it impossible for northern Illinois miners to live, northern Illinois striking miner John Rowe argued indignantly. It "would cut the throats of our fellow miners in Indiana, Ohio, and Pennsylvania, who have got settled on reasonable terms, and we propose to hunger awhile rather than do this, even though Dan McL. calls us knaves." At a special convention governed by Illinois NPU officers, the miners agreed. They not only decided to continue the strike but officially censured McLaughlin "for branding us as knaves and deceivers of the men [of] this district, who are actuated by motives as pure and honest as those of any man."[83]

But honesty meant little when coal flooded the market. Neither the NPU nor NTA 135 could financially support the hundreds of striking families. Consequently, as union miners broke the strike in the northern Illinois mines, hundreds of desperate strikers traveled to the nonunion mines in Egypt to find work. Both groups mined coal below the scale, and both sent their coal to the Chicago market. Although both claimed to be "brave fellows" fighting for what was right for them and their families, both were also deemed "blacklegs" by other miners who claimed that their willingness to mine coal rendered the strike ineffective.[84]

By December, most northern Illinois mines had resumed work. The Illinois strike officially ended when Spring Valley miners signed a new contract accepting a 7½-cent-per-ton reduction and increased dead work with two men to a room. Dead work taken into consideration, the reduction averaged 10 cents per ton rather than the original 20 to 25 cents that operators originally sought to impose. Within days, the last Indiana mines on strike conceded as well.[85] Both northern Illinois and Indiana miners condemned the unions for betraying their cause.[86] Dishonesty and selfishness, they recognized, existed on both sides of the union line. Acknowledging the dissatisfaction, labor leader William Scaife attempted to mollify the embittered workers. The terms were unfair, he conceded, but the miners' struggle was no longer a fight between right and wrong. Instead, it was an ongoing choice between "the least of two evils."[87]

The national market contorted understandings of honor and morality, complicating workplace conflicts in ways that sometimes turned workers against one another. Efforts to generate larger personal profit were never limited to the big businessmen and bankers that rural producers condemned. Though on a smaller scale, producers engaged in similar acts. As small mine owners, they extracted their profits by decreasing their neighbors' incomes, making it impossible for a national union to overcome local interests. For farmers, laborers, and owners, from cooperatives and joint stock ventures to blacklegging, the concessions that national market competition demanded remained the same. To fight debt and exploitation, producers had to compromise their sense of what was moral and fair. Miners and farmers gambled, cheated, and stole. They cried "blackleg" when dishonest labor threatened their own livelihoods but accepted terms that they knew would "cut the throats" of their fellow miners, breaking their strikes, filling their contracts, taking their coal cars, and ignoring their scales. It was the lesser evil than subjecting their families to hardship when income was within reach.[88]

But it was still an evil. Miners everywhere looked in disgust at the 1889 strike failure, observing the markets, declining wages, union officers, strikebreakers, and the families who survived the summer on little more than bread and water. To them, it was a fresh reminder of the immorality inherent not only in their employers' business practices but in the practices of their own neighbors. "In the past we have sown to the lust of flesh and we are reaping [a] harvest of evils," miner "Pumpkin Smasher" said of the 1880s conflicts. In training the farmers that overcrowded the mines, flooding the market with coal, and accepting more reductions, he observed, the miners contributed to the dire circumstances they faced. "[Our craftsmen have become so greedy of pelf that they sell their souls to get a dime more," he continued. Such a phrase was a reminder of the cost dishonest labor demanded. If operators were "soulless" for demanding higher profits at workers' expense, workers forfeited their own souls when they injured their own neighbors.[89]

Few miners, least of all those defeated in 1889, believed the NPU or NTA 135 could end this cycle. But their experiences convinced the miners that they needed a way to live according to the honest principles they claimed, to love their neighbors without starving their families. To many, national unity between the vying unions seemed the only viable option. Union officers "have shown their inability to look after the interests of their craftsmen," Indiana organizer William Houston acknowledged, yet he remained convinced that unionization was "the only rock and foundation to build upon for the salvation of all."[90] As the strikers returned to work in December 1889, miners throughout the nation expressed this same hope, willing the national miners' union to be reborn just one month later. But even as they formed the new order, the problems of the 1880s remained. Competition and wage decline intensified, more farmers entered the mines, and miners remained skeptical of union leadership. Cutthroat competition remained steadfast and threatened the miners' trust in their new organization before they could unite.

CHAPTER THREE

"Judases"

Union "Betrayal" and the Aborted 1891 Strike

I dislike to speak against those who claim to be engaged in the service of labor reform, but he who wears your colors and professes to fight on your side, and then turns his sword against you in the thickest of the fight, is the most cowardly and miserable of all traitors.

—Thomas Faulds

The Indiana block miners were ready to strike. The coal they mined, primarily in Clay County, Indiana, was more valuable than the bituminous coal mined elsewhere in the Midwest, but their local unions answered to the same state UMW leaders as the rest of the state. The block field was the most thoroughly unionized region in the state and when their employers were positioning to break the fall 1891 contract, the block miners intended to fight it. When they notified the state officers of their plans, however, the UMW officers' response was not what they expected. "Everyone was struck dumb when they heard the telegram read," nineteen-year-old block coal miner John Mooney reported. UMW national secretary Patrick McBryde had telegrammed to notify the miners that the national officers forbade their proposed November 1891 strike. The miners were selfish fools for even considering the endeavor, McBryde wrote. The UMW would offer no assistance in enforcing the contract, nor would the miners have the union's support if they proceeded with their strike.[1]

The silence in the meeting hall quickly gave way to vocal rage. McBryde's orders came just months after national officers abandoned a nationwide strike effort the previous May. The May strike was supposed to be an easy victory, but the national officers called off the strike before it even began. Their decision to abandon their national May 1891 strike triggered a wave of wage reductions that eventually pushed miners in Mooney's district to consider the local November strike that McBryde now forbade.[2]

"Do our national officers know what they are doing? Are they aware of what they are doing? If not they will have to define their position and explain their reason for such conduct," Mooney demanded.[3] His anger reflected the animosity many miners felt as the UMW, barely a year old, implemented a more centralized structure to regulate a national but decentralized industry. Interstate competition between coal mines demanded a strong and centralized national union that would negotiate and regulate the wage scale, but doing so often came at the expense of local concerns. As UMW leaders joined other labor orders in centralizing their power structure, their efforts placed them at odds with the rank and file. More than ever before, the new union structure forced UMW leaders to look after national interests and larger mining regions like the western Pennsylvania field rather than the issues of smaller mining regions and areas like Mooney's block field.

To block miners like Mooney, however, the UMW's inability to cope with its overburdened load looked more like betrayal. Accustomed to the union mitigating local grievances against their employers, Mooney and his coworkers were furious that their dues went to an organization that seemed to continually dismiss their workplace concerns. As a result, their experiences in 1891 persuaded block miners like Mooney to throw away their UMW membership cards. But their rejection of the UMW was neither a simple move nor an outright rejection of union principle. In fact, the Indiana block miners' rejection of the UMW began while they were still in the union. Although they were unhappy with the order, they remained in the UMW months after the 1891 strike cancellation. Yet, by November, instead of following McBryde's orders, they, along with the other union miners in Indiana, decided to continue with their planned strike. "We have blacklegged long enough," Mooney explained. The miners believed that following union orders and accepting depreciating terms made them indistinguishable from the "blacklegs" who broke strikes. More importantly, the miners felt that McBryde's orders, and similar orders, represented an abandonment of union principles. True union miners fought for fair treatment in the mines, Mooney argued, "and if the national officers do not help us out[,] let them keep hands off and we will fight our own battles."[4] With that, the Indiana miners began an effort that, within a matter of weeks, resulted in abandoning the union they believed had gone astray.

Although surviving counts of rank-and-file membership are too sparse to produce exact numbers of membership decline during this period, officer reports of membership decline indicate that the Indiana rejection of orders from the UMW national officers in November 1891 was not an isolated event. As a result, the Indiana miners' frustration with the May 1891 strike cancellation highlights an understudied aspect of labor conflicts that often contributed to union membership decline. Studies of strike situations typically focus on the conflict of workers and unions against employers with support from sympathetic government officials.[5] But the conditions that drove workers to strike could also place them at odds with their union. Historians typically attribute this weakening "solidarity" to worker disillusion with unionism after union failures or due to pragmatic decisions to leave the union when it was more beneficial to work as nonunion labor.[6] But Mooney's assertions show that workers did not always join or abandon unions based solely on union potential for success or lack of faith in collective action. Instead, Mooney and many others remained in the union long after major organizing failures even though they disagreed with union leaders and their actions.

In many respects, the UMW's experiences in the early 1890s are crucial because of what *did not* occur rather than what did. The fallout from the UMW's canceled May 1891 national strike demonstrated that membership numbers were not necessarily a reliable indicator of faith in the union or belief in its strength. Although the year-old UMW claimed to be seventy thousand members strong the February before the canceled strike, only a fraction of that number was willing to strike just a few weeks later.[7] Consequently, the UMW's decision to cancel the strike was not because of antagonistic employers but because tens of thousands of miners would not honor union orders. Yet, even when leaders canceled the strike and acknowledged the UMW's frailty, miners did not immediately abandon the union, as might have been expected. Moreover, when Mooney and other miners eventually decided to leave the UMW, many still believed in union ideals. They abandoned the UMW not because they had grown disillusioned with organized labor but because they believed UMW leaders had turned away from their original goals.

In the months following the strike cancellation, miners and officers struggled to save the UMW, wrestling with dissatisfied miners and defiant local unions. In officers' eyes, miners who "kicked" or fought against the union by not paying dues, rebuking leaders, and disregarding union orders were "Judases" who "backslid" away from the honest principles they once held. Conversely, miners like Mooney who insisted that the miners could "fight our own battles," believed that the true backsliders were the officers who forced miners to accept wage reductions, leading the union away from its founding principles.[8] Miners throughout the nation questioned whether the UMW's centralized structure and national scope would ever be able to look after all miners' interests. Thousands formed their own local unions that rivaled the UMW. The Indiana miners' actions in the months after the 1891 strike cancellation, then, were part of an ongoing struggle between national officers and local laborers both inside and outside organized labor.

Closely examining the Indiana miners' grievances with UMW officers provides a useful means to understand when and why many rank-and-file laborers abandoned organized labor. These early UMW failures and mining families' responses to them reveal that union decline in the late nineteenth century was not always due to company hostility or worker disillusion with unions' ability to improve workplace conditions. It did not denote a waning faith in unionism at all but was a conscious effort to recommit the union to its own principles and create a union that fit with their needs and visions for their futures.

Misled

Over seventy thousand coal miners were supposed to strike on Friday, May 1, 1891. Instead, fewer than ten thousand struck, and most of that number went out by accident. Planned by the UMW national officers to initiate the eight-hour workday throughout the coal industry, the strike would be the first time all miners walked out in unison. For over a year, officers and organizers trumpeted the strike, promising that it would begin an aggressive campaign for fair treatment in the mines, increasing wages and improving work conditions. Despite months of campaigning and assurances of certain victory, however, UMW leaders called off the strike less than three days before it was to begin. As the officers explained in a circular sent to all locals, union membership was too low and too many miners had declared they would not honor the strike. Considering these factors, it was "impossible to unite the miners of the country in one solid phalanx for any given object of reform."[9]

Although abandoned, the UMW's planned movement was part of a larger push for political and economic reform across multiple industries. Throughout the nation, groups pushed for moral, civic, and economic reforms ranging from temperance to tax reform. Farmers in the South and Midwest, long frustrated with the economic conditions that slighted "producers," gradually built a movement that, by 1890, became a powerful force in several states. State and federal laws regulating workplace conditions and railroad practices and stronger laws against pluck-me stores suggested that the government was on the producers' side. As southern farmers worked to fight jute prices, the Farmers' Mutual Benefit Association along with midwestern Granges mobilized wheat farmers to stand against the "twine trust" that charged exorbitant prices for the string used to bind wheat.[10] After years of organizing, groups like the Knights of Labor and Farmers' Alliance forged farmer-laborer alliances to challenge railroads and monopolies.[11] By early 1891, producers planned to meet in Cincinnati to form a third political party that would reform the nation.[12] Meanwhile, the AFL made headway securing the eight-hour workday, helping the carpenters gain it in 1890 and planned to extend the push into other industries.[13]

The UMW added to this excitement when it formed in January 1890. After years of fighting, the miners' unions had finally united, creating one of the largest unions in the nation. Learning from failures, the new union's structure dissolved neither the NPU nor Knights' NTA 135. The UMW promised to smooth past differences between the two orders by creating a flexible framework that allowed Knights to remain over their local assemblies while the NPU miners followed the AFL. Both groups answered to the UMW's national executive board members, who were required to hold membership in both orders. This board made all decisions for the UMW, including which strikes the union would support and how much aid the strikers would receive. The officers and many of the rank and file believed the centralized power of the union would give it the strength to confront the competitive coal market, adding mine reform to the growing list of producer-led transformations at the end of the century. The UMW's decision to join the AFL's fight for the eight-hour workday only seemed to further confirm this promise that change would come soon.[14]

"I never so much regretted that the best half of my life is past as I do now, when I see what grand possibilities lie in the years to come," Laurene Gardner wrote excitedly. The forty-two-year-old miner wife had never been a union member herself but followed both labor and political issues closely. Her interest began at age thirteen with the American Miners' Association in the 1860s and continued when she married a coal miner and settled in southern Indiana. As she raised her three sons and two daughters, she watched miners' unions come and go, reading union proceedings "while rocking the cradle" of her children. She raised them "to take no mean place in the grand march of liberty to the worker." Gardner saw this as her duty, and she did it well. Her sons, she bragged, "have never been called blacklegs yet."[15]

For Gardner, a white woman who was both a part of, and apart from, political and labor movements all her life, the mobilization of the UMW and the Populists gave her hope for the future. But the enthusiasm Gardner expressed and successes she witnessed were short-lived. State after state became enmeshed in battles over the constitutionality and enforcement of their new workplace laws. Meanwhile, Populists failed to establish their third party at their 1891

Cincinnati convention. Worse, economic conditions continued to deteriorate for producers across the nation.[16]

Amid this decline, the UMW called off its nationwide strike. Known by the miners as "the first of May," this reversal stood in sharp contrast to what organizers had proclaimed only one week earlier. The miners, then, saw the aborted strike as more than evidence of the UMW's inability to look after miners' concerns. To them, it was proof that the officers had misled the rank and file by pushing a movement that failed *while* lying about union strength. In joining the union, miners had risked their jobs and sacrificed their pay for what the *New York Times* dubbed a "May Day fizzle," a movement that failed before it began.[17]

Those who were ready to strike expressed more outrage at the officers' misleading actions than at the union's abandonment of the eight-hour workday movement. Miners in Flagler, Iowa, expressed "great dissatisfaction" at the strike's cancellation. "We are open to confess the calling it off is something we don't really understand," they wrote, noting that the miners had voted in favor of the strike at the last national convention. In the minds of the Flagler miners, only a mass vote of delegates could countermand the strike call. "Thus the Executive Board would have no right to declare the demand off without very grave reasons," the miners reasoned.[18]

The problem was that UMW officers had explicitly announced that a May 1 victory was certain. The miners had not been alerted to any "grave" situations that caused the cancellation. To them, the change indicated that either the leaders were too cowardly to fight or were lying about their strength. "I believe there has been too darned much blowing and bluff indulged by the delegates to conventions which have been held during the past eighteen months," Indiana miner "M.F." complained. Officers, he and other miners reasoned, should have been more straightforward about the limits of the union's success prior to their eleventh-hour strike cancellation, but instead the *UMWJ* had proclaimed certain victory right up until the strike was canceled. "Are they all imbeciles, or are they all traitors?," M.F. asked of the UMW's national officers. For many miners, the answer to this question did not matter. The Flagler, Iowa, miners reasoned that the "Executive Board certainly should have known, if they did not know, the strength of this order previous to the last moment."[19] That the officers refused to acknowledge the true state of affairs, or at least hid them from the rank and file, seemed disingenuous and preyed on the hopes of miners who had paid into a cause that never came to fruition.

Miners throughout the nation demanded to know why the *UMWJ*'s early issues trumpeted the eight-hour rallying cry if defeat was so imminent. For many, the answer was that UMW officers used the official organ as a propaganda tool to boost worker faith in the movement without building actual strength. Indiana miner F. J. Llewellyn called such efforts "thunder" that, sounded threatening but never generated a true storm. Instead, it produced "a Don Quixotic effort" that only hurt the miners. "Truly a glory shared in by none except the authors and creators of the great U Mean Wind paper organization. What magnificent victories we have won—on paper! What grand things we shall do—in the future! But in the living present, what?" All the officers offered for the present were their continued orders for miners to accept reductions, Llewellyn fumed, "but do so with the mental reservation that in the fall we shall give them hell! Pah! Such advice makes one tired."[20] Leader William Scaife found that the miners in his home state of Illinois shared these views. Even after their 1889 defeat, they stood behind the new union, but the latest retreat was enough to "disgust the members and make them swear they will never belong to a national union."[21]

UMW vice president Phil Penna confirmed Scaife's assessment when he toured the northern Illinois coalfields in 1891. By then, the thirty-four-year-old was no novice to organizing. Born in England, Penna arrived in the United States in the early 1880s and settled in Linton, Indiana, where he began mining coal.[22] His fiery speeches and short temper for nonunion miners soon made "Little Phil" famous in the Indiana miners' unions and propelled him to national leadership when the UMW formed in 1890.[23] Penna had given thousands of speeches and organized hundreds of locals by the time he combed through the Illinois coalfields in the summer of 1891. Yet as he traveled from town to town, Little Phil discovered that even he could not fully persuade the miners to return to their union. Rather, he found that "miners have disbanded their locals in some instances, while nowhere could I find a place thoroughly organized." Instead of pride in unionism, he found "deep seated discontent" with the UMW's actions.[24]

Backsliding

Union leaders like Penna regarded the angry miners with contempt. If it were not for such "ilk there would be no need of an organization at all," the organizer wrote, indicating that the miners' worst enemies were not their employers, but their coworkers who claimed to support the union and then turned away. According to Indiana-Kentucky District president Michael Commesky, these "chronic kickers" no longer believed in the principles the UMW advocated. Instead, they opted to "sit like a gnat on a log" in union meetings and "preach[ed] their scabism to whoever will listen to them" when union victory came slowly. Their hostility toward the order, he argued, had hardened their hearts to organized labor's call. "When men make up their minds not to be converted they will always be sinners," he wrote.[25]

Commesky was not alone in his assertions. Other leaders and union affiliates, including many miners' wives, considered such behavior "backsliding," a term designed to shame the people it described.[26] Backsliders had once believed in the leaders' message but had fallen away. In this sense, the term *backslider* became a double insult. It acknowledged that those carrying the term did not behave in moral and respectable ways. This fact was made worse because the backsliders knew better. They sinned not out of ignorance but simply because they did not care to act morally. In short, while those who had never been converted were simply immoral, a backslider was an immoral traitor.[27]

Officers were not the only union affiliates who cried traitor in the months following the May cancellation. Thousands of miners who joined the UMW grew frustrated when the new union fell short in reaching its goals. Officers, they believed, had not only become less committed to regulating the national market, but even their limited efforts favored some groups of miners over others.

Miners did not have to look far for proof of this favoritism. Many miners complained that the UMW focused most of its attention on the Ohio and Pennsylvania coalfields at the expense of the other miners.[28] "A Beginner" miner from southern Illinois asserted that no UMW officer had even bothered to visit his mining region since they organized, causing the miners to wonder if they even had officers any longer.[29] It was a valid question for the southern Illinois miners to ask. Although they were technically members of the Miners' Federation when it merged into the NPU in 1888, no organizer notified them of the merger by telegram, letter, or visit until nearly five months later. According to Illinois labor leader William Scaife, such tendencies caused thousands of miners west of Ohio to believe "that our organization is an eastern one."[30]

The miners found additional proof for their suspicions in the executive board's own circular detailing the April 25 and 27 meetings when the officers decided to call off the strike.[31] Although the UMW had over one dozen active districts, only five district presidents attended the first day's meeting in Columbus, Ohio, to discuss the strike cancellation. Four of the five were from the Pennsylvania districts and the other was from Ohio. The board summoned Indiana and Illinois district presidents for the second day's meeting, but only the Illinois president arrived in time. After two days' debate, the six district presidents and the executive board decided to cancel the strike and send the UMW's May 1 strike fund to aid an ongoing strike in Pennsylvania coke mines.[32] The balance of the nation's miners would have to wait until the UMW was strong enough to fight on a larger scale.

Indiana

Southern Midwest miners were no strangers to weak unions, but by 1891 they were tired of their unions turning tail to the fight, especially when the union supported strikes in the East. This sentiment was particularly strong in the Indiana field. The block coal miners, who suffered through the 1889 strike with little support from the NPU or NTA 135, expressed no interest in joining the UMW when it formed one month after their 1889 strike failed. Even the bituminous miners who joined when the UMW formed were dissatisfied long before the 1891 summer. Their anger with the national officers began a year earlier when the officers failed to secure their desired wage scale with operators in May 1890. Although the Indiana bituminous miners were among the best organized in the nation and were ready to strike, the national officers ordered them to accept the terms, including a wage reduction.[33]

Jackson Hill Coal Mine No. 2, Sullivan County, n.d. Courtesy of the Coal Town and Railroad Museum, Clinton, Indiana.

The miners' frustration was offset with the promise of the May 1891 strike. National officers assured the miners in Indiana and elsewhere that the strike would bring fair wages along with the eight-hour workday. Consequently, when they learned the 1891 strike was canceled, Indiana miners were furious. But their anger was due not only to the UMW national leaders' reluctance to fight. The short notice of the May 1 strike cancellation prevented Indiana UMW officers from being notified of the cancellation, so thousands of Indiana union and nonunion miners walked out of the mines believing that miners in neighboring states had done the same. UMW Indiana-Kentucky district secretary John H. Kennedy was as shocked as the miners when he heard that the national UMW office had canceled the strike: "I may say right here that the officers, as well as the organized miners of this state, were in favor of the move for eight hours and I fear the change of policy will be a great drawback in perfecting the organization in District 11."[34] Kennedy's assessment proved true. A week later, most Indiana mines remained at a standstill not because miners were striking for the eight-hour day, but because operators had imposed another wage reduction on the miners' return.[35] "The miners of this portion of Indiana were prepared for an honorable defeat, but not a dishonorable retreat, and we have been both and not a blow struck!" exclaimed F. J. Llewellyn.[36] The miners, he insisted, were accustomed to fighting losing battles for a just cause, but to be abandoned by the union hours before the scheduled strike felt like betrayal. The UMW had left the Indiana miners at the operators' mercy as other states' coal filled their contracts.[37]

Despite the miners' defeat and anger at what they saw as the UMW officers' abandonment of the cause, few Indiana union miners abandoned the UMW because of it. They remained in the union but stopped paying their union dues. Actions like this were often a way for miners to show their disdain for union decisions contrary to their interests. Organizer Tim O'Malley, for example, observed that two Knights of Labor miners' assemblies refused to pay dues to NTA 135 in 1887 but continued to support the Knights' General Assembly.[38] In instances such as this, decisions to not support specific union levels or branches spoke volumes to organizations that continually operated on small budgets, making dissatisfaction abundantly clear to union officials.[39]

Officers repeatedly encountered this sentiment in the weeks following the First of May as they traveled the coalfields to assuage miners' frustration with the cancellation. "The month just gone has been one of disappointment and trouble," reported Ohio organizer W. C. Pearce in June 1891. They "are wanting something unreasonable out of the organization," he wrote frustratedly. "In almost every mining locality in Ohio there has been more or less kicking and fault-finding regarding the settlement of the 1st of May. . . . Every day letters are received stating men will not pay their dues until some of the [national] officers come and explain the present conditions." Ohio organizer and national executive board member Richard L. Davis confessed that only two-thirds of his district's union men paid their dues. "The others refuse and some of them say that no matter [what] they will not pay another cent to anything. They say they have paid and paid and have never reaped any benefit and it is impossible for any one to try to show them any good that has been done." UMW vice president Phil Penna found similar conditions when he toured Illinois that summer. Local unions and assemblies there unabashedly told the national officer that they "will oppose sending another cent to the national while the present executive board have control."[40]

Although no monthly detailed national dues receipts from the UMW's early years have survived, Indiana-Kentucky district secretary Kennedy's meticulous weekly reports, which included the amounts the district received from each local, offer a window into miner dedication to the UMW. Because Kennedy was the only union organizer who printed his receipts regularly, it is impossible to compare his totals to other regions. Still, because organizer reports of locals' sentiments were similar throughout the coalfields, it is likely that other district secretaries experienced similar resistance to dues payments from their locals, even if they did not regularly report their dues payments.[41]

In the months prior to the strike, Kennedy's dues totals often ranged between $20 and $90 each week, with the highest amounts collected between March 28 and April 30, corresponding with anticipation for the May strike. This pattern changed in the weeks following May 1. In the first three weeks following the strike cancellation, state dues declined slightly compared to weeks prior, hovering at roughly $40 each week, within the range typical for reports prior to the strike. But by June 4, Kennedy reported only $8.20 for the previous week. In fact, the secretary's receipts for the entire month of June only totaled $70.50, far below the dues received just weeks earlier.[42]

The decline in dues payments for Indiana was likely due to a number of reasons. Some Indiana miners, like the miners the other organizers encountered, were disillusioned by the strike cancellation. Others, however, likely simply stopped paying dues because they were still on strike. Kennedy's reports confirm this trend: miners resumed paying union dues after their summer strikes ended in failure. In fact, Kennedy's receipts for July 1891 showed an *increase* in union dues that surpassed those collected even in the weeks leading up to May 1. If union decline was primarily due to worker disillusion with union strength or ability, Kennedy's dues should have plummeted and not recovered after most

Indiana miners' strikes had failed. Other district officer reports from this period suggest that similar sentiments existed elsewhere as well. The miners were frustrated with the UMW failure and cursed the national officers, but they still saw merit in the organization.[43]

Misplaced Faith

Few miners communicated this sentiment more than those in the Indiana block mines. They had no interest in joining the UMW when it formed and were not members during the May 1 strike cancellation. But lack of membership did not mean the miners rejected union sentiment. Instead, the nonunion block men joined the thousands of Indiana bituminous miners in what they thought was a nationwide strike. Moreover, when the strike failed, the miners did not become disillusioned with unionism. Even though, as block district organizer Samuel Anderson explained, they had "not much faith" in the new union, over 150 miners in Knightsville alone decided to "give it a fair trial" by becoming UMW members for the first time.[44]

The Clay County miners' willingness to join the UMW after a substantial defeat demonstrated that neither low union strength nor the miners' lack of faith in the union was enough to dissuade workers from joining a union. But this did not mean that the new members trusted the union or its officers. Their skepticism came from their long-standing frustrations with larger unions overlooking block district concerns. "Nearly half of the miners of this state are in this county," Anderson complained, but their coal was of a different quality and was mined and priced differently from the coal in the national bituminous market. As a result, block miners paid the same dues as bituminous miners but found that block coal concerns were rarely addressed in the state or national union agendas.[45]

Block miners grew particularly frustrated with the national defense fund. All union miners were expected to contribute to the fund to be used as aid for striking or locked out miners. Unlike past funds, which were controlled by local and state unions, the UMW National Executive Board held sole discretion over how the defense fund was spent. In the weeks following the 1891 cancellation, the board made this authority clear in a circular declaring that "not a cent shall leave the defense fund, during our tenure of office, which is not warranted by a strict compliance with the constitution." The centralization of the funds, much like the centralization of union authority, was supposed to increase union efficiency and curtail strikes until the board deemed the union strong enough to win.[46] Yet in 1891, it seemed that the UMW gave little aid to mines outside

Pennsylvania. For miners who were accustomed to using such funds to help aid local miners who had fallen on hard times due to accident or illness, not having access to aid after loyally paying money into the fund seemed unfair, especially when a distant region reaped all the benefit. "Our most intelligent members began to ask, 'What are [the national officers] doing with the defense fund?'" When Anderson and the other leaders replied that they did not know, "a quiet smile could be seen on some faces and that was the last of them." The miners understood that they would never see the money again.[47]

Despite Anderson's effort to revive faith in the union, the miners wanted nothing of it. "We called two delegate meetings and one mass meeting to discuss the propriety of thorough organization," he recalled. "These were failures." Consequently, as Phil Penna and the other national officers decried the union miners' who "kicked" against the UMW and "backslid" away from it, Anderson, like other local organizers, insisted that it was not the miners who backslid. Instead, Anderson wanted the nation's miners to understand that the Clay County men were neither "dupes" fooled by their employers nor "sinners" who had backslid from the union. "There are as intelligent and good union men here as there are anywhere," he insisted. The union, not the miners, had turned away from honest principles. Although the national market meant that the miners were now competing against other regions, many in the block field believed that a local union would protect their interests better than the UMW. "I believe that when we started to organize we made a grand mistake, for if, instead of sending away our money for taxes without receiving one particle of benefit in return, we had put every cent of money we subscribed into a [local] fund to thoroughly organize Clay county, we then ourselves could have removed the many local hardships we have to labor under and could have joined issues with [the bituminous miners] on a sound basis."[48]

Anderson's anger was echoed throughout the state when the UMW issued its fall 1891 orders for the Indiana miners to reduce wages. Rather than earning 75 cents per ton as expected during winter months, block miner John Mooney and his coworkers—at UMW orders—now earned only 45½ cents. The officers' decision, Mooney asserted, "is as dishonest and false as the system that it is based on. It is impossible to establish a common measure of prices that will do justice to the coal miner." But there was nothing the miners could do. "We cannot fight the men, the operators and the organization."[49]

Frustration turned to hostility when ten thousand miners in western Pennsylvania went on strike for higher wages that fall. The UMW did not order this strike, but because the national officers wished to maintain a unified front, they ordered all miners to lend their support to the Pennsylvania miners.[50] The

Indiana miners were outraged, Mooney explained, because the same officers "gave their aid and sanction to the Pittsburg[h] [Pennsylvania] miners to demand 13 cents per ton above scale rates, and they condemn the miners of Indiana when we are justified in forcing the operators of this state to pay scale rates."[51] In short, the national officers had ordered Indiana miners not only to work at a reduction, but to send aid to miners striking for wages nearly 25 cents per ton higher than what Indiana miners earned.[52] Within days, Indiana miners and officers planned a strike of their own. Their appeal reached the executive board just as the Pennsylvania strike ended in defeat. Facing an exhausted national treasury, National Secretary Patrick McBryde sent the telegram that stunned the Indiana miners. UMW Indiana-Kentucky district secretary John Kennedy rejected McBryde's orders to accept the reduced wage. Siding with the Indiana miners, Kennedy rebelled against UMW commands and ordered all Indiana miners to strike.[53]

It was not in Kennedy's character to disregard orders. Born around 1847 in Scotland, Kennedy moved with his parents to Indiana and began mining at age nine.[54] When he turned seventeen, he enlisted in the Union Army, serving the final months of the Civil War. After briefly returning to the mines at war's end, he reenlisted and served for another twelve years, during which he learned how to read and write. He worked for several years in the Texas coal mines before returning to Indiana, settling in Terre Haute. There, Kennedy began organizing under the Knights of Labor in the 1880s, becoming secretary-treasurer of the Indiana District of NTA 135. When the NPU formed in 1888, he was among the handful of Knights officers to join the new order, where he later assumed the secretary-treasurer position for the Indiana NPU.[55]

Kennedy did not gain these positions through his personality. Unlike most organizers known for their gregarious behavior and charisma, Kennedy was painfully shy, detested public speaking, and often avoided large union meetings. Described as "taciturn" and "morose," the slight man rarely socialized, even during union conventions, where he knew the other organizers well. Still, none could deny that Kennedy was "amongst the most persistent [UMW] organizers that we have ever had." Rather than relying on oratory or grace, Kennedy organized locals by writing letters to anyone interested in unionizing, opting to meet with interested parties only when essential. Even then, Indiana organizer John Kane later wrote, "when a visit is deemed necessary by him, he makes it, and many a time he has [arrived] and gone before anybody knows it."[56]

Despite this, both miners and union officials respected Kennedy. Forceful, with a tireless work ethic and meticulous attention to detail, he applied his military discipline to unionizing. Kennedy diligently reported district news and receipts of dues to the labor papers each week, far more frequently than any other UMW officer in the nation. His efforts and dedication earned him the admiration of union miners throughout the state. During a period when miners were constantly dissatisfied with union leaders and regularly turned them out of office, Kennedy held the Indiana district secretary-treasurer position for over ten years.[57]

No miner or UMW officer doubted Kennedy's loyalty to the union. Yet, in November 1891, Kennedy condemned the organization and its national officers and ordered the Indiana miners to strike. "We are sorry we have to act in opposition to the wishes of our national officers," he wrote in his weekly report announcing the strike, "but we have been sidetracked so often that patience ceased to be a virtue." Kennedy's carefully selected words resonated throughout the state, where miners believed the officers no longer cared for their interests.[58]

The UMW's difficulty distributing strike aid seemed to confirm these suspicions. Although most of the mines who joined the Indiana strike in the fall of 1891 ultimately failed, several mines initially earned their demanded pay increase. As directed by state officers, they forwarded their pay increases to the state treasury to be sent to aid the remaining striking miners. However, because the Indiana mines were so spread out, the miners' aid took days to reach the state officers and even longer to distribute the funds. In the meantime, striking miners wrote letters to the *UMWJ* complaining that they received no aid. Seven weeks into the Indiana strike, for example, "Summit Miner" asked in the journal, "What has become of those men that received the advance six weeks ago and were going to donate us 5 cents per ton for all coal mined and day men in proportion. If we are defeated and have to blackleg are we worse than they?"[59]

For the miners who had already sent their pay advance forward to the officers, letters like Summit Miner's came as a shock. By the time they read the letters, which took roughly a week to appear in the *UMWJ* columns and equally as long for the newspaper to reach the rural mines, their aid had long been sent. Consequently, although Kennedy accounted for the donations, it appeared as though the funds were entirely mismanaged.[60] To the strikers, it seemed that the miners who won the pay advance had abandoned them. To the donating miners, it appeared as though the officers misplaced or stole the money.[61] "If this aid did not reach the men needing aid, what became of it?," asked miner wife Laurene Gardner in response to a claim by UMW vice president Phil Penna that her mining town did not pay the aid they were required to send. "We disclaim owing the striking miners or anybody else anything more than the assistance due one brother from another. In all my knowledge of Ayrshire we have never asked or received either assistance or encouragement from anyone," she argued.

"Yet if our striking brothers need more help we stand ready to give it."[62] Union miners, in her mind, were bound by the principles they shared, not by officer commands.

Gardner's statement indicated the disconnect that ran through much of the labor movement and nineteenth-century society. On one hand, Gardner and others understood and appreciated the need for centralized governing authorities over both union and governmental affairs. Their national structure was essential in an age where businesses and people continually crossed state and national borders. Those affiliated with the People's Party found government regulation of railroads and coal mines essential to establishing regulated rates that, they believed, would benefit both worker and consumer. At the same time, this uniformity also cost residents and local unions their autonomy. It placed their money and futures in the hands of individuals who often lived hundreds of miles from the mines and fields. Centralized boards' actions seemed especially disconnected from rural residents who often remained outside the reach of timely and reliable communication. In instances like the missing telegram canceling the May 1891 strike or the delayed reports of aid the following fall, the communication gap had a detrimental impact on workers' lives and their faith in governing structures. Even those who climbed the union ranks, such as Kennedy, earned their livings through clerical work and politics rather than sweat and muscle like the people they represented.[63] Consequently, placing these leaders in a centralized structure that gave them increased control over union finances and affairs prompted miners to mistrust their leadership even more. In the heat of Indiana's missing aid ordeal, Kennedy reported that he encountered miners who praised the UMW yet "in the same breath" claimed "that dishonesty has been practiced by the state officers in distributing the funds." Miners believed in the ideal of unionism but feared the process of unionism had been corrupted.[64]

Surveying the damage of the 1891 strike cancellation and subsequent failed local strikes, Indiana-Kentucky district president Michael Commesky noted that miners in his district, as well as neighboring districts, viewed the UMW officers with contempt: "At this date I cannot say what effect the strike will have on the organization, but we hope for the best." Despite his attempt at optimism, however, Commesky had his doubts. Instead of closing his letter with his characteristic call for organization or the frequently used "yours for the cause," the union leader ended with "yours for the present," hinting that the future of the organization or at least *his* future in it was uncertain.[65]

Kennedy's dues receipts indicate that Commesky had cause for concern. The union miners faithfully paid dues through the 1891 fall. In fact, by November

1891, the same month the miners struck against UMW orders, Kennedy's receipts totaled $283, a larger amount than had ever been collected prior to the May cancellation. The UMW's condemnation of the Indiana strike, insults against the miners, and the Indiana miners' subsequent failure, however, proved detrimental to the Indiana UMW. The number of locals paying dues fell drastically so that most of the $85 in dues Kennedy reported in early 1892 came from five locals.

The decline, however, was not confined to Indiana. The hostilities and misgivings the Indiana miners expressed paralleled miners' unease throughout the country.[66] Miners and organizers across the nation claimed their experiences with UMW leadership decisions were similar to those of the Indiana miners.[67] The *Bloomington (IL) Daily Pantagraph* reported that faith in the UMW was so low that only fifteen members attended the Illinois District's 1892 convention, and that most of the northern Illinois mines had "withdrawn from the union."[68] "Napoleon" of Iowa observed that if Ohio and Indiana, the "great union states" of the nation, could not function, there was little hope for other regions to avoid such "tomfoolery."[69] The Indiana miners' winter strike became symptomatic of larger problems and misgivings already spreading throughout the UMW rank and file, regardless of region.

The officers' perceived inability to safeguard the miners' interest caused even the most dedicated union families to voice frustration with the UMW. Although Laurene Gardner professed to be a faithful UMW supporter, she was among the first to take up her pen and question the officers' decisions. She had "faith in at least their good intentions," she wrote, "but we know how disastrously they turn out sometimes."[70] For her town of Ayrshire, Indiana, the result was especially disastrous. Mines like the one in Ayrshire that had won the pay advance in their fall 1891 strike were forced to either resume work at the reduced wages or risk the mine shutting down entirely when the strike elsewhere ended in defeat. Ayrshire shut down.[71] Partially locked out and partially on strike against a reduction even lower than what they had originally fought, the Ayrshire miners who had donated their pay to the striking miners just weeks earlier now looked to the UMW for aid. Their strike, however, was not sanctioned by the executive board and therefore was not entitled to a share of the UMW strike fund.[72]

Furious with the UMW officers for demanding Ayrshire pay the union in return for nothing, Laurene Gardner chastised the UMW leadership and practices. "I offer no apology for any suggestions or remarks I may make in these lines," the miner's wife began. With that, she demanded an account of the national executive board and Indiana state board's spending. "Commencing with Ayrshire, how much money has been paid into the treasury and what has become of it? I mean since the United Mine Workers was organized here," she demanded. To Gardner and many others, it seemed "that part of the business is but poorly managed." The UMW's rejection of the miners' need and the inability of miners elsewhere to send adequate aid made this abundantly clear. National officers, it seemed, simply were not capable of handling the miners' funds responsibly. As a result, Gardner joined the chorus of miners throughout the nation who adamantly opposed the "national defense fund." UMW locals should control their own funds, she argued, "instead of sending it out like bread upon the water without even the assurance that it will return again after many days."[73]

Gardner's assertions were repeated in mining regions throughout the state in the weeks following the strike. Although miners liked the idea of a nationally unified body, they did not appreciate needing the approval of the executive board when they wanted to draw on the funds they contributed. Their frustrations, then, lay with the union's distribution of power and its efficiency, not its ideals. Indiana miner John A. Templeton made such an observation when he assessed why the once-solid unions in his region had fractured over the officers' actions in the late 1891 strike. The winter strike failure had "given the organization a blow from which it will not get over for some time," Templeton acknowledged, but miners were more ambivalent about union structures than opposed to them. According to Templeton, "the men are badly split up at Dugger [Indiana], some of them wanting to hold on to the U. M. W. of A. and another lot wanting a local organization and some want no organization at all."[74]

Within weeks, Dugger miners' membership in the "home organization" known by locals as the Nickel Knights grew. According to miner "Dogtown," the Nickel Knights originally formed as the Independent Order of Home Mine Laborers in Washington, Indiana, where miners were upset with the high dues paid to state and national officers without receiving any benefit.[75] Their nickname in part nodded to the principles emphasized in the Knights of Labor. According to Dogtown, the "Nickel" portion of their title came from the five cents the members paid in dues each meeting night, which were kept at home for expenses and local cases of sickness or strike, and not dependent on the sanction of a distant board of officers. Although the miners in the home organization did not seek to organize other locals under their name, the idea quickly spread to nearby mines so that, at least around Dugger, "any organization outside the United Mine Workers has been termed nickel knights."[76]

Dugger UMW leader John E. Griffiths claimed he knew nothing of the order but admitted that many local miners had been dissatisfied with the UMW ever since the strike.[77] Ironically, the locals had sided with the national officers in opposing the winter strike, arguing that the state officers' strike order "was premature and ignore[ed] the fundamental principles of our organization." With their argument dismissed at the state convention, Dugger miners honored the state officers' strike call. Within weeks, however, "a number of men got dissatisfied with the amount of aid received from [the] defense fund and openly declared they would pay nothing into the organization . . . and that feeling grew during the strike until it looked as if organization in Dugger was a thing of the past." Dugger miners "got luke warm" and pulled away from the UMW, unwilling to be part of a body whose individual parts did not cooperate.[78]

UMW organizers, however, viewed such actions with contempt. Phil Penna described the Nickel Knights as "Nauseating Knaves." They were not men, he insisted, but "specimens of which we have everywhere," who had no sense to stay in the union or uphold its principles. The Nickel Knights were "Judases who have sold their manhood" to the company, T. J. Llewelyn argued. According to miner wife Sinthy Snodgrass and many others, most were "pumpkin rollers," or farmers who mined for supplemental incomes and cared little about the trouble they caused. John Kennedy agreed, stressing that he hoped the Nickel Knights would "abandon their evil ways and return to their proper place in the United Mine Worker's [sic] of America."[79] Nickel Knights, they believed, were the backsliders at the heart of the UMW's impotency.

UMW leaders may have seen their organization as an innocent victim, but not all UMW affiliates held the UMW in such high regard. Laurene Gardner first encountered the Nickel Knights when her family was forced to leave their home in Ayrshire and search for work in the mines surrounding Dugger and Linton. Her experiences during the Ayrshire strike, like those who joined the Nickel Knights, caused her to question the UMW leaders' abilities. Although Gardner remained committed to the UMW and vehemently criticized the Nickel Knights, she did not defend the UMW's actions of the past year. She neither claimed those who joined the local organization were backsliders who abandoned their beliefs nor dismissed the Nickel Knights' grievances against the UMW as unjust. Instead, she criticized their methods. "It is a poor way to correct any evil in the organization to pull out," she wrote. In condemning the Nickel Knights this way, Gardner indicated that the true evil was not the rebellious miners, but the organization itself. The Nickel Knights' fault, in Gardner's eyes, then, rested not with any kind of abandonment of principles, but with their unwillingness to run the perceived evil out of the miners' national organization.[80]

Such assertions that evil lurked within the UMW resonated throughout the district. Indiana block miner and mine operator "Old Timer," claimed that the block miners backslid from their principles not when they decided to leave the UMW, but when they first decided to join it. Their decision to reject the UMW and form their own local, then, reflected a return to the principles they once abandoned. "We wandered off to follow strange gods; were led into the wilderness and there left to perish; but thank God, we are coming to our senses again and I expect soon to see our craft in this district organized into a solid block coal union," he declared. Secretary-Treasurer Kennedy's reports confirm that hundreds of block miners shared Old Timer's sentiments. Of the two thousand miners in the once thoroughly organized block district, only a hundred remained in the UMW by April 1892, yet the miners in the district were still sufficiently united to negotiate a contract with the operators.[81]

Old Timer and others defended their rights and principles by *leaving* the UMW rather than joining it. Thousands of miners like Old Timer and the Nickel Knights believed that local unions had a better chance of favorable work terms than the union that struggled to control the national market. Nickel Knights and other "home organizations" settled all disputes with the companies directly rather than waiting for UMW officials to mitigate differences. This proved beneficial for several reasons. First, it allowed workers to settle disputes and return to work quickly. In addition, operators, seeking to keep a national union out of their mines, often granted local organization miners' requests more than those of the UMW miners.[82]

These factors, combined with the miners' growing frustration and mistrust of UMW leaders, caused state and local organizations that rivaled the UMW to spring up across the nation. Northern Illinois organizer Will Hall described a mass meeting in Streator at which miners resolved that a national union was not reliable. With that, they decided "to form a local union, attached to nothing or nobody."[83] Pennsylvania miner M. J. O'Neil described similar sentiments in his own district. "I am not in any organization at present, neither are the miners of this run," he confessed, adding that the miners "one and all have become disgusted even at the word organization."[84] Within months, miners in O'Neil's district planned to establish a new regional union covering the mines along the Monongahela, Ohio, and Kanawha Rivers.[85] UMW miners in Ohio debated seceding from the UMW, leading the movement to return to state-based organizations.[86] These sentiments reached to the South and Midwest, where miners *did* form new state organizations that October. Five thousand Alabama miners joined the United Mine Workers of Alabama, a new state organization that refused to affiliate with the UMW.[87] That same month, Iowa miners founded their own state organization, while Missouri and Kansas union miners considered organizing two "national" unions, one representing the mines east of the Mississippi River and the other with jurisdiction over the west.[88] Although they had pushed for a unified national order for years, by 1893, that structure and scope no longer seemed ideal.

Far from being committed to the national and centralized structure, miners looked at the UMW's shortcomings and suspected that, somehow, miners' organization had gone astray. "It is the most trying time I have seen in my life," western Kentucky miner "Blackbird" confessed. He claimed that most of the miners in his district had abandoned the UMW while those that remained had no money in the union's treasury and made little effort to connect to the national officers. Operators took advantage of the union's weakness and abolished all mine rules that kept miners safe.[89] Blackbird was exasperated. "I have done and am doing my best to lead a christian life and to stand by our organization and lead others to it, but they will not." The miners recognized they needed to restore their union but refused to revive their UMW. Instead, they organized on their own. "It troubles me to see men go astray like this," Blackbird continued. In his mind, neither UMW miners nor their officers had remained faithful to the UMW. "I sometimes feel like exclaiming my God! where are we drifting to?"[90]

Blackbird's question was an old one that touched the heart of many Americans' deepest concerns. From the time the nation began to industrialize, many citizens expressed anxieties over the concentration of wealth and power in the hands of a few and the greed, corruption, and moral decay that seemed to follow in its wake. "Whither are we drifting?" became as much a warning as a question in reaction to the rapid changes in economics, society, and culture. Freeman Otis Willey popularized the phrase in a book that pointed out how the United States had gone astray. While the country was founded upon making moral decisions for humanity, he wrote, complacency had let selfishness and greed steer the nation off course. Inequality ran rampant, leading to injustice, and lack of freedom, which would only grow worse if left unchecked, Willey argued. This idea of good entities drifting astray resonated in the coalfields. It inspired miners like Blackbird to apply this idea to his peers, but it also gave miners and wives a way to voice their frustrations with the structures that, though claiming to support freedom and equality, had drifted away from those goals. "Inquire a little more into the question, 'Wither are we drifting, as a nation,'" miner wife Margery Jones wrote. The United States was not a desirable place to live "if in a land like this, blessed as it is with a keen, discreet and enterprising population, the perversity, avarice greed and selfishness of man is to succeed in subverting liberty and independence except to those who by the most diabolical schemes have possessed themselves of nations wealth and opportunities." To Jones, Blackbird, and others like them, society had shifted its priorities and it seemed that no one was interested in honest work, or helping the honest worker.[91]

In a period when worker justice seemed to fade, such concerns reached into nearly all reform movements of the period. It caused workers to question whether leaders were holding fast to the cause or if they had grown complacent in upholding these goals. Increasingly, groups of members within all orders clamored for their organizations to focus on action in politics as well as the workplace. Although ideas of voluntarism circulated through the ranks of organizations like the AFL, the majority of workers, both inside and outside the unions, had little use for such rigid policy. Those who remained outside the union did not abide by "pure and simple unionism" ideals. Many of those in the union joined because it offered the best means to secure their goals and believed that unions should do all within their power to affect change, including enter politics. Labor organizations' reluctance to enter partisan politics, for many workers, was a sign that leaders had drifted away from the cause of doing everything within their power to benefit the worker.[92] But, even political organizations seemed to go astray. Just as union miners divided over whether local, state, or national unions could best protect their interests, neither midwestern workers nor their farming counterparts could fully agree on a political party or agenda. The few Populist proponents, though convinced that the nation had gone adrift, remained split over whether a third party was the best way to steer the country back on course. Like thousands of the nation's miners and the new union, they refused to fully commit to any political body, even if they sympathized with its stance.[93]

Such confusion over who was faithful to the cause and who had gone astray also applied to major labor organizations like the Knights of Labor and the AFL. As the UMW licked its wounds from the 1891 failure, its officers began to see larger implications that the aborted strike had on organized labor as a whole. The Knights and AFL had forged a shaky alliance uniting miners' national unions into a single order, but the UMW's retreat from the AFL's eight-hour fight threatened to upset relations on both ends. In a public interview and a subsequent circular, AFL president Samuel Gompers claimed the cancellation was due to the Knights of Labor's unwillingness to support it. Knights of Labor general master workman Terence Powderly, Gompers claimed, "has been strutting before the wage-workers of the country" for too long. The failed strike was proof that, eventually, "the mask of hypocrisy . . . will be torn from his face." In turn, Powderly and his fellow Knights leaders retorted that Gompers was nothing more than a demagogue bullying the nation's workers to strike when they were not ready. They claimed that, in his treks across the country assuring workers victory was certain if they would only strike, Gompers misrepresented the strength of the movement, especially since neither the Knights nor the AFL had enough funds to support all the strikers. Such "reckless disregard" for the miners' welfare, the Knights claimed, was the hallmark of Gompers and the AFL. The UMW's misfortune had become fodder in an ongoing war between labor organizations, both using it as proof that the other was not committed to the workers' interests.[94]

The UMW officers responded with outrage. In a *UMWJ* editorial, the officers insisted they acted alone, rather than at the will of Gompers or Powderly, and ordered the vying leaders to "attend to the business of your organizations," or in the very least, "for goodness sake don't make the United Mine Workers the medium of exchange." In forming the UMW, the miners had put the Knights-AFL debate to rest, officers argued, and the "mud slinging" between the two organizations threatened to reopen old wounds.[95] "We are like a man with two wives, said wives having legions of relatives. And strange as it may seem this plurality of wives is a barrier against the displeasure of the husband to either of his spouses," Indiana organizer John Kane wrote. Both orders charged the UMW with "the blackest lie" that the UMW was guilty of "favoring and befriending one [organization] to the detriment of the other." This "spirit of antagonism," Kane feared, would only allow the two orders to drift further apart, rending the UMW in two once again.[96]

Despite the UMW officers' requests, however, hostilities only intensified as UMW membership declined. NTA 135 delegates to the 1892 General Assembly of the Knights of Labor were shocked to hear Powderly condemn the mine workers' union, claiming it had drifted away from the Knights' driving principles. Based on a report given to him by Knights' general secretary John Hayes, Powderly stated that the UMW favored the AFL at the expense of the Knights, that the miners had stopped paying dues to the Knights, and that their willingness to set a wage scale rather than abolish the wage system contradicted the ideals the Knights professed. With that, Powderly ordered an investigation into the UMW with the added suggestion that NTA 135 withdraw from the UMW and restore the miners' union to its original goals.[97]

For miners who already questioned where their dues went when they paid them to national officers, Powderly's claims only added to worker doubts regarding UMW leader propriety. Although L. V. Deloche of Ohio was sorry to hear Powderly rebuke the UMW, he wrote that "I am now glad" that the master workman was so harsh, "for it will perhaps be the means of bringing some members of the Knights of Labor and United Mine Workers of America to a sense of duty, for surely some must have been neglecting them, or the general master workman would have had no occasion to mention the matter." If the UMW truly was adrift, this, he believed, would allow the officials to "live up to the agreements made at Columbus" when the UMW was formed.[98]

But living up to the goals outlined at Columbus in 1890 proved even more difficult than smoothing differences between warring unions. The Knights and

AFL were not the only threats to the UMW's national identity or scope. Success hinged on the miners seeing the order as an organization for their interests so they would join and follow the orders issued by organizational leadership. President and Master Workman John Rae described this in his final convention report. Noting the numerous local strikes called against national leaders' orders and the dozens of anti-UMW locals, he asserted, "it is plain that while our miners cry for national organization, they continue to practice local methods."[99] For Rae, who tried to uphold the union's national scope while appeasing local interests, this duality cost him supporters on both sides of the UMW divide.

Just as miners favoring local autonomy criticized Rae for not fully supporting them, miners who supported a strong centralized union condemned Rae for tolerating miners who disregarded national orders. The 1892 UMW convention sided with national leaders in their decisions to not support the winter strikes in Pittsburgh and Indiana and insisted "stricter methods must be adopted" in enforcing national authority over the mining districts.[100] Rae's leniency, Tim O'Malley and others believed, created "the criminal blunders of last year." The miners "like to be tickled with taffy occasionally," O'Malley wrote, but as much as they liked flattery, they also wanted a firm hand at the helm of their organization. Rae may have tried his best to keep the peace in the UMW, but "in their hearts [the miners] despise him, and admire the man who has convictions and the courage to express them, even if it does not suit them at the time."[101] Recognizing Rae's difficult position, Illinois leader William Scaife expressed sympathy for the leader that, he noted, could not act without the support of a unified rank and file. "These have been troublesome times," he wrote as he surveyed the events of the past year, "and it has been another case of damn you if you do and damn you if you don't. With Brother Rae, no matter what he done, he was certain to be damned."[102]

As Rae's predicament demonstrated, defending rights, even for unions, proved difficult. Establishing a centralized national organization that looked after specific regional concerns demanded more manpower and better communication than the young UMW could provide. It involved bringing together disparate groups across a vast region, and in most cases, it demanded sacrificing the needs of some for the good of the whole. For miners who looked to the UMW for salvation from workplace ills, Rae was not a casualty of the strike cancellation; instead, his overstatement of union strength and his inability to tend to all miners' concerns damned him in the miners' eyes. These actions, combined with those of the other officers, tainted miners' trust for the entire order. By January 1893, membership in the three-year-old union had tumbled to barely twenty thousand members and continued to fall.[103]

Far from a solidified force, union miners' criticisms of leaders were part of a battle over how to stop organized labor from drifting away from its original purpose of protecting the laborer. For some, this task required forming new unions while still others believed that the surest way a miner could look after his interests was to stay out of unions entirely until one was strong enough to uphold its principles. Although officers dismissed these varying views as an abandonment of union principles, mining families disagreed. Their dedication to unionism never waned, but they believed UMW officers' devotion to the union had.

CHAPTER FOUR

Outsiders

Race and the Exclusive Politics of an Inclusive Union, 1892–1894

Fewer than fifty miles of rugged countryside separated the miner "Willing Hands" and miner wife Laurene Gardner of Indiana. In many respects, their backgrounds were very similar. Both were deeply connected to the coal industry, originally from the Upper South, and both had moved north to the Indiana coalfields. They were ardent Populists and were two of the UMW's strongest advocates during a period when rank-and-file discontent with UMW action and policy was widespread.

Despite their advocacy, however, neither Willing Hands nor Gardner fully fit with the miners' union and their relationship to the UMW reflected how lines in late nineteenth-century unionism contorted to simultaneously include and exclude the same individual. Gardner, a white woman, was neither a coal miner nor union member, but she and her "fellow craftsmen" considered her a part of the UMW. Willing Hands, a black miner, *was* a UMW member but wrote repeatedly that he was excluded from the UMW's main body.

Coming of age in the southern coal mines, Willing Hands knew that race and class issues were deeply entwined.[1] Fears of corporate and political corruption, increasing wealth gaps, and poverty were interwoven with lynching, convict labor, and Jim Crow. He watched in horror as racial hostilities intensified throughout the nation, including the coal mines. Like thousands of producers, Willing Hands maintained that slavery still existed, but the enslavement he witnessed involved more than poor treatment and low wages. It involved literal chains, forced labor, segregation in mines, railroads, and coal cars that were all fortified by the growing power of "the lynching club of the South." Consequently, when miners began discussing the best course for the UMW to revive its dwindling membership, Willing Hands vehemently argued that the UMW needed to defend black miners instead of neglecting them. "You can never get your union strong as long as you ignore the Afro-American as a coal producer against you," he challenged.[2] Arguing that the UMW only stood to gain by speaking out against convict labor and other Jim Crow–related systems practiced in and around the mines, Willing Hands expected the UMW to fight for racial equality in addition to economic justice. When it fell short, he and thousands like him asserted that the UMW offered the nation's black coal miners little more than membership.[3]

Not all agreed with his forceful stance. "I notice our friend 'Willing Hands' seems much troubled about the interests of his race," Gardner noted in her weekly letter to the *UMWJ*. A white miner's wife born on the Illinois-Kentucky border in 1850, Gardner believed that the economic inequality all miners faced should be the UMW's focus, not questions of racism. Her effort to promote unity over racial equality echoed white conversations taking place throughout the nation. As citizens voiced concern over the nation's fragility and expressed fears of another civil war, laborers, wives, and union officers expressed similar alarm with the disasters within organized labor. By 1892, employer and government hostility to labor, combined with major strike losses, rattled union foundations across the board, including the young coal miners' union. Gardner, like many white union miners, wanted to maintain the fragile unity the young UMW had built. "No side issue, race creed, sectionalism or anything else should divert attention from the common doom of slavery that is hanging over us all," she later declared.[4] If the miners could pull together and secure better conditions, justice and equality for black miners would follow, she and other whites believed, but they thought the key was to stand united on their common ground. Consequently, much like the northern and southern reconciliation that came at the expense of African Americans, the UMW, in a similar quest for unity, eclipsed these questions as well.[5] "We have seen the results of divided action in the last year's record of local troubles," she wrote. "Not until the order will move as one harmonious whole will victory crown our efforts."[6]

The discussion involving a black miner and a white miner's wife in the pages of the *UMWJ* highlighted several crucial aspects of the UMW's function in the late nineteenth century. Neither looked like the typical white male union coal miner, yet miners and officers alike encouraged Willing Hands and Gardner to write their opinions to the journal.[7] During a period when black voices were systematically, legally, and violently silenced and when women had limited voice in the public arena, Willing Hands and Gardner were welcome to participate in a white male–dominated forum of a white male–dominated organization.

This kind of partial inclusion is seldom reflected in the scholarship of Gilded Age organizing or society. Instead, scholars have framed questions of racial acceptance more in terms of accepting membership or participation. Perhaps most famously, these questions led to the debate between historian Herbert Gutman and attorney Herbert Hill over UMW inclusiveness toward black miners. Describing the life of black Ohio UMW organizer and officer Richard L. Davis, Gutman argued that the UMW's willingness to accept all races and ethnicities gave black miners like Davis a glimmer of hope that equality could still be achieved during a period of rampant racism. Hill disagreed, claiming that Gutman gave the UMW too much credit. The order offered miners of color little more than membership, he argued. To him, black miners found racism among white unionists more often than any sense of hope for greater equality.[8]

This central conflict can be found in examinations of other unions as well. Scholars of the period have carefully observed the politics of ethnicity inherent within unions, political organizations, and greater society. They have described how unions and political parties included and excluded groups of workers or potential constituents based on immediate need. In particular, they have shown that skill-based hierarchies in workplaces often corresponded with ethnic and gender backgrounds that gave preference to English-speaking white men. In most cases, it resulted in outright exclusion of black and immigrant workers from skilled positions and from unions.[9]

But Willing Hands and Gardner do not fit within these patterns of exclusion any better than they fit within the union they defended. When literal skill met the politics of late nineteenth-century society, they became both a part of, and apart from, the whole. Because she had never mined coal, Laurene Gardner was banned from full membership and from attending union meetings. However, her skill in raising a family on a miner's meager wages and raising children to follow the union were commendable qualities to a union facing a dwindling budget and an unruly rank and file.[10] Although it did not formally include her, she included herself in the UMW when she spoke of the miners and the union officers, using phrases such as "we need" and "our officers." More importantly, no one challenged Gardner's claim or her right to pen letters to the *UMWJ*. Union miners at times took issue with her opinions on union policy and politics, but in doing so they included Gardner in their ongoing debates instead of ignoring her.

While Gardner's inclusive wording indicates that she was *of* the UMW even if she was not *in* it, the language Willing Hands used demonstrates that, although he was *in* the order, he was not *of* it. Unlike skilled jobs where employers created stratified hierarchies, the drive to lower coal production costs made it more advantageous to force all miners regardless of color, language, or experience to compete against one another for jobs. As a result, any union that wished to regulate wage rates needed to include all miners without regard to ethnicity as well.[11] Organizations like the UMW therefore regularly tried to recruit black and non-English-speaking miners. In 1892, Willing Hands was a member of the UMW through the Knights of Labor's NTA 135. But in his letters, which were often directed toward white UMW miners, he often referred to the UMW as "your union" and used the word "you" to describe the miners. His use of "we" seldom referred to a collective body of miners or organized producers, as Gardner used the word. Rather, "we" described black miners whose interests and experiences, Willing Hands believed, differed from those shared by white miners and their wives. The UMW may have accepted any creed or color, but Willing Hands remained culturally ostracized from the miners' organization. He was a member and heavily involved with the UMW, but, in his mind, the UMW was a white union.

In many respects, Willing Hands's assessment was correct. Understanding the importance of inclusion, the UMW avidly reached out to organize black and non-English-speaking workers. If these workers could be "taught" the value of unionism, many white English-speaking officers believed, they would remain loyal to it.[12] Yet, while white English speakers expected faithfulness to the union from these groups, much of the rank and file stopped short of treating minority groups as full equals in the order. The predominantly white and English-speaking union paid little attention to the concerns unique to its minority members unless the goals also served white English speakers' needs. White miners opposed convict labor because it competed with their own wages, but they cared much less about confronting the systemic discrimination minority groups received. This discrimination encouraged the workplace exploitation that forced desperate black and non-English-speaking miners to accept lower wages for the same work.

While UMW miners and officers understood this problem and avidly supported pulling these groups into the ranks, they often remained blind to the problems that forced minority groups to accept depreciated terms. Instead of confronting this discrimination or fighting the rampant ethnic inequality in the workplace as minority miners like Willing Hands demanded, white English-speaking miners blamed minority workers, who they perceived as particularly immoral, careless, and unskilled.

Keeping such workers out of the mines became a goal shared by many white English-speaking miners. Union leaders claimed the organization included all laborers of the craft, but in practice the UMW was frequently more welcoming to women like Gardner or to the hundreds of English-speaking farmers who mined than to the nonwhite and non-English-speaking laborers skilled in the mining craft. Despite its claims of wanting to protect the miners, the UMW's efforts ran along ethnic lines rather than those of skill, tearing through the organization's already riddled ranks and pushing away its minority members.[13]

Involved

Excitement buzzed in Linton, Indiana, as news spread at John McBride intended to come and speak. By the time of his fall 1892 visit, UMW membership was already on a fast decline, but Linton, a small town not far from Eugene Debs's home of Terre Haute, remained one of the last well-organized UMW strongholds in the nation. Yet, as the day of McBride's visit approached, several miners' wives were outraged to learn that their husbands would not allow them to attend the meeting.[14]

For several days, Linton men and women debated whether wives should attend the meeting, prompting miner wife "Observer" to settle the issue by asking the *UMWJ* editors to decide. If these meetings were open to the public, she reasoned, women had every right to attend. "Where is the difference between a man taking his wife to hear one of his own craftsmen speak in a hall on things to his interest (and I hold what is . . . hers too) or taking her to that same hall on that same night to hear politics discussed?" Although they agreed with Observer's point, the editors were reluctant to give a clear answer. Noting that mass meetings were open to "the whole body or congregation," the editors responded that wives could, hypothetically, attend a mass meeting, "but it all depends upon what is considered the whole body," they concluded, leaving the final decision to local unions.[15]

The heart of the Linton debate did not rest on whether women could participate in union affairs, but *where* women could respectably participate in these affairs. Not only did no one question Observer's right to write her opinions to the *UMWJ*, but she and several other miner wives *did* attend the meeting. Observer's frustration came from the fact that many other husbands did not allow their wives to attend. Her challenge, then, was not for the expansion of women's rights in the union, but a demand for the union to publicly recognize and support the authority many wives already held.

Wives' authority in their communities was expressed many ways. As with farmers' wives, rural laborers' wives were accustomed to helping balance family budgets. Their involvement in their family's economic decision-making often extended into the public sphere in ways not available to middle-class women during this same period. Farmers' wives' involvement in their homes had long granted them membership in the Grange, and by the 1890s wives often spoke in Farmers' Alliance meetings and wrote to farmers' papers, while Mary Lease, Annie Diggs, and other women entertained largely male audiences with their organizing efforts.[16]

This inclusion extended to women associated with industrial labor. Even when women were not granted membership, they often remained involved in informal ways. Leonora M. Barry, for example, joined and rose through the ranks of the Knights of Labor in the 1880s. She actively organized women's assemblies but also became involved in aiding male-dominated industries like coal mining. Mary Harris Jones, also known as Mother Jones, likely became involved with the Knights around the same time as Barry. Although she was not a laborer herself, Mother Jones was informally connected to organizations like the Knights of Labor and the UMW. In the 1890s, she helped organize for the miner's union, gave speeches encouraging strikers and their wives, and, long before women's auxiliaries formed in the UMW, Jones organized striking miners' wives and daughters to taunt and intimidate strikebreakers.[17]

Most women's contributions were more subtle than Jones's and Barry's. Women were often involved in strike decisions, helping their husbands decide when to strike and when to remain at work. Local newspapers regularly reported wives aiding their husbands in strike situations, sometimes getting shot in skirmishes between strikers and company guards. Other times they raised money to support strikers. On one occasion, a group of Terre Haute, Indiana, wives attacked a local newspaper editor who slandered UMW secretary-treasurer John Kennedy. On another occasion, wives intimidated strikers themselves, ordering them to step aside from guarding the mine entrance so their husbands could break a strike.[18]

Incidents such as these were often only mentioned in passing in the media and in union reports. Taken together, however, these passing references indicate that many wives were actively involved with their husbands' unions, even if their efforts were relegated to the background. Their efforts were often overlooked, but their constant involvement with their families and communities meant that their opinions were listened to when they wrote to official newspapers like the *UMWJ*. Most wives, if they wrote at all, wrote only once or twice, but some, such as Laurene Gardner, wrote once a week for several years. This prolific writing makes Gardner unique. In fact, Gardner wrote to the newspaper more regularly than most men. Still, it is important to note how readers reacted to her involvement. Instead of ignoring or discouraging her, readers engaged with her letters just as they did with other letters. Her words attracted the attention of then Vice President Phil Penna, who paid her a visit during one of his trips through the coalfields to thank her for her letters, and when she died in 1896, miner Eugene Merrell sent an obituary to the *UMWJ* on behalf of the miners in her town.[19] "She early recognized the fact that the wives, mothers and sisters, were equally interested in the miners['] struggle for existence," Merrell wrote commenting on her "bright and newsy" weekly letters to the journal. "Her labors to better the conditions of the miner . . . endeared her to every coal miner in our country."[20]

Merrell's words about Gardner indicated the kind of acceptance wives experienced. They were never completely included in their husbands' organizations or had any official say in its decisions. Still, wives remained actively involved and, in a sense, were included in the miner's union, even if it was often only in the background.

Not all of those associated with the mining industry were so welcomed, however. The UMW may have accepted the involvement of non-miners like Gardner or Mother Jones, but actual miners who were not white, or who lacked the English-language skills that Gardner and Jones had mastered, often found themselves ostracized from the organization that claimed to include them.

Separated

Black experiences in the mines and trouble with the UMW frequently centered on issues of morality, and in mining regions this question of morality in the mines was closely tied to the convict labor system. For black miners, the immorality came from the exploitation they endured, but white miners believed the immorality came from the black miners themselves, who, whether they labored as convicts or wage laborers, threatened white miners' livelihoods by working for less.[21]

The end of slavery, coupled with the dramatic increase in rural industrialization, set the tone for racial relations in the workplace and society. Landowners' desires to keep former slaves on plantations coincided with the increasing demand for laborers in rural industries like turpentine, railroad, and coal, which required grueling work at low production costs. For many white business owners, convict labor became a viable way to cheaply industrialize rural regions while reinforcing the racialized social structure that kept black labor at the bottom of social and workplace ladders. Harsh laws targeted the black population, causing the convict labor force to be overwhelmingly black, and allowing those who leased their labor to have little regard for convicts' well-being. They performed unskilled and semiskilled trades on roads, mines, brickyards, and lumber camps, where, historian Douglas Blackmon observes, laborers languished in "nightmarish human suffering and brutal retaliation." Disease, illness, malnutrition, bad water, torture, and frequent beatings were just as deadly as the dangerous work conditions. Hundreds of prisoners died each year. For example, between 1888 and 1889, 34 percent of the 648 prisoners perished in one mine outside Birmingham, Alabama. The exploitation present in the convict labor camps set the tone for how many black miners were treated in the mines and how white miners reacted to them.[22]

As deplorable as these conditions were, the cruelty black miners endured was not the source of many free miners' outrage at the convict labor system. The forced labor and dangerous working conditions meant that the coal mined by convict laborers could be priced more cheaply than that produced by miners who worked for wages. As a result, convict laborers became an economic threat to free laborers who worked the same jobs. In many cases, such as in Coal Creek, Tennessee, in 1891, coal companies replaced striking workers with convict laborers. Doing so increased company profits and often forced striking miners to accept wage reductions. From the outset, then, many white miners despised convict labor not because they saw it as immoral, but because it endangered their livelihoods.[23]

White anger toward black labor in the mines also extended to black wage laborers, who, like white wage laborers, were willing to change mines or regions for the sake of better opportunities. Miner W. J. Kelso argued that free black workers' desire for steady work became a lucrative business opportunity for several white miners in the mines around Birmingham, Alabama. This group of white miners gathered "crews" consisting of former convict miners and black men who had never mined before, and hired them out to local mines where they worked for depreciated wages. In doing so, the white miners-turned-businessmen monopolized the jobs in area mines, causing "A Would-Be-Knight" to note that in the mines they controlled, it was "nearly impossible to get a job without friends, and there is some of the dirtiest work done there you ever heard about."[24]

This trend was echoed in other mining regions as well. Although convict laborers were often used as strikebreakers, companies also used free laborers as strikebreakers. Workers were recruited to move to mines from other regions, often under the pretense of earning high wages. Hundreds of black men and women were brought to striking mines, lumberyards, and brickyards,

and turpentine camps each year, both voluntarily and by force. Some know-
ingly came to break strikes, while others came unaware of "labor trouble" but
lacked the funds to return home.[25] In cases like these, black miners had little
choice but to work under depreciated terms. Kentucky miner W. J. Smith reported that at his mine in Madisonville, miners "lost cars all the time and one
colored man claiming a car talked plain about it and the weighmaster shot
him." Black miners' decisions to fight wage reductions, push for fair weights,
and, as in the case of Madisonville, object to operators stealing cars, not only
made them especially susceptible to losing their jobs, but also increased the
risk of losing their lives. "This is why they won't have organization in Hopkins
county," Smith concluded. There was no point in joining a union that could not
protect its members.[26]

Black mine organizer and union officer Richard L. Davis faced a similar situation in his Ohio district.[27] A group of black miners carefully considered accepting
an operator's offer to put a majority of black miners in the No. 3 mine. "Some
claimed that they thought they ought to have a majority in one mine, at least,
that the whites had the majority in every mine in the valley," Davis reported.
A black majority mine would not only offer more jobs to black miners but also
allow black miners to be elected to represent the workers' concerns, but Davis
had reservations about the plan. "I can remember the time when this mine was
altogether colored, all the other mines were for the whites," he wrote. "Now then,
for No. 3, the colored man's mine at that time, all the other mines in the valley
had the $1^1/_8$ inch screen, the screen at mine No. 3 was $1^1/_2$ inches; at all the other
mines the men were paid for dead work at mine No. 3 they were not paid for
this class of work." Racially dividing the mines would not solve black miners'
problems; discrimination would follow them no matter how their numbers
were configured.[28]

Despite Davis's efforts to push for integration to further dissolve the color line
in the mines, racial divisions remained steadfast. Miner F. H. Jackson responded
to Davis the following week, explaining the black miners' frustration: "The
white miners of Mine No. 3 refused to work some three weeks ago because they
thought they had to work under a negro boss, which was very wrong to them.
It caused my race in this valley to feel very angry over this action of my white
friends." Learning of the dissatisfaction, the mine boss promised he would "fill
Mine No. 3 with negroes and give them eight and nine months['] work, and it
would be best for them." Although Jackson insisted that the tactic was a ploy to
divide the miners and their union by race, he also acknowledged that the offer
was a tempting one for black miners, who seemed to get no protection from the
UMW regarding steady work or promotions in the workplace.[29]

Situations like this became a source of racial hostility and struck at the heart of white laborers' perceptions of skill. In many cases, literal job experience did not matter as much as white laborers' assumptions regarding whether a black laborer could perform the job honestly.[30] White laborers and farmers may have been just as willing to accept lower wages for steady work when pressed to provide for their own families, but they held little sympathy for the black laborers who did the same.[31]

Such sentiments seeped into union practices, even if the order allowed all ethnicities to join. "The colored men often kick because white men do not treat them right, and say we don't give them a chance," white former Illinois union leader Dan McLaughlin wrote from his new home in Indian Territory. "Just as long as the colored man allows himself to be shipped around the country in gangs for the purpose of driving white men away from their homes and lowering wages, just so long will the prejudice and hard feeling exist. Let him be white or black, we have no use for the man who insists on going down into the ditch and dragging us with him."[32] McLaughlin's statement revealed a disjunction that ran throughout workers' ranks.[33] The old union leader who had ordered union miners to break the 1889 strike in Illinois spoke of strikebreaking in general, condemning all who broke strikes and worked below scale rates. In his mind, the problem plaguing black miners and the UMW was not one of race, but of ethics. White miners' anger against black miners, he insisted, was not due to their skin but to black miners' willingness to drive down wages. Yet, McLaughlin's claim also reveals the racist sentiment rampant in union ranks. McLaughlin's unapologetic words indicate that he and other white UMW members would discriminate against *all* black miners as long as *some* black miners broke strikes. Even though white union and nonunion miners frequently broke strikes and compromised their labor principles to provide for their families, the strikebreaker, in many white miners' minds, was black.[34]

In some regions, miners were able to integrate their locals despite this stereotype. Historian Daniel Letwin observes that although hostility to interracialism remained, locals in Alabama were particularly successful in this endeavor.[35] Still, as in many other industries, many white miners resisted opening their locals to black miners, who whites presumed to be dishonest based on stereotypes of black convict labor and black strikebreaking.[36] Illinois miner "Pro Bono Publico" observed this in his own town. Like many unionists, he saw this exclusion as a stumbling block for UMW strength and pushed miners to put aside racial differences. Urging readers to "treat every man as white," he ordered them to cooperate with each other regardless of whether a coworker may have broken a strike or might have once been a convict. "It is a business matter," not one of racial sentiment or morals. "Christianity or morality don't dig coal," he argued, reminding miners that "the coal produced by the immoral man is just worth as much money in the market as that produced by the moral man or church member." For that reason, he continued, "it won't do for us to hold aloof from another man because his life has not been all that could be desired previously." Rather, "the only way to make those men better and at the same time make yourselves better is to get into the union with them . . . and urge upon them to do better in the future than they have in the past."[37]

To black miners, however, simple inclusion was far from equitable. All miners were accepted in the miners' union, and, by 1891, the UMW had added a provision to the constitution that "no person be hindered from securing work on account of race, color or nationality." Still, thousands of unionized white English-speaking miners refused to work with black miners. NPU organizer John Young reported that, although black and Italian miners in Braidwood, Illinois, were interested in the union, they still refused to join. "They say that they would be in the union if they get the same show as other men, and there is a great deal of truth in it," he wrote, acknowledging that black and non-English-speaking miners' interests were frequently neglected even after they joined the order. Recognizing a similar situation, Kentucky miner and organizer W. H. Foster reported that the union was "going down" in his region because "the white man is doing all he can to down the Negro and the Negro is doing all he can to down the white man." Willing Hands's own assembly in Bevier, Kentucky, dissolved over the very issues Foster described, yet he offered no apology for the black miners' unwillingness to work with the white miners. "When everything is smooth you object to our color, which is unconstitutional and contrary to the will of our National, state and general officials." Given this inconsistency, Willing Hands argued that it was only logical that when white miners went on strike "out of revenge we, the bulk of the Afro-Americans go to work for spite."[38]

Not surprisingly, during the widespread frustration with UMW authority, when locals throughout the nation broke away from the UMW and formed "home organizations," many black union miners did the same. Tired of UMW officers who did little to end the racial discrimination in the mines that hired white miners over black and, learning that the region's five hundred white miners in Leavenworth, Kansas, were planning to strike, black miners of Leavenworth broke from their white counterparts to form an "anti-strike organization." In doing so, these miners curried special favor with their employers, securing the fair treatment and steady work the UMW did not provide.[39]

The African American miners of Leavenworth demonstrated a crucial component of worker hostility toward unions. Black laborers in other industries such as farming and railroading took similar antistrike pledges because they were treated unfairly.[40] Leaders like UMW Missouri-Kansas district president F. B. McGregor may have insisted black miners were "led by the nose" away from proper organization and morality, but to the miners who joined the antistrike push, it was a way to secure what the national union neglected. As such, their anti-UMW order became a means to not only secure higher wages in their workplace but to also hit back at the order that disregarded them.[41]

For black miners, this disregard took many forms. Even when white miners were willing to join the same local, white miners seldom wished to follow black leaders. Richard Davis endured countless threats from both white and black miners for his firm stance for miners to unionize and cooperate across the color line.[42] Miner T. H. Rollins demanded to know why black miners "are never elected to any position that there is any honor or pay in?" To Rollins, the practice of accepting black miners but denying them leadership smacked of hypocrisy. "I feel that we have as much at stake as our white brothers," he wrote, echoing white union miners' claims that all miners had an interest in improving the mining trade. But while white miners used this as an argument for black miners to cast aside concerns for racial equality within the union, Rollins used it to push for black rights within the order. "I know that I speak the sentiments of my colored brothers at large," he wrote. Black union miners were as willing and competent as whites to help guide the union but were seldom given the chance.[43]

Rollins was not the only worker who used the union as a means to achieve racial equality in addition to economic equality. Black laborers often used their unions as vehicles to expose racial injustice.[44] "Brothers, buy and read a few Afro-American papers, to see just what the negro has to fight," Willing Hands wrote, encouraging white miners to sympathize with black miners' concerns. His words referenced the trouble "that not only the Afro-American gets in the South, but all over the land, both North and South."[45] He regularly called readers' attention to lynchings, reminding them that such happenings were connected to the use of black convict laborers. "I appeal to you to do something against such outrages," he wrote. Using "supposed Afro-American criminals" as laborers, employers kept African Americans pressed down while forcing all miners to "work for a song." "It is not social equality I want," the miner wrote, "but it is right and justice that I want for the African race and the only way to get it is through and by the Knights of Labor and the United Mine Workers' laws being strictly enforced." It was in the white miners' best interest to join the antilynching cause, he argued. "Laborers you will suffer the same fate that we Afro-Americans are if you don't become more solid, for it is you next that the despots will mob." Willing Hands's point was clear: if the white miners wanted to improve their own condition, they had to help improve the conditions the black miners faced, but doing so required white miners to take a stand against racism. "We must all go up the ladder of fame together or go to poverty arm in arm," the black miner charged, "and it is left for you white brothers to take your choice as to which you will do."[46] If unions truly intended to fight for the worker, Willing Hands, Rollins, and many other black laborers believed, they needed to treat racial injustice as a threat to everyone, not just to people of color.

White support, however, only went so far. Although white workers supported laws forbidding convict labor, they explained that their support came from concern for their own economic wellbeing rather than a desire for racial justice.[47] Laws that dealt with broader aspects of racism that had indirect implications on mines received even less support. Segregation, black miners' inability to safely express workplace grievances, and lynching all affected black miners and organization, but few could convince white miners or the UMW to push for new laws. White miner "Mike," for example, replied to Willing Hands's plea for UMW action against lynchings with a joke. Referencing the lynchings of two black men accused of rape in Nashville, Tennessee, Mike sarcastically quipped that it was "too bad" the men were lynched. Instead, the men "should be taken to the World's Fair and exhibited to Sunday school scholars as models of innocence."[48] Mike's callous reply indicated not only his disregard for the problems black Americans faced, but also his presumption that the fate of the lynching victims was just.

Mike's response, however, appeared in the same *UMWJ* issue that contained black mine organizer Richard Davis's report of a trip through West Virginia. Traveling with two white men to organize the region, Davis faced hostility at nearly every coal town they visited. Denied access to the boardinghouse, he was expected to sleep in a run-down cabin far from town and eat his meals outside, separate from his fellow travelers. In each case, his companions spoke to their hosts and usually secured Davis better accommodations, or at least access to a bed and a dining table. Still, Davis could not help but wonder what would have happened if he had made the trip alone. He presumed he probably would have been arrested, "for I felt like cursing and I would have used cuss words had I been by myself."[49]

Outraged at the irony of the two columns, Willing Hands once again urged readers to pay attention to the violence blacks faced, "for it will not be long until a Virginia mob will have an Afro-American labor organizer hung." With that, he condemned Mike's words, asserting that the violence African Americans endured was no joking matter. "Further," he continued, "it is not possible for you to wish the organization success as long as Afro-Americans are left at the mercy of others, as I fear that you would have done R. L. Davis should you have been in company with him."[50]

For his part, Davis cautioned that this ongoing racism against black miners would only hurt the UMW. "For take the negro out of the organization and you have a vast army against you, one that is strong enough to be felt and feared," he wrote.[51] Racism in the workplace and the union deterred hundreds of black workers from joining the UMW, but even those who, like Davis, saw value in the UMW believed there was much more to achieve. UMW membership was simply not enough to be included in the order. Even within union ranks, as many black miners understood it, the line between white and black, "you" and "us" remained.

Unskilled

Racialized distinctions between "them" and "us" extended to miners who did not fully assimilate into US culture. In most cases, those ostracized were newly arrived immigrants who spoke little English. In the late nineteenth century, when the United States experienced a dramatic increase in immigrants from non-English-speaking European countries, particularly those in Southern and Eastern Europe, many of these new arrivals to found work in the coal mines. Like many of the "old" immigrants from the British Isles and Ireland who came to the Americas with prior mining experience, these new immigrants came into the United States already knowing how to mine coal and hoped to continue working in the mining industry. The difference was that, by the late nineteenth century, English-speaking immigrants were welcomed into the miners' union and frequently served as respected labor leaders and union officers. Newer immigrants did not receive such acceptance in the mining communities or in the miners' union.[52] To many English-speaking miners and wives, including Laurene Gardner, these "imported laborers" were more dangerous than those who came from Western Europe. Like black miners and convict laborers "imported" into mining camps to lower wages and break strikes, Gardner and others maintained that non-English-speaking miners were "imported" into the nation to achieve the same goals.[53]

Often collectively called Bohemians, Slavs, or Huns, these new immigrant groups were racialized in ways that set them apart from other immigrants. Anthropologist Paul Shackel noted that the social Darwinist explanations popular in the Gilded Age often extended into the mines, allowing entire mining communities to discriminate against non-English speakers and treat them more harshly than English-speaking immigrants. These new groups were often

classified as not white and considered somewhat primitive, dishonest, ignorant, culturally backward, and violent. Consequently, both native-born and
native-English-speaking immigrant miners looked at these new immigrants
with disdain.[54]

Nonnative-English-speaking miners became a threat in many English-
speaking workers' minds for several reasons built on racialized assumptions.
First, English speakers feared that their communities would be overrun with
men and women who did not adhere to local customs and disregarded local law
while driving wages lower. Indiana-Kentucky district secretary John Kennedy,
who hailed from Scotland, made a careful distinction between immigrant miners from the British Isles and those who arrived from Eastern European countries. Unlike other immigrants, these new immigrants "could live and work on
a piece of bread half the size of his hand and a glass of water for twenty-four
hours."[55] Though hyperbolic, such a claim horrified English-speaking immigrant
and native-born miners who understood that denying basic necessities resulted
in a wage reduction that would cascade into their own homes. These notions
were made worse by the belief that the "pauper laborers" arriving were "unin-
telligent" and "unskilled."[56] Not only did these new miners not speak English or
understand US customs, but, according to most assimilated miners, they did not
know how to mine coal. As a result, many assimilated miners maintained that
the new miners would degrade the mining trade by lowering wages, making a
mockery of the skill required to perform the job safely, and placing all miners
in danger underground.

For thousands of native-English-speaking miners and other residents, trouble began with the new arrivals' inability to speak English. "It is quite a common
thing to lay the blame on the number of those who work in the mines who do not
understand the English language," one Braidwood, Illinois, miner explained of
the declining wages and failed unions. Although many non-English-speaking
immigrants honored strikes while English-speaking miners broke them, he
acknowledged, the stereotype remained.[57] John Kennedy conceded that "those
non-English-speaking people were not to blame" in recent strikes. Still, "it was
through them and on account of them that the strife and bloodshed was brought
about." Even if they did not break strikes, they were responsible for lowering
wages, he insisted. All the "ignorant Poles," were good for, according to Kennedy, was driving down wages and pushing honest laborers out of work.[58]

These claims were not limited to the mining industries. A *Harper's Weekly*
column on Pennsylvania coke workers described Hungarians as "the most difficult class of laborers," in part because of their association with violence but
also because of their unfamiliarity with the English language or US workplace

culture.[59] Likewise, a survey conducted by the Kansas Bureau of Labor and Industrial Statistics revealed that workers in dozens of unskilled and semiskilled trades feared that immigration weakened the quality of work and therefore its value. "We are in an era of cheap, shoddy labor," one painter declared, and competition from immigrants, he and many others believed, was the root of decline.[60]

These stereotypes continued even after a nonnative-English speaker learned English. Native-English speakers often assumed that an immigrant's lack of English language skills was additional confirmation of the immigrant's lack of trade skills. In short, native-English-speaking miners assumed that if an immigrant did not speak English well, they could not mine well. Charles Fisher, for example, learned how to mine coal in France but was working in the No. 2 mine in Frontenac, Kansas, when it exploded in 1888. With over seventeen years' experience mining coal, the thirty-three-year-old knew proper mining practices, including how to ventilate a mine, and on the day of the explosion could tell simply by the sound that a "blown out shot" was the source of the mayhem that followed.[61] But when Fisher was called as an expert witness in a trial to determine who was at fault for the 1888 explosion, he sat on the witness stand and was confused at the court proceedings. Each time the plaintiff asked him a question, the defense objected before Fisher could answer. By the time the plaintiff asked him to tell the jury whether the company supplied "brattices" to direct the mine's airflow, the Frenchman neither knew whether he was allowed to answer the question nor what the plaintiff meant by his question. As the jury awaited his answer, Fisher voiced his exasperation to the court. "You must explain this to me," the miner demanded. "I can't understand very well the English language; I want you to explain so I understand."[62]

The problem was not that Fisher could not speak English. He could. Although Fisher was an immigrant himself, prior to the explosion, French miners not fluent in English went to him for assistance when dealing with mine management. Fisher spoke on their behalf, requesting new rooms for some men or, on the morning of the 1888 explosion, demanding better ventilation in the rooms. His fluency in English and knowledge of the common complaints in the mine likely explain his inclusion as an expert witness for the plaintiff in the trial.

Fisher's confusion came when counsel for the plaintiff asked him whether the company supplied brattices to control air flow in the mine. Most miners familiar with the term "brattice" knew it as a wooden frame placed in a mine doorway that, by itself, had little to do with controlling air flow. The heavy canvas cloth coated with tar that hung from the brattice controlled the flow. Only miners of British descent called to testify during the trial voluntarily called the curtain and frame together "bratticing." The other miners, including Fisher, simply knew it as a "curtain" or "canvas" and never used the word "brattice." This was especially important, since the Cherokee and Pittsburg Company often provided the wood for the frame but did not provide enough curtains to hang from them. The plaintiff's question regarding whether the company supplied brattices, as Fisher likely understood it, made no sense.[63]

The misunderstanding, which resulted from the attorneys' unfamiliarity with mining terms and practices, however, reflected poorly on Fisher in the courtroom and drastically altered his treatment during his testimony. In response to Fisher's confusion, the attorney for the plaintiff rephrased the original question and asked whether the company provided "curtains." Although defense attorneys frequently objected to the questions asked of all witnesses as a tactic to muddle the plaintiff's testimonies, the grounds for objections to Fisher changed after his outburst. In the other testimonies, and before Fisher's outburst, the defense's objections were that questions were "too suggestive" to the witness or "irrelevant" to the case. The objections, like those for other witnesses, were quickly overruled and the trial continued. But after the outburst, the objections grew more frequent and the defense often charged that "the witness has not shown himself competent to express an opinion with reference there to." Much to Fisher's frustration, as he tried to recount his experience during the explosion, the defense argued he was incompetent to do so. "I can tell it if you let me," the miner insisted as he grew more restless, but it was no use. Unlike the objections to other witness testimonies, several objections against Fisher attacking his competency were sustained.[64] Nearly two decades of working in the mines was not enough to be recognized as a mining expert by the Kansas courts. Credibility hinged on more than one's ability to mine coal; it also demanded impeccable proficiency in the English language.

Despite his actual skill, Fisher's lack of English fluency placed him on the fringes of the workplace and society. Throughout the coalfields, immigrants like Fisher were cast as "ignorant" and "unskilled" despite their experience in the coal industry. As in the United States, European mining techniques often varied from mine to mine based on coal quality and surrounding rock composition. However, native-English-speaking miners frequently assumed that nonnative-English speakers, particularly those from Eastern European countries, were unskilled in "modern" mining techniques, namely blasting the coal with explosives. In reality, mines in Eastern Europe were as likely to use explosives to blast the coal as mines in Britain, so they had more experience in mining coal than the local farmers who also worked in the mines. Nonetheless, the stereotype of the unskilled "Hun" remained steadfast. Much of the nineteenth-century mining society refused to believe that the nonnative-English speakers could ever be skilled in the mining trades.[65]

In a report circulated throughout the mining districts as well as labor newspapers, Ohio chief mine inspector Robert Haseltine claimed that "Slavonic and Latin races" possessed "intense greed" that "create a constant menace to the lives and health of themselves and their fellow workmen. These people . . . are entirely ignorant of the science of mining and as a result are continually working in peril." Not only did they not know how to mine, he continued, but they could not be taught. "Their lack of knowledge of our language precludes their being warned in time of danger or of being instructed as to the mode of applying the remedy, until many times it is too late."[66]

Claiming to protect the mines, miners clamored for tighter laws such as one Pennsylvania law that was allegedly designed to keep inexperienced workers out of the Pennsylvania anthracite mines. The law required miners to prove they had at least two years of experience as a mine laborer and had to pass an examination (in English) proving that they were skilled in the mining craft.[67] Although it was passed under the guise of keeping experienced miners safe, the law did not target inexperienced miners. Instead, the real goal of the law was to eliminate the miners who English-speaking miners *believed* were the most inexperienced and dangerous in the mines. Still, English-speaking miners in other states looked at the anthracite field with admiration for their new law. "If other states will follow this example," the *National Labor Tribune* wrote, "the miners will be similarly protected; if not, they will be subjected to the competition of not only the Huns and Italians who have drifted there under ordinary circumstances, but will have also those that Pennsylvania will refuse to take."[68]

The trouble was that the law did not work as the miners envisioned. Anthracite miner "A Delving Serf" insisted that it was ineffective because it "has not stopped one Polander or Hungarian from filling the place of a miner." Non-English-speaking miners hired translators so that they could understand the exam and accepted the two years' required labor as a mine laborer. Native-English-speaking miners, however, refused to work the two years as a mine laborer. Knowing they could immediately mine coal elsewhere, new arrivals from Western Europe and miners living in the United States simply avoided the anthracite field. Instead of attracting more desirable miners, the *Collier Engineer* noted, the law allowed "the undesirable classes [to] have the field all to themselves." Irate, Delving Serf continued to say that he witnessed miners receive mining certification "who could not tell in English where they were born, what their names were, or how old they were." Worse, Delving Serf insisted, one local operator had three of his Polish employees go before the board in hopes they would be appointed to the mining board, "and lo and behold, Mr. Polander was appointed, when to my certain knowledge miners of at least twenty-one years' experience who were applicants were passed by."[69]

Delving Serf's statement, which contrasted "Mr. Polander" with experienced "miners" indicated that, in his mind, one could not be Polish and an experienced miner. Such an understanding emerged not just from simple expectations of white, English-speaking entitlement. It demonstrated a fundamental belief that those who could not speak English were incapable of being honest skilled workers. The Pennsylvania law "increased the trouble it was to relieve," *Age of Steel* noted. Others agreed. "Even after serving two years as laborers, many of them are too ignorant to be truthfully called miners," the *Collier Engineer* reasoned, and those who claimed they were miners in their home countries "lie about their experience."[70]

Such concerns prompted thousands of native-English-speaking miners and wives to find new ways to keep specific immigrants out of the mines. The "intelligent foreign born miner" should not be offended at UMW efforts to stop immigration, Laurene Gardner argued. If "he is ready and willing to avail himself," to assimilate, unionize, and mine with care, he was welcome to stay. But those who did not were "one evil that organization was meant to check," she insisted.[71] Citizens in Hymera, Indiana, agreed. Attendees of a mass meeting at the Hymera Baptist Church demanded on behalf of the miners that all immigration be immediately prohibited, "except [for] persons who can read and write the English language and who bring with them the means to make a home in this country."[72] Although thousands of farmers and laborers in the United States were already impoverished to the point of desperation, could not read or write in any language, and owned no property, non-English speakers were deemed to be far more dangerous than any other group. The fact that so many native-English-speaking workers failed to meet Hymera's criteria was clearly not an issue to those at the Hymera meeting.[73]

The UMW in the Pennsylvania anthracite field made a similar overture to block specific immigrant groups from the mines. When the original examination law failed to keep Eastern Europeans from the anthracite mines, John Fahy, an Irish immigrant and the president of the UMW anthracite district, worked to find a way to carry out the true intent of the law. He pushed to forbid the use of translators on the mining exam so that passing the exam not only hinged on mining knowledge but also on understanding the English language. By 1897, Fahy was using his position in the UMW to lobby for companies to be taxed for each nonnaturalized worker they hired. This tax, which received the support of the UMW, was passed as the Campbell Act. Companies passed the "alien tax" on to their nonnaturalized workers, causing them to work for lower wages than their naturalized coworkers. The tax was later ruled unconstitutional, and Fahy eventually began to successfully organize the Eastern European miners in the region, but not before nineteen immigrant miners were shot by a sheriff's posse in Lattimer, Pennsylvania, for protesting the tax.[74]

English speakers may have accepted non-English speakers into their ranks, but such actions left no doubt where their true sentiments lay. For thousands of nonnative-English speakers, such hostility gave them little reason to support an organization devoted primarily to native-born and English-speaking interests. Swedish miners in Oswalt, Iowa, for example, took pride in the fact that they kept their entirely Swedish-speaking Knights of Labor assembly strong when the English-speaking miners' assembly faded.[75] Still, by summer 1892, miner Oscar Anderson voiced uncertainties about NTA 135 and the UMW to Knights secretary John Hayes. As one of the two organizations that comprised the UMW, NTA 135 was supposed to have a say in UMW affairs, but it held little influence. "In fact," he wrote to Hayes, "135 is dead as far as Iowa is concerned." To the Swedish miners of Oswalt, this was a problem. "The Mine Workers organization is so much mixed up in the *Federation* of *Labor* that our members positively refuse to pay them any Tax" (original emphasis).[76] Already angry that the UMW only sent one cent to aid their local in the May 1891 strike where they secured the eight-hour day, UMW's close ties to the AFL further distanced the local from the national miners' union. Like thousands of English-speaking miners who refused to pay dues to organizations that did not respect their wishes, Anderson and the Swedish union miners of Oswalt wanted nothing to do with a labor organization that voiced increasing hostility to immigrant labor. The Knights of Labor General Assembly, Anderson believed, was far more accommodating to their interests. With that, he requested that Hayes transfer the Swedish local's charter from NTA 135 to the General Assembly, and to send all Knights material to the local in the Swedish language. To UMW leaders, Anderson's request, which pulled the assembly out of the UMW, was similar to the Indiana miners' decision to form their own unions apart from the UMW.[77]

The instance revealed a more complicated dynamic between the rank and file and the union than many union leaders acknowledged. Severing ties to the UMW, to UMW leaders, would have looked like the collapse of a local and the miners' rejection of the union, even though the miners remained affiliated with the Knights. It is likely that UMW officials would have dismissed it as such and even cited it as evidence of immigrants' ignorance or antiunion sentiments. The instance in Oswalt, however, indicated that, in at least some cases, the English-speaking miners' claims that non-English speakers were too ignorant to join or stay in a union were unfounded. The Oswalt miners' decision to leave the UMW but remain in a union better suited their interests. Regardless, when nonnative-English-speaking groups questioned unions or union leadership, their claims were often dismissed as a product of their alleged ignorance.

Irate at being called an "ignoramus" for opposing UMW officer decisions, French miner Louis Goaziou sarcastically played into this stereotype. "What little English I can speak and understand I have learned in or around the mines, and the little I can read and write I have learned at home in the evening, so you can easily see that having such an ignoramus as myself for teacher it's no wonder that my education is very imperfect." Perhaps he *was* incapable of understanding how the union functioned, he continued, but many miners "not as ignorant as myself" nonetheless agreed with his assessment. Several miners rushed to Goaziou's defense, but the miner's statement still made it plain that his words against the union were dismissed by many native-born and English-speaking immigrant miners who saw him as an immigrant incapable of understanding the union, making his grievances against the officers less legitimate than those of native-English-speaking whites.[78]

Goaziou's claims were not unfounded. Phil Penna noted in his travels to Ladd, Illinois, in 1891 that, of the estimated 250 miners working in the town, half were from Poland. "Of the remaining one-half there are about thirty in the organization. The other forty would join, but they have not got time, being engaged in cursing the d——d Poles."[79] Ohio miner "Union" claimed that Goaziou and other immigrant miners who complained against the officers or refused to pay dues until the union acknowledged their grievances were behaving unreasonably. Although miners of all backgrounds and ethnicities withheld dues or abandoned the union when it did not suit their interests, nonnative-English-speaking miners who did so were seen as particularly hostile to the union throughout the nation. "Some of the foreign-speaking people have told us that they are in the majority and they do not intend to be ruled by the American or English-speaking people," Union explained. He implied that such demands were illegitimate. When their requests for equal treatment in the union were denied, immigrant miners abandoned the union. "I feel sorry that our foreign-speaking brothers are responsible for such a state of affairs," Union continued. "Let us have unity and we shall prosper; without this we will get farther apart." The claim blamed the union's failure on nonnative-English-speaking miners, who were refused a full voice in the miners' organization. For Union and thousands of other English-speaking miners, "unity" came only when these miners accepted the leadership of white, native-English-speaking miners and dutifully paid their dues to an organization that begrudged them.[80]

Inclusion and Exclusion through Legislation

The treatment black and nonnative-English-speaking miners received differed greatly from how farmer-miners were treated. But unlike black and nonnative-English-speaking groups imported into the mines, farmers were often well-embedded in the local community, were native English-speaking, and white. As a result, farmer-miners became, to the miners, a quieter threat compared to the hysteria that followed other minority mining groups. Practical miners, or year-round miners, recognized farmer-miners' presence in the mines as a danger. Still, for many white English-speaking practical miners, the perceived threat of black and non-English-speaking miners eclipsed the farmer-miner threat. Despite constant complaints from mining regions throughout the nation, miners never implemented any major initiative or policy to keep the farmers out of the mines.

Farmer-miners' presence in the mines intensified in mid-1893, when the Panic of 1893 and depression shattered the already crippled economy in the coalfields. As Mary Lease allegedly urged Kansas farmers to "raise less corn and more hell," hundreds followed the first part of the advice and made up for the difference in the mines. They "crowded out" the practical miners during the winter months when wages were highest. Their presence in the already full mines slowed the turn and lowered earnings for everyone. It was unfair, the *National Labor Tribune* wrote, that the farmer-miners "take from the soil during the season of farming, and when winter demand sets in for fuel they cut a fat streak out of what the regular miners should have." Miner John Neal complained that his mine continued to take on farmer-miners until the mine was so crowded the miners could not earn a living.[81]

The problem with farmer-miners did not end with "crowding" the mine and slowing the turn. In fact, many of the problems practical miners had with the native-born, white farmer-miners were the precise problems white English-speaking miners had assigned to black and non-English-speaking miners. Farmer-miners often knew enough about mining to claim a spot in the mine but were often less likely than non-English-speaking miners to understand mining techniques. Working six months a year in the mines, farmer-miners simply did not have the skills of "reading" mine faces, cracks, and other danger signs that might prompt a practical miner to use a different technique to blast or otherwise loosen his coal.[82]

Indiana miner and operator "Old Timer" considered farmer-miners a liability on multiple fronts. Noting that Elijah Bridgewater, an inexperienced local farmer-miner, injured himself in the mine, Old Timer reminded his readers not only of the typical mining dangers, but also that the danger increased when working with less skilled men. Still, Bridgewater's injury, caused by a slate fall, was likely at least partly the company's fault. The company seldom supplied enough timbers to prop up the mine, and Bridgewater had good evidence to prove that the company's neglect caused his injury. However, Bridgewater "knew but little about mining," and the defendants highlighted his inexperience on the witness stand when the farmer-miner moved to sue the company. The jury sided against Bridgewater ten to two. Not only did Bridgewater's presence in the mines place other miners in direct danger, but as a witness he unwittingly aided the company's escape from responsibility for the fruits of its neglect, allowing unsafe workplace practices to continue.[83]

In this sense, white assimilated miners' fears of unskilled miners being used by the company proved true. The danger, however, came not from non-English speakers, but white, English-speaking farmer-miners like Bridgewater who tended to rise to higher positions in the industry faster than other minority groups in the mines. Farmer-miners were often favored by companies. Not only did they work for low pay but, because they did not mine regularly, farmers were often unfamiliar with safety laws and standard mining procedures in the mine. To operators, this made farmer-miners' ideal candidates for jobs such as mine foremen or mine inspectors. As foremen, they would follow company orders without fully understanding safety implications. As mine inspectors, farmer-miners would be less likely to spot or care about a violation than a practical miner holding the position. "A Miner" wrote that nearly two dozen workers in his Missouri mine died in a fire because the mine inspector failed to report the lack of an escape shaft. "He is a farmer and does not know anything about a coal mine," Miner wrote. Even after the fire, the inspector still reported no violations in the mine. Such negligence outraged Miner, who insisted that the inspector "should be removed or thrown into the mine and roasted with the twenty-three men that were burned to death . . . either would suit the miners so they get rid of him and get a competent inspector to do his duty."[84] Miners were at risk due to inexperience in the mines, but farmer-miners whose favor with companies put them in authority positions often posed a greater threat than other groups.

UMW leader John Kennedy noted that farmer-miners were "useful [to operators] in strikes" and were often hired as strikebreakers.[85] Even when forced to join unions in strongly unionized areas, they did not see the benefit in remaining loyal to a union of a trade they performed only a few months each year. As a result, if farmer-miners joined a union, they stayed in only for the period that they mined, seldomly paying dues. And while in the union, Kennedy observed, they still caused problems for the practical miners. "During the strike of 1889 in the block field our chances of success looked favorable up till the time the farmers had their crops put away, and then they swarmed down on us and we must either divide our small resources with them or they would go to work in the mines," John Kennedy recalled, noting that the same conditions applied four years later. Because they had joined the union, the farmer-miners were entitled to the same meager aid the union provided to practical miners. "Every week when the amount was a little smaller than usual they would come to the commissary, draw their rations and the same day or the next morning go to the boss and tell him they were ready to go to work although they had worked on their farms and had [a] year's provisions stowed away in their homes."[86]

The threat farmer-miners posed was strikingly similar to the problems white English-speaking miners associated with black and non-English-speaking miners. However, while many practical miners could agree with miner and small coal operator "Old Timer" that "miners must dig the coal and the [H]ay John must grow the corn and raise the pork and beef," they were ambivalent about how to achieve this goal.[87] "If we were organized here and charge these winter coal diggers about $20 for the privilege of taking our living from us, we would not be bothered with many of them," miner John Neal suggested.[88] Although few suggested a fee so high, Neal's plan was an old one. One of the first resolutions the UMW passed was an "anti-'corn-husker' resolution" proposed by an Illinois miner stating that "men who only work part of the year in the mines must pay all dues and abide by all conditions of our organization and should they fall in arrears during the time they are out of the mines they must pay all arrears before they can be allowed to work."[89] Such stipulations meant little, however, when the UMW could not force the practical miners who remained in the union to pay their dues. By mid-1893, UMW was too weak and divided to implement any national policy, whether it pertained to wages or to farmers in the mines.[90]

Practical miners railed against the "cornfield mechanics" for injuring their livelihoods. According to T. J. Llewellyn, these "Benedict Arnolds" tore apart the miners' union. "These 'coal butchers'" would be the first to sign iron-clad agreements to keep unions out of the mine. "Were it not for the good men who will suffer through the action of the 'things' who are supposed to have been created upright, but who haven't backbone enough to make men, I would cheerfully say that 50c a day is enough for these poor, miserable traitors, who are busily engaged in tearing down the bulwark between themselves and slavery."[91]

Llewellyn's was just one of the statements that left little doubt that farmer-miners who worked against the union were seen as deplorable coworkers, yet the quotation also indicates that they were also viewed very differently from the black and non-English-speaking miners who were associated with the same behavior. Whereas black and non-English-speaking miners were viewed as naturally inclined to dishonest labor and therefore were ostracized within their organization and not entitled to fair treatment, farmer-miners, like white, English-speaking practical miners, were expected to know better. They were "Benedict Arnolds," traitors to their own people. In identifying them as such, Llewellyn identified farmer-miners with the interests of the UMW, even as the farmer-miners acted against the order.

Many practical miners would have agreed with Llewellyn that the farmer-miners were a problem, but their dislike for the farmer-miners was different from what black and non-English speakers received. White native-English speakers seldom understood black or immigrant struggles in the mines but fully understood farm life. In fact, when a series of local strikes ended in failure in part due to farmer-miners strikebreaking, Indiana district secretary-treasurer John Kennedy once again complained about the trouble farmers caused. When miner "Salamander" replied that the farmers needed to be organized, a frustrated Kennedy replied that the farmers did not respect the union despite his numerous attempts to encourage them to do so. Instead of agreeing with Kennedy, many practical miners expressed sympathy for their farming neighbors. "I have been one of them [a farmer] in times past and was a farm laborer for a good many years, and I am sure they would be much easier organized than any other class I know of," Indiana miner "Salamander" replied. "Tow Row" of Ohio agreed, claiming that not only were the farmer-miners good men, but their actions should be emulated. "I think it would be better still for all of us to own farms, and work on them, too, when the scale of wages did not suit us." In her reply to Tow Row, Laurene Gardner expressed her own sympathy for the farmer-miners: "I wish every coal digger owned . . . a little patch [of farmland], for that would give me one, two or three, in fact." She merely opposed their willingness to rob miners of work. Whereas this behavior was enough to persuade white English-speaking miners to stereotype black and non-English-speaking miners as dishonest, the farmer-miners were only guilty of being industrious and hard-working. English-speaking practical miners may have condemned their actions, but still counted the farmer-miner as one of their own.[92]

White English-speaking miners' willingness to tolerate unskilled mining practices among some groups while lobbying against black and immigrant workforces in the mines shows how the politics of skill played out in the Gilded Age. Acceptance in the mines depended on more than skill; it drew from stereotypes of race and ethnicity that included some while excluding others, regardless of how experienced they were in the mines. Although the UMW professed to be an inclusive organization that embraced all miners regardless of ethnicity, it pushed aside black and nonnative-English-speaking miners, dismissed their concerns, and berated their abilities. Instead, groups that did not fit with the white, English-speaking, experienced-miner mold were accepted into the union more out of a desire to make them obey union doctrine rather than a genuine interest for their well-being. White native-English speakers neglected legislation that would help black miners and embraced legislation that would keep specific immigrant groups out of the mines and the nation.

These positions stood in contrast to the miners' stances on farmer-miners, who, though not welcome in the mines, did not suffer the same degree of hostility. Instead, white English-speaking practical miners looked on the farmers with alarm but also with sympathy, judging that their placement in the mines was due to the same hardships all white English speakers faced in an economic depression. Whereas skilled black and immigrant miners were pushed away from the order, white native-English-speaking women like Laurene Gardner and farmer-miners blended in with it. Consequently, official inclusion in union ranks meant little.

When concepts of skill met the politics of the nineteenth century, loyalty only worked one way. UMW officers demanded loyalty from its rank and file. At the same time, minority groups remained underrepresented in union offices and terms like "skilled laborers" more accurately referenced a person's ability to speak English clearly rather than their competence in the mines. Black and non-English-speaking miners, then, were expected to fall in line with white orders or be branded as immoral and ignorant foes to labor's cause. Black and immigrant concerns of fair treatment and safety, however, never quite became a concern for the UMW as a whole. As a result, black and nonnative-English-speaking miners looked warily at the miners' organization and the double standard that permeated its ranks. As long as the union did nothing to resolve this issue, true "unity" would not be attained.

Ultimately, these various groups that did not completely fit with the UMW frayed the already unraveling union. Still, many believed the organization remained miners' best hope to further their interests. This was the common ground for Willing Hands and Laurene Gardner. Despite their disagreement regarding who belonged to the UMW and what the organization's priorities should be, both remained confident that it was the best labor organization to achieve their respective goals. Yet, as the depression continued, even the most steadfast believers began to question the union's strength. As officers abandoned the organization and the Knights of Labor disintegrated, it seemed that the UMW and what remained of the miners' unity was on the brink of dissolution.

CHAPTER FIVE

Unsettled

Nonunion Mobilization and the 1894 Strike

From district to district, miners' reports of their strike success rolled in. "We are right in line to call for the general suspension," Missouri miner "Sunshine" wrote just a few days after the UMW's first nationwide strike began in April 1894. At his mine, "every man stopped at noon." Indiana officers reported that the state had nearly shut down its entire coal production. From Illinois, "Calamity" boasted, "all solid in this county; men all out, will stand by the national officers win or lose; organized to a man—300 to 500 at every meeting." J. H. Adams proclaimed that the "prodigal sons" of the Indiana block district "have returned to their father" and, with over two hundred members, they were "more determined now than ever before" to fight for better pay. Even nonunion Iowa miners, who reluctantly had joined the strike, were not only still strong six weeks in, but had decided to reorganize UMW Iowa District Thirteen.[1] Miners in Ohio were firm and stronger unionized than ever before, "waiting patiently for the final suspension to come to a close at 70 cents, and nothing less," W. S. Moke reported.[2] In nearly every state, miners echoed his claim. "There must be no receding, no backsliding, if it takes all summer and next fall to fight it out," declared one Pennsylvania miner.[3] Wages had fallen too low not to fight; on this point, nearly 150,000 striking bituminous mine workers agreed.

Such a solid standing caught both union miners and officials by surprise. There were only thirteen thousand miners in the UMW when the strike commenced, and even those members questioned the logic behind a summer coal strike in the middle of the largest depression to date. The 1893 depression crippled rural industries, skyrocketed unemployment, and sent prices for raw materials into a tailspin.[4] Still, the prospect of facing a new wage reduction caused thousands of union miners to reluctantly join the effort. Significantly, most of the strike force came from the thousands of nonunion miners who saw merit in collective action despite not belonging to the union that organized it.

The success marked a crucial juncture in 1890s labor organizing, where two distinct efforts coalesced. On one hand, the enormous turnout for the bituminous strike was part of a movement that swept the countryside in the summer of 1894. Farmers and laborers, whose paths often crossed in the rural workplace, were accustomed to forming informal and temporary local committees to confront immediate concerns. In 1894, they became a disorganized mass that mobilized on the grassroots level in response to hard economic times. Not directly affiliated with any specific occupation or organization, this conglomeration of disaffected rural workers brought locomotives and factories to a standstill. Thousands of farmers and laborers marched to Washington, DC, with Jacob Coxey and other leaders demanding government intervention, demonstrating the angst and frustration they felt during the depression.[5]

These grassroots protests coincided with organizational efforts to confront the same economic concerns, but with a centralized union structure. The Knights of Labor, UMW, and American Railway Union all mounted independent endeavors to address workers' wages and the socioeconomic wellbeing of the nation. Organizations, such as those affiliated with the AFL, turned more intensely to negotiations and arbitration during the 1890s. As railroad corporations and coal dealers negotiated contracts on a national scale in centralized markets, unions joined these negotiations and evolved their structures to better accommodate arbitration tactics. Typically, unions centralized their hierarchy to mirror that of businesses so that union leadership had the power to negotiate and make decisions quickly on behalf of the rank and file. This "business unionism" approach was not new in 1894, but the miners' strike was among the first instances in which union officers determined the outcome without consulting their rank-and-file base.[6]

Efforts to centralize union authority in the coal industry began before the UMW formed. Miners in NTA 135 were accustomed to being loosely associated with the national structure of the Knights of Labor, even if the locals remained fairly autonomous.[7] Recognizing that local and state organizations could not affect the national market, the founders of the NFM proposed a centralized body that would govern state organizations. State federations had little to do with each other, but each of these orders were federated under one organization when the NFM formed in 1885. The NFM Executive Board had little control over the state organizations, often letting state conventions settle debates regarding the mining trade.[8] These state organizations gave way to "districts" when the NPU formed in 1888, signaling, on paper at least, an effort to create a more solidified national body than a federated one. Still, even this order failed to clearly grant decisive authority to the executive board and failed to merge with NTA 135 into a single miners' organization. The mining trade remained wholly decentralized despite organizer efforts to unify it.[9]

The UMW emerged amid these efforts. During this period, hosts of national organizations—both worker and employer alike—moved to grant increased power to the heads of the orders. Organizations like the AFL became more proficient in both business unionism and lobbying while employer organizations like the National Association of Manufacturers formed to block worker union gains.[10] The UMW was one of the orders at the head of this turn, successfully pulling the Knights and NPU into one central order under the authority of a powerful executive board, at least compared to previous incarnations of the miners' union. The new miners' union had an executive board that could determine on behalf of its membership when and where to strike, but, as evidenced with the miners' reaction to the UMW's 1891 and 1892 executive orders discussed in chapter 3, the national organization did not exercise this power effectively. Officers hoped to change this trend in 1894 with the attempt to orchestrate the first nationwide coal strike. If it succeeded, the union would, for the first time, demonstrate national solidarity. It would prove that the miners' union was disciplined enough to act on the orders of its executive board rather than by votes of delegates.[11]

As historian Warren Van Tine observes, the culture of fraternity and democracy in unions had long conflicted with centralization of power, but this shift toward hierarchy intensified in 1890s labor organizations. Conventions and delegations continued to give workers' voice, but final decisions increasingly rested with the officers prized for their administrative and negotiating skills.[12] Still, relatively little is known of how these shifts looked to the average worker. The new rule that granted executive authority to a centralized board ran counter to decades of union procedure. While the decentralized structures of old unionism often contributed to union ineffectiveness in regulating the national market, many workers believed this shift away from autonomy diminished the democratic aspect of union decision-making. For individuals accustomed to mass meetings, votes, and appointed delegates to represent localized interests at national meetings, this shift was a move *away* from the unionism they knew and a step *toward* the very centralized structures they mistrusted. Consequently, although union restructures in the 1890s greatly increased unions' abilities to negotiate with employers, the change also intensified discontent among these workers, who wanted to maintain greater local autonomy. This shift, then, directly influenced rank-and-file membership and their allegiance to their unions.

In 1894, the workers' goal to earn higher wages briefly aligned with officers' efforts to stabilize and centralize union authority. The growing angst among rural producers primed them to push closer to collective mobilization precisely as organizations like the UMW announced their industrial strikes. Organizers marveled at the labor militancy of the formerly staunchly nonunion workforce and saw it as proof of the miners' endorsement of the union and the leadership at its helm. Consequently, when the miners earned a roughly 10-cent-per-ton wage increase during a depression, the success was enough for UMW officers to declare the 1894 strike a victory, because the union had increased miner wages and mobilized the miners as a unified national force.

But many miners disagreed. The strike settlement, which was roughly 10 cents per ton *less* than the miners had demanded, was decided by UMW executives before the masses could vote. To the rank and file, then, the strike did not mark their first national victory over the competitive coal market. Instead, it seemed a defeat delivered by the leaders of the miners' organization. The

"Miners and woman at an unidentified mine," Vermillion County, Indiana, n.d. Courtesy of the Coal Town and Railroad Museum, Clinton, Indiana.

officers' tactical decision to negotiate with operators while the strike force was at its strongest looked like betrayal to the miners, who believed that union leaders had "sold out" their best chance to earn a fair wage. As such, this defeat that leaders presented as a victory did more than highlight the challenges of union building or the complex reasons rank-and-file workers joined the movement. It also demonstrated the importance of leadership taking rank-and-file concerns to heart. Not doing so, union leaders learned, alienated the rank and file who, despite agreeing to strike, did not place blind faith in the union or its leaders.[13]

Reorienting the Labor Movement

The tumult visible in the 1894 strike was a product of several changes that transformed the late nineteenth-century labor movement and reflected two fundamentally different views of how a union should function. Most rank-and-file unionists were accustomed to using local strikes to settle workplace disputes. While many saw the need for a strong national union by the 1890s, they expected to use the national organization to settle disputes on the national level similar to how their local unions settled local disputes. In short, many expected special conventions where local unions sent delegates to vote on settlement terms on the national level.

In their minds, the goal of collective action was to secure better wages and workplace conditions, not necessarily to form long-standing workers' unions. Creating a centralized union structure with a large base that followed leader orders, then, was not a priority to many miners who saw no problem with the special conventions and delegations that had settled terms in the past.

This outlook ran counter to what many labor leaders envisioned. To them, sporadic union membership without a decisive leadership was not enough to effect change in an increasingly national industry. The miners needed to be strong and unified or their efforts would not succeed and, many leaders believed, this would be impossible without consolidating union authority under a central head.

Few people understood this need for centralization better than labor leader John McBride. Born outside Massillon, Ohio, in 1854, McBride knew the coal industry all his life. His father, Thomas, was an Irish-born sailor who eventually settled in Ohio, where he mined coal and briefly owned a share of a local mine. In the 1860s, Thomas McBride served as the head of the eastern arm of the American Miners' Association, the first nationwide union of coal miners. Thomas McBride's life as a miner, owner, and labor leader likely instilled in his son an appreciation not only for what miners faced but also the national market concerns that vexed mine operators and labor leaders alike. Consequently, when John McBride entered the mines at eight years old, he was poised to follow his father's lead and, by age eighteen, he took an active role in labor organizing.[14] McBride earned national attention in 1884 as the president of the Ohio State Miners' Union when the mines of the Hocking Valley area consolidated ownership and entered into the national competitive market. As wages decreased, McBride led nearly four thousand Ohio miners in a six-month strike that ended in defeat.[15]

That defeat convinced McBride that localized strikes were ineffective when mines competed against each other for coal contracts. Like many rural producers, then, McBride understood how various industries intersected to decrease producer wages and firmly believed that market forces were a greater threat to the miners than their employers' greed. A local strike against employers, he believed, would no longer prevent wage decline; too many dependent factors always seemed to conspire against the worker. As a result, McBride took a different approach. As businesses and governments established centralized bureaucracies to instill order out of chaos, McBride believed a centralized structure would also give unions strength. His business unionism tactics relied on the union's ability to act like a business and negotiate terms in boardrooms rather than picket lines. Consequently, as employers struggled to implement modern machinery and tactics to mine coal more efficiently, McBride and other union leaders strove to mirror this shift by employing a machinelike union structure that would strengthen the union through uniformity.

Like the mining machinery that promised more progress in the mines than it could deliver, the progressive bureaucracies of the late nineteenth century often proved too cumbersome to negotiate change efficiently. The year following the Hocking Valley strike, McBride took a stance similar to other producer organizations dealing with nationally competitive markets. As leaders like Charles Macune looked to use the Farmers' Alliance to regulate industries like grain and cotton, McBride helped to pioneer the first joint meetings between unions and major coal operators to nationally regulate the coal trade.[16] Ultimately, the standard scale of coal prices that McBride and the NFM set with operators in the mid-1880s proved impossible to enforce, but like the Hocking Valley strike, the failure reiterated to McBride the importance of a strong and centralized national trade union. Frustrated with the ongoing divisions between the leadership of the NFM and NTA 135 of the Knights of Labor, McBride aided in both attempts to merge the two orders, serving as NPU president in 1888, and presiding over the Columbus convention that formed the UMW in 1890.[17]

By the time he became president of the UMW in 1892, McBride had spent nearly a decade trying to unite the nation's miners into a strong union that could regulate the national coal market. With strong Populist sympathies, the labor leader was more convinced than ever that organization and politics went hand in hand to secure market regulation, but even with the UMW, his business unionism tactics were less than fruitful. As UMW president, McBride inherited a union full of members who were frustrated with the 1891 strike cancellation and who cursed the centralized executive board that McBride wanted to strengthen further. Learning from the Hocking Valley strike, McBride condemned local strikes and vowed that such endeavors would have neither the sanction nor the financial aid of the miners' union. To the miners like those in Indiana, such a stance seemed to sacrifice local workers' livelihoods to keep the national union alive. Many abandoned the union, some of them forming local unions that rivaled the national. As a result, by the time McBride called for the 1894 strike, the UMW had already lost thirty thousand of its fifty thousand members.[18]

The loss of membership numbers had other implications for union strength. McBride's efforts to further centralize the UMW were part of a larger trend taking place within organized labor. The scrutiny that the UMW Executive Board faced was felt in many centralizing orders, including the Knights of Labor and the AFL. The result was an exodus like what the UMW experienced in the months following the 1891 strike cancellation. Facing dwindling numbers, groups like the Knights of Labor and the AFL grew increasingly hostile as they fought to steal membership from the opposing order, reinvigorating old divides. Smaller organizations with dual membership like the UMW were injured by what UMW leader John Kane called "a spirit of antagonism" created by the two vying orders that threatened to pull their support from the miners' union unless it cut ties with the opposing order. By the time McBride assumed the presidency, relations between the UMW, the Knights, and the AFL were already so fragile that UMW vice president Phil Penna complained that the national meetings of both the Knights and the AFL were "oppressively heavy" to the miners' union. Yet even as the orders threatened to rend the UMW in two, Penna remained convinced that the union would "hold together, and if the big dogs will fight, let them go."[19]

Tensions had also escalated due to Terence Powderly's charges against the UMW in the 1892 Knights of Labor General Assembly.[20] To the miners, the Knights' claims that the UMW had neglected to pay dues to the Knights seemed to confirm the dishonesty many had long suspected from the union leaders. McBride, recognizing that Powderly's charge threatened to undo nearly a decade's work in unifying the miners, immediately contacted Powderly to sort out the charges.[21]

After weeks of correspondence, the two labor leaders determined that the trouble originated with Knights general secretary-treasurer John Hayes. Hayes had inflated NTA 135 membership numbers and informed Powderly that the UMW had not paid the correct amount in dues.[22] Enemies of Hayes claimed that his unfounded report to Powderly was an effort to crush the UMW and bring all UMW miners, including those of the NPU, under the Knights' exclusive control.[23]

Even as Powderly insisted the UMW was loyal to the Knights, the Knights made it clear they were no longer loyal to him. Internal dissention riddled the Knights' ranks long before 1893. When charges of impropriety surfaced that Powderly had used the Knights for personal gain, Powderly's enemies, including a faction led by Hayes, unseated Powderly as general master workman at the November 1893 General Assembly. James Sovereign of Iowa took his place at the helm of the order, and, at the behest of Hayes, suspended Powderly from the Knights entirely the following May.[24]

The coup set the tone for 1894. The centralization of labor union leadership gave the rank and file clear figureheads to blame for the anxiety over the 1890s depression and increasingly competitive national markets. Convinced that corruption and selfishness resided at the top of centralized hierarchies, frustrated producers united to purge their governing bodies of the most visible threats to their livelihoods. The rank-and-file mistrust that Hayes had exploited, then, was like the angst that encouraged folks to march with Coxey and urged Populists to form a third party. For many union-affiliated workers in industries like coal and railroads, this led to efforts—from both officers and rank and file—to reorient organized labor. To the rank and file, this meant "purifying" the order of dishonest union leaders who had "sold out" workers' interests for personal gain while for leaders like McBride, it required fashioning a centralized union with enough authority to control the coal market.[25] The 1894 nationwide bituminous coal strike would test this agenda, and, as McBride soon learned, the goals of establishing union strength and securing union authority aligned almost as often as they did not.

Mobilizing the Masses

Much of the 1894 unrest came from a bad economy and wages that had declined since 1891. In 1891, bituminous miners in competitive regions earned an average 70 cents per ton for screened coal. By 1894, they earned 50 cents per ton for the same labor.[26] Many miners believed that the declining price resulted not only from miners' willingness to work for low wages, but also from too much coal. For years, many union leaders and miners called attention to the surplus and insisted that the only way to raise coal prices was to decrease the supply. Some proposed lessening the supply through a process known as restriction, where miners limited coal production either by producing a predetermined tonnage or shortening work hours.[27] Still, given miners' actions, like accepting free clicks and other means of making extra money, it was unlikely all miners would honor restriction.[28] Worse, the overcrowded mines and slow turn meant that, even if all miners restricted their output or hours, operators could maintain production rates by adding more men to the mine, further slowing the turn to the point that it forced miners to work more in order to feed their families.

For thousands of miners, then, the only way to decrease the US coal surplus was to stop mining entirely so that the coal supply would be depleted, which would force coal prices to increase.[29] The UMW chose this course in summer 1894, when operators announced a new wage reduction in bituminous mines. Miners throughout the nation were to quit work until every operator agreed to keep wages at the 1893 scale of 70 cents per ton. But the young union had little power to enforce its goal. Unlike previous strikes, which allowed individual mines or regions to return to work as soon as they reached a settlement, the suspension required all bituminous mines, both large and small, to cease production simultaneously and not return until every mine agreed to pay the scale. Consequently, even if an individual operator was willing to pay the demanded scale, the miners were forbidden to accept the offer. In keeping with McBride's goals to create a centralized union authority, the suspension would only end when the UMW Executive Board declared it over. No local settlements or loading coal for any reason would be tolerated, regardless of the wage amount. All miners would work for the same price or not at all.[30] Success therefore depended on all practical miners, farmers who mined, and other migrant industrial workers to obey national orders and remain above ground until the UMW leaders declared the strike over.[31]

Placing such power in the hands of a leading few marked a tremendous break from past union practices and demonstrated a conscious effort, at least among UMW leadership, to centralize union authority. However, such efforts were met with substantial unease from the rank and file, who feared that the 1894 suspension would meet with the same defeats as past years. A strike at any time was a gamble. A coal strike during the summer months of a depression was especially risky.[32] Many miners feared that the strike would benefit only the operators, who could sell their surplus coal at a higher profit if the miners stopped production.

In fact, even before the strike began, several operators encouraged their miners to join the UMW strike. The Missouri Bureau of Labor Statistics and Inspection even noted that some coal operators purposefully lowered wages so much that the miners had no choice but to strike.[33]

Even among miners who supported the strike, there was unease. "Mr. Editor, how much longer is these hard times going to last in this country?," one Missouri miner asked in his letter to the *UMWJ*. His questioning reflected the desperation many rural "producers" faced during the depression and the indecision many had regarding what to do about their situation. The Missouri miner never endorsed the strike. He did not write excitedly about certain victory but wrote that he thought there was nothing else left for the miners to do. "I sincerely hope that this general suspension all over the country will prove beneficial to us miners," he wrote, "for if it doesn't, I don't know what is to become of us."[34]

Such ambivalence stretched throughout the nation. A host of rural workers felt the brunt of the mid-1890s depression and, while their discontent was not new, it reached a boiling point in 1894. Rural residents in coal, agriculture, and railroad industries increasingly discussed political reform. Discussion of the People's Party increasingly crept into these debates throughout the coalfields.[35] Although these discussions seldom ended with any agreement, let alone any mass commitment to a third party, they did lend to broader conversations about social change. Much as the Knights turned out Powderly because they believed he used the office for personal gain, so the "Army of the Commonweal" demanded that officials elected to the government act on behalf of the people they represented. Reformers like Ohio businessman Jacob Coxey found kindred spirits in the coalfields where Coxey's demands for government assistance in securing higher farm profits and fair-paying jobs resonated with producers in both agriculture and industry.[36]

The farmers and laborers who marched had no central leader or organization. Although Coxey was the most famous, he was one of many reformers who led "armies" to Washington D.C. in 1894. In many cases, their only common ground was that, like the Missouri miner ambivalent about the coal strike, they had nowhere else to go. As such, the industrial marches loosely bound individuals together through a collective discontent. To the marchers, formal organizational ties or even a centralized leader were not necessary.[37]

The 1894 coal suspension shared a similar pattern. From the outset, the effort was not unified. Many miners were divided over whether to join. Delegates to the Iowa state convention, for example, voted to join the strike by a vote of sixty-six to fifty-eight. When it was clear that the masses favored the strike, the fifty-eight miners who had opposed the effort agreed to honor it, even agreeing to recast the vote so that the vote to strike was unanimous.[38]

Even those who agreed to join the effort disagreed with UMW officers regarding when they would walk out of the mines. Rather than follow the UMW officers' orders, some, like miner "Blind Robin," suggested that the strike commence a week earlier than officers ordered to prevent operator stockpiling. Others, such as those in the Indiana block district, voted 726 to 1,349 to not join the strike until May 1, when their 1893 wage contract expired and the 1894 reduction went into effect. Organizers had reasoned that the suspension was a tool to deplete the coal supply rather than a weapon against individual employers, and therefore ordered the miners to walk out before the 1893 contract ran out. Still, to miners in Indiana and in Illinois, striking before May 1 meant breaking their contract, which they believed was dishonest. To many miners, then, joining the strike effort did not mean they needed to follow the UMW officers' orders. They simply did not recognize the authority McBride tried to exercise over the strike.[39]

Actions such as the miners' decisions regarding when to walk out indicated the role the masses played in the movements of 1894. Just weeks after the miners' suspension began, and days after Coxey reached Washington, the American Railway Union (ARU) launched a strike against the Pullman Car Company. Railroad workers walked out en masse. Led by Eugene V. Debs, an already well-known organizer and Populist sympathizer who hailed from the Indiana coalfields, the ARU enjoyed support from miners throughout the country. Together, the demonstrations seemed to be proof that the producers could be mobilized from grassroots. Coxey and other reformers may have classified these events as a collective push from the Army of the Commonweal, but this effort was not as unified as leaders had hoped.[40]

The Suspension

The strike began as a success. Although the UMW only had roughly 13,000 miners in its ranks, mostly concentrated in Ohio, the nonunion miners' own frustrations allowed them to join the strike, even if they would not join the union.[41] By May 1, roughly 125,000 miners were idle and more joined in the following days.[42] Missouri and Iowa almost entirely shut down their industries; Indiana and Illinois shut down by three-fourths, with more expected. Ohio, Alabama, Indian Territory, and New Mexico slowed their production to a crawl. On traveling through the partially unionized Kentucky mines, J. Carter, like dozens of other union organizers, found the miners' faith in the UMW revived as the strike continued. "Even the women here are helping us," he wrote excitedly, "they say they will desert their men if they go back on the old wages."[43] By May 10, John McBride proudly announced that within five days "there will not be 5,000 bituminous coal miners at work in the whole country."[44] After years of defeat, the overwhelming success inspired thousands to believe for the first time that national solidarity was not only possible, but within reach.

The major problem with the suspension was that its success depended on no coal being mined, but many mines ignored the orders and continued working. Mines in Earlington, Kentucky, ran full-time, mostly with black miners who had no interest in aiding the UMW-led suspension and instead filled southern Indiana contracts.[45] Virginia, Maryland, and substantial portions of West Virginia, Pennsylvania, Iowa, and Colorado all refused to join the suspension.[46] Missouri miner Philip Veal claimed that most of Kansas ignored the suspension because state organizer and mine operator M. L. Walters and other officials ordered them to remain at work. "The miners in Kansas in most places have seceded from the union under Mr. Walters, their leader (which Benedict Arnold and Judas Iscariot must envy)," Veal wrote.[47] According to Veal, Walters told the miners that "Kansas was not invited to join the national movement," and that the suspension would only benefit the eastern mines. Even when Missouri miners marched across the state line to encourage the miners to quit, they were met by a crowd of angry miners, wives, and strikebreaker-sympathizers who chased the strikers out of the state.[48]

In other regions, farmers abandoned their fields for the mines, unwilling to turn away high-paying work, even during the normally busy summer farming months. "[The miners had] done everything they could to persuade them to quit work a couple of weeks, and put in their time cultivating their farms," John Kennedy wrote, "but as there was nothing human about them except their shape of course they could not be persuaded to quit work."[49] This refusal to honor the suspension would damn the effort despite how successful it was in some places of the country. The miners would not be able to dry up the coal supply if so many places were still digging.

Pennsylvania and Kansas fields shipped coal to railroad depots across the country while Kentucky and other unsuspended mine regions began sending their coal to fill the Chicago market demand. Dozens of striking miners and wives in coal towns throughout Ohio, Illinois, and Indiana stopped trains and uncoupled coal cars to sidetrack them. Even though the railroad workers eventually initiated their own strike a few weeks later and requested a general sympathy strike for their cause, many railroad workers had no sympathy for the coal suspension and quickly rehooked the cars, allowing the coal to continue to Chicago. Nothing, it seemed, would prevent coal from going into the market, especially as several state governors ordered troops to keep the trains running.[50]

Meanwhile, operators throughout the nation, eager to turn a profit from the strike, appealed to their employees to return to work, offering the scale price and, at times, even more than the miners asked. By mid-May, hundreds of miners, having suffered for months, accepted the offer and returned to work while others remained torn between honoring the strike and accepting the 70 cents per ton that the miners had already declared as their goal.[51]

Between the growing number of miners abandoning the strike and the increasingly violent hostilities between the miners and strikebreakers, it seemed wise to settle quickly rather than hold out any longer.[52] UMW leaders called for a special convention but warned all miners that the UMW would not be able to reimburse travel expenses. If miners wished to send a delegate, they had to pay for his travel. The expenses of the May Special Convention, and the difficulty of getting all delegates to Columbus in time made it clear that the miners would not be able to hold another special convention. Consequently, when the delegates failed to settle on a scale, they passed a resolution allowing the national officers and the UMW State Presidents to settle on the delegates' behalf. Within a month, the officers settled with the operators, but not for the 70 cents the miners and delegates expected. Instead, McBride ordered the miners back to work for 60 cents per ton.[53]

For union leaders, the suspension was a victory. "Under all the circumstances I think you have done remarkably well," Terence Powderly wrote to UMW national secretary Patrick McBryde. With so many farmers and miners willing to break the strike, leaders believed they had no choice but to settle while the union was strong enough to negotiate with operators. Powderly hoped the balance of the strikers would see this point and "have the good sense to accept the terms you have won."[54] The labor leader's words recognized that the miners joining the UMW-initiated strike did not necessarily mean they were willing to follow union leaders' orders. The rank-and-file dissatisfaction that Powderly referenced, however, ran deeper than leaders could comprehend at that moment.

Renegades

McBride declared the 1894 settlement a victory, but many miners saw little to celebrate. Instead, miners like "Incog" declared it a "great fizzle" and a "grand fiasco."[55] Those who returned to work early on the 70-cent scale were reduced to the settlement rate of 60 cents, angering those who had stood by the strike and refused to work despite high wage offers. "We are beaten, and that badly, by ourselves, after having been idle only two months," miner Alfred Broad of Illinois wrote. During their brief suspension, they had "paralyzed" the country and caused "everyone . . . to realize that they cannot do without the coal miner." It was "a noble move defeated (in my mind) almost before we had [time] to look around." To Broad, canceling the suspension was not only premature but a surrender of what the miners had gained. Deflated, the miner wondered, "Will we ever be so near victory again?"[56]

Broad's sentiments were held by miners throughout the nation. "To simply say that we don't like the settlement signed by our officials would not give the readers to understand just how bitter the dose is for us to swallow," Indiana miner W. J. Winterbottom wrote. Although the miners in his region returned to work as ordered, many Indiana miners believed that the officers "abused the power delegated to them at the Cleveland convention." As it stood, Winterbottom noted that, in his region at least, "feeling against our officers who signed the compromise runs high with no signs of abatement; nothing short of their resignation and its acceptance will satisfy us." Writing on behalf of the nonunion men who were UMW members before the strike, one southern Illinois miner declared that "John McBride is the greatest scoundrel on earth, and Penna and Fahy have been consigned to hades long ago." These sentiments manifested in a more literal format in western Pennsylvania, where miners at a mass meeting burned McBride in effigy before declaring they would not accept the settlement terms.[57] McBride, in their minds, was a traitor who had "sold out" the miners' interest and dismantled a strike that he did not have the authority to govern.

The trouble did not come directly from the low settlement terms, but how the terms were settled. From the outset, union miners did not expect a victory and even the excitement of the initial successful weeks was laced with the skepticism of miners who had faced defeat so many times in the past. The miners' anger came from the officers' decision to settle the strike without seeking grassroots rank-and-file consent. The miners, not the leaders, would have to work under the new terms, yet the UMW leaders did not seek the miners opinion when settling. Such an action was unthinkable to union miners who were accustomed to mass meetings and votes to determine a union's course—a procedure McBride moved away from as he centralized the UMW's power structure.

To many miners, this effort to centralize union authority was a way to preserve the union at the miners' expense. "Our noble leaders told us all to go in the same boat, and all sink or all swim," one Pennsylvania miner said of the strike. Yet, he observed, when the officers deemed the strike's goal unachievable, "our captain tells us to do for ourselves." The miner and several others in his region were blacklisted and kicked out of their company-owned homes due to the settlement, leaving them scrambling for work after weeks of being idle. Their captain, McBride, he noted, did not have to deal with issues such as this. "He, I think, got a life preserver," the miner joked bitterly. UMW officers may have made "the rottenest settlement," but they got to keep their jobs and their homes. "[I'm] wishing they would have to go on the road with me and look for work and not one cent to go with." To him and many others, centralizing union authority only intensified the disconnect between leaders and those they represented. To them, if the union was going to be for the miners, the miners needed a say in union decisions.[58]

This stance was markedly different from what UMW leaders expected. While both leaders and many miners appreciated the need for a nationwide structure, the two groups envisioned its function differently. McBride believed the union needed a centralized structure with a constant and strong membership base, but miners saw the national union as a tool that could be used at the will of the masses. Just as miners formed and disbanded committees to settle disputes with local employers, the UMW's nationwide infrastructure became a useful means to settle a national dispute. In many miners' minds, this was a tool for the workers to wield, not a bureaucratic machine run by an officer several years removed from the mine shaft. McBride's decision to strengthen the union bureaucracy in the name of efficiency only aroused anger from the miners who wanted to make their own decisions apart from employer and labor leader alike. As a result, the same trends that allowed the UMW to mobilize workers beyond their own rank and file also proved a liability. The nonunion miners joined for a strike, not to pledge lifelong membership to the miners' union. Neither faithful union miners nor their nonunion compatriots were willing to recognize McBride's authority as the head of the strike, even if he was the head of the union that orchestrated it. His decision to settle the strike was completely out of place and beyond the authority many miners thought they had given him.[59]

Union bureaucracy and centralized power meant little to the striking miners who viewed the settlement terms not as an executive order but as an option for them to accept or reject. Far from following UMW national orders as McBride expected, nearly every UMW district involved in the strike resumed old strike settlement practices and called for special conventions to determine whether they would accept the terms the UMW had already formally accepted. While some locations decided to accept the terms upon learning the officers' reasoning behind the settlement, many others decided to settle their own terms. Four thousand miners at a meeting in Carnegie, Pennsylvania, refused to even listen to the addresses from their district officers, resolving instead to continue the strike. They asked that those who signed the 1894 settlement submit their resignations.[60] A mass meeting of more than a thousand outraged miners in Ohio resolved to continue the fight for the scale and requested the resignations of the entire UMW Executive Board that signed the compromise.[61]

Missouri miners were equally dissatisfied, "Justice" complained, arguing that "east of the [Mississippi] river are all that were considered when it came to a settlement."[62] Such disregard was enough for delegates to the Missouri-Kansas convention to declare that national officers had no authority in Missouri-Kansas District Fourteen any longer. Rather, they ordered "that the legislative power be placed in the hands of the local unions."[63] At their own convention, Illinois miners resolved that, even though they believed the officers acted within their authority to make the settlement, they would disregard the officers' settlement and continue the fight for the 1893 scale.[64] Such actions demonstrated that even if the rank and file believed the officers acted justly, they were unwilling to blindly follow the orders of a bureaucratic organization. In their minds, union agreements with employers required the consent of the workers in order to be legitimate.[65]

Consequently, Ohio state president A. A. Adams won the admiration of thousands of miners in Ohio and elsewhere when he refused to sign the 1894 settlement on behalf of the Ohio miners. Instead, he condemned the officers for overstepping their authority in the strike and called a special state convention for the miners to decide the fate of their strike on their own terms. McBride, furious at Adams for placing the state with the largest UMW membership at odds with the national officers, publicly condemned Adams's decision. The strength of the union hinged on its ability to present a united front against coal and railroad companies, McBride argued. "But let our forces become divided or our organization lose the respect of the Hocking Valley operators and they will jump at the chance of reducing wages to 40 cents, as they did in 1884." From there, he noted, the western Pennsylvania mines would follow suit, tearing down all that the UMW had built.[66]

The states had little use for the labor leader's words. Indiana mines, too remote to hear news of the settlement, were among the last to receive word of the terms. Miners in Sullivan County, one of the densest mining regions in Indiana, first learned of the terms four days after McBride announced the settlement. The miners immediately called for a special state convention to discuss the UMW leaders' actions. Although most of the Indiana miners had not yet learned of the settlement, let alone the special convention in response to it, the Sullivan miners issued a formal statement on behalf of the Indiana coalfields. Not only did the miners reject the settlement and plan to "continue this fight until we get last year's price," they also issued a harsh condemnation of the UMW leadership. Indiana District Eleven president Joseph Dunkerly "had no right whatever to sign that scale without first consulting his constituents," the miners. They went on to claim all national officers and district presidents "have violated the trust reposed in them by the miners of the bituminous districts of America" and "crippled our chances of success in the greatest and only true fight of our lives." With that, the miners joined the ranks of other miners throughout the nation asking for the resignations of Dunkerly and the other officers who had signed the settlement.[67]

Few Indiana mines had learned of the settlement by the time the Sullivan miners removed Dunkerly from office on behalf of the miners in the state. Yet, as they learned of the convention, more locals endorsed its outcome. "The removal of President Dunkerly has met with general approval throughout this district," W. J. Winterbottom reported. He insisted that anyone who condemned "the coup" was a traitor to the UMW.[68] Winterbottom's sentiments were confirmed in a second special convention called to allow miners throughout the state to participate in the decisions. After passing a motion that forbade any person who had signed the Columbus agreement from speaking or voting at the convention, the miners set about determining their stance on the suspension and Dunkerly's actions. Although the miners accepted the new scale under protest, they refused to reinstate Dunkerly and continued to request the national officers' resignations. They would tolerate low pay, but an untrustworthy officer was unacceptable.[69]

The rejection of Dunkerly was not the only problem that threatened unionism among Indiana's miners. Block miners had long complained that Indiana District Eleven officers looked after bituminous interests at the expense of the block and frequently complained that "it was an evil day for the miners of Clay Co. when we allowed our charter to be absorbed by [NTA] 135."[70] The strike settlement, which improved conditions in the block district, only intensified this divide. Ordered by state officers to remain on strike, the block miners were once again expected to sacrifice their livelihoods for the benefit of the bituminous men. As a result, District Eleven's 1894 rebellion against the UMW gave the block miners enough reason to make good on their long-standing threats to secede from District Eleven. "In the name of common sense, why should we be taxed to pay men that we would not recognize, believing that they [the Indiana District Eleven officers] not only violated our constitution, but violated every sense of honor, equity, and justice?," block district leader Samuel Anderson asked, defending the block miners' secession. With the endorsement of McBride and the other national officers, Anderson and the block miners formed a new Indiana district, District Eight, and elected Anderson district president.[71]

The fracture that caused Clay County block miners to rebel against District Eleven and District Eleven to rebel against the UMW was one result of the chaotic hostilities that ran throughout the nation in the 1894 summer. As Coxeyites found themselves held up in cities by troops, Pullman railroad strikers proved no more able to hold up the trains than the miners could choke the coal supply. By mid-July, Grand Master Workman James Sovereign ordered the Knights of Labor to immediately launch a strike in sympathy with the Pullman strike, but to no avail. Like McBride, Sovereign's authority as leader was undermined by a rank and file accustomed to a more democratic process. The *Scranton (PA) Tribune* reported that less than fifteen thousand workers joined the Knights' general strike, demonstrating Sovereign's lack of authority over the order. "The grand master workman has no power to order a strike without the action of the general executive committee," one official at the Knights of Labor's national headquarters declared. Disregarding Sovereign's order, the Knights of Labor officers appealed to all district and state assemblies to join the strike but did not command them to do so. If the Knights assemblies decided to participate, they did so not by executive order but by rank-and-file vote.[72]

The limits on authority that prevented Sovereign from calling a strike and McBride from settling one indicated that the rank and file did not necessarily value the centralization their unions underwent in the late nineteenth century. McBride and other leaders may have exercised their national authority in executing the settlement, but for the masses the strike was one launched *with* the UMW. It was not necessarily under UMW control. For the thousands of miners who supported the strike more than the union, the UMW was a vehicle to achieve a goal that came from the workers themselves, not an entity that required or deserved unequivocal loyalty.

The problem was that these competing views over who had the power to call and settle strikes created havoc on the strike effort. With the national officers unable to establish the scale the miners wanted, and the miners unwilling to accept the scale set, the state conventions' resolutions to fight for a better price was not practical. Those who resumed work at the 60-cent scale stood at odds with those who remained out for the 70-cent scale, breaking the hold the strikers had on the coal supply.[73]

As coal returned to the market, the miners who held out for 70 cents gradually returned to work in defeat. "No matter what some men pledge themselves to do[,] they can soon break their promise," one miner from Mount Olive, Illinois, wrote. The miners in his town, once a "standard bearer in the fight for right and justice" who were "sure that they would hold together till victory was won," were shattered when the UMW accepted the settlement terms. Although the miners rejected the UMW settlement and formed a local committee consisting of miners and citizens to negotiate a localized settlement and although the committee reached a new settlement with the company, the company ultimately refused to adhere to the terms. Instead of paying the promised price and assuring no miner would be blacklisted, dozens of miners found themselves out of work. The miners appealed to the UMW's Illinois state president J. A. Crawford to settle the dispute, but the officer never came. While this neglect deepened Mount Olive miners' frustration with the union, one miner noted that many of the men had "lost confidence in our state officers" even before Crawford refused to come. In their minds, the union was worthless "and we have not got any of them to believe otherwise." The miners had fair reason to think so, the miner observed; in their mine, the UMW's 1894 settlement had encouraged further wage reductions for those allowed to return to work.[74]

The story that the Illinois miner conveyed to the *UMWJ* was similar to what thousands of miners experienced in the weeks following the strikes.[75] The practice of blacklisting union men had long been implemented in the coalfields, but it grew more widespread after the suspension. The strike was unsuccessful at securing the miners' desires and ensuring their dedication to the UMW, but it did demonstrate the UMW's strength. The organization did not have large membership, but the 1894 strike showed that the UMW could mobilize workers outside its ranks and shut down the coal trade.[76] This potential for power was enough to concern coal operators, who now saw the union as a viable threat to be eliminated before it grew stronger. As both capital and government became more hostile to workers, repression snuffed out any remaining hope for raising wages. Iowa miner "Peace" noted how common this situation had become. "I notice in the paper that we are not the only men that have got blacklegs," he wrote. After ending the strike, the miners returned to the shaft only to learn that two of their union leaders were replaced by "eleven scabs, five of whom were union men, but will be so no longer." Illinois District leader W. J. Guymon found similar circumstances throughout his state. "When the strike ended the union expired," he observed. After the settlement, "operators told the men that they would have to give up the union or they could not work." Such concern for "victimization" forced workers to choose to protect their livelihoods over their union. As a result, local unions and assemblies shrank as workers surrendered their union cards to return to the shafts.[77]

Employer efforts to quash the UMW after the 1894 strike were largely unnecessary because membership was so low. Although the UMW proved it could mobilize the nation's miners, the sharp decline in membership—often even before the blacklisting began—indicated that the rank and file had little faith in the UMW after the 1894 strike, even if their employers did. For miners who were inspired by the turnout of thousands of miners willing to work together, the officers' settlement indicated that leaders could not be trusted. Some believed it confirmed that the UMW was not an organization capable of defending mine workers' interests. Perhaps more importantly, Dunkerly's overthrow and the rebellion of the State Districts marked the beginning of a reinvigorated battle between officers and the rank and file. John McBride and the other leaders had briefly succeeded in mobilizing the masses, but now the masses seemed to turn against them.

CHAPTER SIX

Wolves

Fractured Unions in the Gilded Age, 1894–1896

> We cannot expect to make a success of any movement until, when we elect men to office, we place explicit confidence and give it to them so long as they prove worthy.
>
> —William Scaife

"We have been knocked out," Philip Henry Penna remarked to a *New Orleans Daily Picayune* reporter, referring to himself and his fellow UMW officers.[1] In all his travels as vice president of the UMW, the former Indiana coal miner never planned to be turned out by an organization he helped build and sustain. Yet in November 1894, Penna and six other UMW leaders, the delegates for NTA 135, were barred from Screwman's Hall in New Orleans while the Knights of Labor conducted its annual General Assembly.

NTA 135 had served as the Knights' arm in the UMW for nearly five years by the time its delegates were shut out of the 1894 assembly, but relations between the Knights and UMW had long since soured. For years, the Knights and the AFL had been embroiled in a fight for worker loyalty that extended to the UMW organization, threatening to tear the miners' union apart. This conflict intensified when Knights general secretary John Hayes declared that the UMW's close relationship with the AFL threatened the Knights' already declining numbers.[2] UMW president and master workman John McBride's decision to challenge Samuel Gompers for the AFL presidency in December 1893 only confirmed Knights concerns that the miners' union favored the AFL. Although McBride was unsuccessful, there was little doubt he would attempt to unseat Gompers again in 1894.[3] More importantly to Knights leadership, it was well-known that the miners' delegates were part of a coup to unseat General Master Workman James Sovereign and his administration.[4] Charging that NTA 135 was nothing more than a "sideshow" to the UMW, Hayes renewed his 1892 allegations against the miners' union and insisted that NTA 135 had no right in the Knights' General Assembly unless it severed ties with the UMW. After giving the miners fifteen minutes to state their argument for remaining in the assembly, Hayes ordered a vote and barred the miners from participating in the decision. With a vote of 25 to 37, the six miner delegates were shut out of the convention, guaranteeing reelection of the Hayes-Sovereign faction.[5]

The representatives of NTA 135, then, became the latest casualties in the war within the Knights that had ousted Powderly just a year before. But the tumult that turned out Powderly and the miners was not limited to the withering Knights of Labor. Instead, it reflected the unrest that ran throughout organized labor and politics in the final decades of the nineteenth century. The upheaval that helped mobilize the laboring masses in 1894 pitted labor unions against each other and turned seemingly unified orders against themselves. Although historians have observed the fractures between major organizations like the Knights of Labor and the AFL or the infighting within these orders, few have examined how closely these battles were related to each other or how they affected the potential rank and file.[6] Close examination of worker responses to these fights indicates that the infighting among union leaders not only weakened the power structure of unions but also directly contributed to membership decline.[7]

As workers returned from the 1894 strikes, wars within the unions continued on multiple fronts, intensifying the "purge" that began when the Knights cast Powderly out of office. Dissatisfied with their leadership, the remaining rank-and-file workers waged a war against leaders, including former Indiana district president Joe Dunkerly, while power struggles among union leaders led to additional coups. Just weeks after the miners were "knocked out" of the New Orleans Assembly, the miners were at the center of a second coup, this time in the AFL, when McBride unseated Gompers as president.[8]

This unrest came from a host of sources, from personal ambition to varying opinions of how address the economic forces that hurt laborers. But for workers who already saw treachery in the 1894 strike settlements, it was unclear which organization or leader to believe. Many rural producers would have agreed with "Old Miner" of Kansas who claimed that a "wolf in sheep's clothing" lurked among them.[9] By the time he wrote those words in 1894, many miners were unsure who the "wolf" was. Instead, they distrusted across the board government officials, mine operators, and union leaders who claimed to act on behalf of the miners' interests. As the unions turned against themselves, the career labor leaders who were bogged down in ongoing battles became more suspect to the rank and file. It became increasingly difficult for workers to discern who still upheld honest labor principles and who had sold out, using the organization for personal gain. These fights did more than undermine leadership decisions; they broke apart seemingly strong unions.

Divided Forces

In many respects, the 1894 bituminous coal settlement crushed the enthusiasm the strike had inspired. Thousands of miners who had joined union ranks during the suspension threw away their union cards. But even those who remained in the union were far from content with their unions or the leadership. Instead of blaming employers or the market, many miners blamed the UMW for the failure. "I always thought the United Mine Workers were formed for the benefit of the miner," one Pennsylvania miner wrote after his mines returned to work at a reduction, "but at Anderson's it is for everybody but the honest organized miner."[10]

The miner's distinction between the UMW and "the honest organized miner" was one that many miners made in the weeks following the settlement. Such sentiments were what caused the Indiana miners to oust Dunkerly as their state president. The same day the Pennsylvania miner's letter was printed in the *UMWJ*, a letter from Indiana miner Lee Erwin also appeared. With similar emphasis on officer dishonesty, Erwin claimed that Dunkerly cared little about the miners' disdain. "He is somewhere on his junketing tour through Europe enjoying himself better than most of us since we have got 60 cents per ton," Erwin wrote. "The complaint [of Dunkerly's expulsion] all comes from such as [UMW Indiana District Eight president] Sam Anderson, P. H. Penna and their kind that think if they can't have their way everything goes wrong." Still, Erwin insisted that "old [UMW Indiana district] eleven" remained "doing her part for justice and right," even if her officers did not.[11]

Phil Penna denied that Erwin's claims of Dunkerly's travels were true, noting that the ex-Indiana district president had been working in the Indiana mines since being ousted by the miners. But the accusations Erwin and the other miners lodged against the leadership were indicative of the growing mistrust between union leaders and the rank and file. Indeed, while Indiana debated Dunkerly's honesty, Illinois miners questioned whether their state secretary treasurer, W. J. Guymon, had stolen money from the union. Regardless of whether Dunkerly truly toured Europe while miners suffered, or whether the

Illinois secretary-treasurer took money from the union, many miners found the accusations credible. Leaders like Dunkerly, Guymon, and Penna seemed too far removed from, and unconcerned with, miners' problems.[12]

In the midst of these discussions, state UMW president A. A. Adams of Jacksonville, Ohio, emerged as an authority on the allegations of officer misconduct when he opposed the UMW officers who signed the 1894 settlement. Prior to his 1894 stand he served as the president of the Sunday Creek Valley miners and tended to be more radical than most of the state and national leaders. Adams had openly criticized Ohio and national officers for instructing Ohio miners to accept scrip payments at irregular intervals on top of a wage reduction in 1893. But Adams was not the only union man upset with these terms. Ohio miners' grievances against the officers were enough for Ohio UMW miners to vote nearly every member of the Ohio Executive Board out of office in the next election, resulting in what the *Coal Trade Journal* called "a rebuke to the officers for being so conservative."[13] Adams defeated former President John Nugent by fewer than three hundred votes of the more than seven thousand cast.[14]

By the time Adams refused to sign the 1894 settlement, then, he had built a career on rebuking and challenging the more conservative business unionism tactics that UMW president John McBride advocated.[15] Indiana miners ousted Dunkerly for following McBride and joined Ohio miners in praising Adams for his condemnation of the settlement. The Ohio leader received even more attention when he claimed that the officers likely accepted bribes to end the strike. According to Adams in a later interview printed in the *Journal of the Knights of Labor*, McBride secretly met with mine operator William P. Rend while Rend's superintendent approached Adams and presumably the other members of the executive board to end the strike. If Adams agreed, the superintendent reportedly promised Adams would receive "$600 and the assurance that the operators would give me a fat job for all time to come." When Adams refused, he was offered "$1,000, and a position with the operators." The money, Adams was told, came from "the railroad companies" and "that they had furnished lots of it." Adams claimed that he rejected the offer, but the fact that the other officers had accepted the settlement was, to him, grounds for suspicion of corruption. "Whether Mr. McBride got any money I cannot say, but I was offered money to do just what he did."[16]

Adams's allegations that the officers had sold out the miners' interests tapped into suspicions already held by the rank and file. By then, the settlement and the way the officers had reached it had caused thousands to abandon UMW ranks. Those who remained tended to be more forgiving of the officers, but the latest accusations gave even loyal unionists reason to question the integrity of the officers.[17] These rumors, similar to the claims that Dunkerly was vacationing in Europe, seemed credible considering past circumstances, casting doubt on all national officers. "If that be true it is a scathing comment on the miners who put him in office," Indiana miner wife Laurene Gardner wrote of McBride when she first heard Adams's claims in July 1894. This was not the first time McBride had been charged with "selling out" the miners, she observed. "As for Phil," she continued, "I haven't the slightest doubt of his sale."[18]

For many UMW affiliates, including staunch supporters like Gardner, the question of the officers accepting bribes became one of confidence rather than of outright guilt. In a letter that forgave the officers for the 1894 settlement terms, Indiana miner "Incog" addressed the lingering charges of officer impropriety, breach of authority, and bribery allegations. Insisting that the union was ineffective if the miners did not trust their officers, Incog called for "an expression from the men." He suggested that each miner vote in favor of the officers or against them, with the checkweighman at each mine sending the results not to the state officers but to the *UMWJ* for publication. If the miners still favored the officers, the leaders could remain in office, but if the majority opposed them, the union needed to call a special convention and the officers needed to resign. "But, by all means, let us do something to settle this feeling of unrest and distrust to have confidence restored." "A Miner's Wife" from Indiana agreed. "Unless something of this kind is done, there will always be dissatisfaction, for I am told a great many locals say they will surrender their charters before they will pay any more per capita tax until the national officers are removed." Taking a vote of confidence in the officers was essential, she argued, and "if the national officers do not agree to this, they must undoubtedly be stuck on their job."[19]

For stalwart union supporters, even votes of confidence could not be given without more information. To reject the officers without a convention, investigation, or informed vote was "little short of treason," one Ohio miner wrote, noting that the "miserable cry of 'our right sold for money by our national officials'" was as disastrous to the union's reputation as miners who disobeyed union orders and destroyed company property during a strike.[20] Such caution eventually won out, with the miners resolving to hold a formal investigation at the 1895 UMW National Convention.

The UMW was not the only union divided over charges of impropriety. As McBride and the other UMW officers came under fire for their actions, the Knights of Labor, in its own turmoil, divided over the allegations against their former Grand Master Workman. Consequently, Powderly's battle, and the miner's role in it, became a touchpoint for the confusion that ran through the ranks of multiple organizations by the mid-1890s.

"National Executive Board of the United Mine Workers of America, 1897." Standing: Fred Dilcher; W. C. Pearce, secretary; R. L. Davis. Sitting: Patrick Dolan; John Kane, vice president; M. D. Ratchford, president; J. H. Kennedy. Henry Stephenson and J. M. Carson not pictured. Reprinted from Chris Evans, *History of United Mine Workers of America*, 2:480.

Cast Out

After being unseated by James Sovereign as grand master workman of the Knights of Labor at the 1893 General Assembly, Terence Powderly set out to clear his name of the charges that Knights secretary-treasurer John Hayes lodged against him. Conditions deteriorated further when Powderly and other Knights leaders were formally suspended from the order that May, on the charge that they were planning to hand what remained of the Knights of Labor over to the AFL.[21]

Within days, Powderly fired back against the claims. In a pamphlet issued to Knights members, he refuted Hayes's claims point by point. "It is a conviction with me that the intention [of Hayes] is to disrupt the order, disgust the membership, drive true men and women out of it, and then its valuable property will fall to those who remain," the former master workman wrote. "There can be no other reason assigned for such a suicidal policy as we are now witnessing."[22] As with the charges against UMW officers, rank-and-file members of the Knights were confused over which charges to believe, but the rumors around informal secret meetings led the *Scranton (PA) Tribune* to speculate that "there is an awakening in favor of Mr. Powderly."[23]

The officers of NTA 135 were among those sympathetic to Powderly's claims. NTA 135 had been the Knights of Labor's arm of the miner's union since the UMW's founding. Hayes had waged a war against the union as early as the 1892 Knights of Labor General Assembly when he gave Powderly misinformation regarding NTA 135 membership and loyalty. The charges threatened to tear apart the UMW, causing many leaders to see Hayes's war as a liability to their already feeble organization. As a result, while miners demanded the UMW officers' resignations, UMW officers conspired with Powderly to remove the Hayes-Sovereign faction from power at the 1894 General Assembly in New Orleans that November.[24]

Hayes would not surrender control easily. It was no secret that the miners who were part of the group conspiring with Powderly and that their delegates, combined with the Powderly sympathizers from other assemblies, might be sufficient in number to push the Hayes-Sovereign faction out of office. By October, the former general master workman informed his sympathizers that Hayes had a plan to retain control of the Knights. "Every District and State Assembly supposed to be friendly to me, or opposed to them, that has elected a representative to the New Orleans session is to be disfranchised," Powderly warned.[25] Still, he wanted as many supporters as possible to attend to make a stand against Hayes, even if they no longer represented their home orders. "John McBryde [*sic*] should be at New Orleans if he has to walk, even if they [the miners] have thrown him out," Powderly stressed to UMW national secretary Patrick Mc-Bryde. The statement reflected the instability of multiple labor organizations as members sought to overturn their leadership.[26]

No one was surprised, then, when John Hayes renewed his 1892 charges against NTA 135. Powderly traveled to New Orleans in anticipation, ready to stop the proceedings with a court order at the first sign of illegal action. Hayes denied seats for the miners' delegates as well as those in LA 300, convincing the other delegates, with the help of Daniel DeLeon and the Knights' socialist faction, to forbid them from entering the assembly with a vote of 25 to 37. The decision to bar the miners divided the assembly. Knowing this, the expelled delegates hoped that the twenty-five who claimed the act was unwarranted would convince other delegates to turn against Hayes and reinstate the miners in time to vote for the executive officers. Still, Hayes had enough support to hold the officer election before the assembly could move against him.[27] "Come to think of it," Powderly later reflected on New Orleans and the election, "[Hayes] was not the only rascal, he was simply preeminent in his role that was all."[28]

Such a line between "honest" officials and "rascals" was not as clearly defined to rank and file. In the weeks following the New Orleans Assembly, local assemblies received a barrage of circulars from the Knights and UMW. On behalf of the Knights, Hayes published the charges against the UMW officers and ordered that NTA 135 be reorganized solely under the Knights.[29] UMW officers refuted the charges and insisted that reorganizing NTA 135 outside the UMW would dissolve the UMW.[30] "Judging from the letters I am receiving from the local assemblies of the United Mine Workers of this state the men are at a loss to know what to do," Indiana district secretary John Kennedy wrote in his weekly report. "They claim they are receiving circulars from the [Knights] general assembly and circulars from the [UMW] national office and that they do not understand them," he continued, noting that he was equally confused. "I am not furnished with copies of all those circulars, and even if I were, I do not know that I would be able to advise."[31] Even the officers did not know whom to trust.

As UMW delegates voiced their outrage over the New Orleans Assembly, the AFL faced its own upset. Workers frustrated with Gompers's reluctance to endorse the 1894 Pullman strike and refusal to pull the federation directly into partisan politics divided AFL membership. By mid-1894, most AFL unions had voted in favor of socialist Thomas Morgan's plan to forge a political alliance between populist and radical workers. Over three hundred trade unionists ran for office, mostly as People's Party candidates. Gompers had backed away from the plan. His decision cost him the support of the AFL ranks and, by the December 1894 convention, opened the door for McBride to successfully unseat him. In the AFL, the coup signaled a push toward political action not possible under Gompers's direction and indicated the growing divisions and unrest within organized labor as a whole.[32]

Doubts

In some respects, McBride's victory over Gompers added to the ongoing confusion among the UMW's remaining rank and file. Recrimination among the rival organizations mattered little to the rank and file, and divisions between the Knights and AFL meant more to organizational leadership than its grassroots. Still, the suspicions these matters aroused influenced rank-and-file thought.[33] There was little doubt that McBride's 1894 success came from the fame he gained through the suspension. For many miners who faced blacklisting, wage reductions, and broken locals, it seemed that McBride gained more out of the settlement than the miners themselves. Knights of Labor secretary John Hayes's cries that the UMW was aligned more closely to the AFL than the Knights also found fertile ground as McBride handed the UMW presidency to Phil Penna in January 1895. That same month, while the UMW officers waged a war against the Knights of Labor, Ohio UMW officer A. A. Adams gave a public interview printed in multiple newspapers detailing the events leading up to the settlement and the bribe he was offered.[34] The scandals were all connected, the *Journal of the Knights of Labor* insisted in an editorial supporting Adams's claims. "Some of these [officers] are the men who demanded seats on the floor of the General Assembly of the Knights of Labor and were refused, and have since sought to disrupt the Order," the editorial charged. This impropriety with the strike settlement reinforced Hayes's claims that NTA 135 was corrupt and "will strengthen the opinion of many that the General Assembly was not very far from right."[35]

The charges Knights and UMW officers brought against one another strengthened the misgivings thousands of laborers had regarding the centralization of the unions and the decisions of labor leaders. For decades, those within the labor movement fought over how unions should function and who would have control over the central structure. Glassworkers, for example, spent most of the 1880s attempting to consolidate their regional unions into a single national entity. Divisions over union strategy during a strike in 1887, however, bitterly divided the ranks of the unions.[36] More familiar was the split of the cigar makers within the Knights in the mid-1880s that resulted in the formation of the AFL, or the subsequent fight within the Knights over the Home Club and its function. Divisions and fights for control, then, were not isolated to the Knights' war against the UMW but were symptoms of a common and reoccurring problem that ran throughout organized labor.[37]

Following the New Orleans General Assembly, UMW officials ordered locals to not pay the per capita tax to the General Assembly until the miners at the UMW national convention could decide on a course of action. For miners who had refused to incriminate UMW officers in the 1894 settlement without a more thorough investigation to the corruption charges, such commands to reject the Knights without any proof of the Knights' guilt seemed untrustworthy. "As long as the miners are in the dark[,] our officers are secure," George Richards of Bevier, Missouri, wrote to the *Journal of the Knights of Labor.* Although Richards was a miner and attended the New Orleans General Assembly, he was not among the NTA 135 delegates unseated at the convention. Rather, he sided with Hayes and voted the delegates out. He had "voted as a Knight of Labor" based on the evidence that was presented, but the UMW officers offered no such evidence to the NTA 135 rank and file. "Are the miners consulted? No, but an ORDER is sent out: 'Pay no more per capita tax to the General Assembly.'" Richards saw this as confirmation that the Knights had acted correctly, that UMW officers cared more to kill the Knights of Labor than to aid the miners. "In order to retain their present offices," Richards argued, UMW officers "set the miners quarreling with each other, organization to fight organization, create strikes, or anything else that will tend to keep them in power." In his mind, their expectations for miners to "blindly" follow UMW orders would only worsen the miners' condition. His words linked the ongoing fight between union leadership to the resentment from the 1894 settlement, suggesting that the UMW's centralized structure—and the leaders' position at the helm—pulled the organization away from its original goals. "My God! miners, what are we coming to?" Richards asked, "Are we not fit to be consulted on such grave matters as this? Are officers when elected to assume the powers of dictators, and tell you that you must do so and so, whether you want to or not?"[38]

Not all union miners agreed with Richards that the UMW officers were wrong, but many did agree that the ongoing battles between unions came at the detriment of worker interests. It was clear to many that at least one set of officers, if not both, cared little for rank-and-file concerns. The trouble was that it was not clear which organization was more trustworthy than the other. If a miner wished to remain a loyal "union man," he had to choose the organization to which he would remain faithful.[39]

Rank-and-file misgivings came to a head as the UMW prepared for its own national convention. In addition to holding the annual UMW officer elections, a committee would investigate Adams's charges, and the delegates belonging to NTA 135 would decide whether to side with the UMW or the Knights of Labor. The officers up for reelection were the ones who had signed the 1894 settlement. They were under investigation for bribery, overstepping authority, and corruption, and were currently embroiled in the UMW-Knights conflict. The fact that these same men were involved in so many controversies caused many miners to question "would it not be best for us to have a new set of officers entirely composed of men that have not held any office in the national before?"[40] Noting that resentment over the 1894 settlement remained strong in his district, Indiana miner Sim Cooper suggested that Phil Penna decline the nomination for president. "Now, Mr. Editor, Phil is not the only man by a great deal," Cooper continued. "Secretary McBryde is in the same box, and all that signed the compromise last June, and I think that Pat [McBryde] ought to decline, too, and let us see if the order can run one year with a new set of officers."[41]

Cooper and the other union miners' demands for new officers did not come from frustration with the 1894 settlement alone, but officers' seeming preoccupation with affairs that had little to do with the average miner. Many miners believed the "trouble between our delegates to the General Assembly and general officers of the K. of. L." had no bearing on local concerns. In fact, few state officials and local correspondents even commented on the events in New Orleans or the fight between UMW and Knights leadership that followed. Instead, their debates centered on whether their union dues were too high, if they should establish a defense fund for strikes, what to do about the constant wage reductions, and how to reach the Eastern European miners alienated from the union.[42] These were the issues that miners wanted addressed. According to many miners, however, officers' "jealousies," desires for control, and personal grudges came at the expense of these concerns, just as they had in years past. "It seems to me that when labor officials devote their time fighting each other for supremacy, that the interests of their constituents are sadly neglected," miner "T.T." wrote. Such a revival of the old "rule or ruin" policy, they believed, would only cause further injury to the already hurting rank and file.[43]

"The sooner we are rid of such officers the better it will be for the laboring men of this and every other country," T.T. declared. These concerns stemmed from the neglect that many miners felt while the officials waged their war against each other. "Think of it!," T.T. exclaimed. "Ten thousand miners in Ohio on the verge of starvation. Fifteen thousand in Pennsylvania attempting to avert a reduction in the present rate of mining. And yet we have some labor leaders who appear anxious to precipitate a war of extermination between the K. of L. and Federation miners. Shame on such men."[44]

T.T.'s claim highlighted how far removed officers were from the rank-and-file members. In similar accusations, miners pointed to the officers' salaries to demonstrate officers' disconnect from rank-and-file concerns and placed the salary question among the items to be discussed at the 1895 UMW convention. Although wages continually declined and UMW numbers shrank, officers' salaries, which came from UMW funds, never decreased.[45] Even the 1894 settlement made by the officers on behalf of the miners did not affect officer salaries, causing one Illinois miner to quip that union miners were "paying officers a salary to neglect their duties."[46] When union leader Tim O'Malley defended the officers, claiming that they did not accept their pay during the strike and instead donated "several hundred dollars" to the strike effort, miner Louis Goaziou quickly responded that this was further damning evidence that the officers earned too much. "What about the miner who don't earn $1000 in three years and suffered the pangs of hunger to uphold a principle? I know some who fed themselves on boiled bark and leaves sooner than to give up the fight," the miner continued, adding sarcastically, "But the well fed officer who goes a little into his own pocket, knowing very well that he will get it back, that's the real hero, and I suppose the hungry miner who foots up all the bills, he is a darn fool."[47]

Other miners echoed Goaziou's claims. By early 1895, one group of Ohio miners found that officers already made five times more than the average miner in their district and another reduction for the miners was pending. They believed paying the officers flat salaries would not only bankrupt the miners and their union, but also make the leaders complacent. "We believe that the nearer the officers can be kept on an equal footing with those they represent the better it will be for us," the Ohio miners declared.[48] To them, union affiliation meant little if the unions could not aid the miners, but time and again officers seemed unconcerned with the instability of the union.

Distrust of leadership flowed into other aspects of late nineteenth-century rural life. It reached into farmers' organizations and political parties, anywhere the rank and file was expected to trust someone else to usher in changes for the laborer or farmer interests. Like labor activists, farmers' organizations and political parties also learned that common goals were not enough to create a unified movement and that organizational feuds only further alienated the grassroots base. Rank-and-file producers wondered whether they should hold to the goal or cut their losses.[49]

Arguments came from all sides. Some producer organizations advocated for the People's Party while others pushed against it. Democrat Hermann Lieb appealed to the German residents of Decatur, Illinois, by claiming that no good would come from voting for the Populists. "We will never again see the day when wheat will be worth $1 a bushel," he argued, noting the competition for wheat was too strong for the price to rise. Illinois Germans, then, would do better "to vote straight democratic this time at least."[50] Such claims added to the producers' uncertainties about voting for a third party and contributed to the ongoing debate over whether it would be best to fuse with a larger party.[51]

While such arguments caused producers to question which group could best look after their interests, it also fed a suspicion that at least some of the vying entities were less than truthful about their professed intent to aid the rank and file. Concerns like these soon ran throughout politics and labor organizing, weaving them together in a web of distrust. As labor organizations like the Knights and the AFL continuously worked to undermine each other in the eyes of the rank and file, this mistrust bled into politics. Rural producers cast a wary eye at any organizer or candidate claiming to fight for the common man. In 1892, Populists in Alabama expressed concern that the Alabama Republicans' endorsement of Populist James Weaver was part of a scheme aimed to split the Democrat vote for Grover Cleveland. That same year, Terence Powderly and other Knights leaders allegedly used Republican funds to send Knights organizers into the South to generate support for Weaver at the expense of Cleveland.[52] Powderly made similar charges in 1894 when he complained to UMW secretary Patrick McBryde that the then-vice president Phil Penna received funds from the Democrat Party to organize Pennsylvania Republican miners into People's Party clubs in order to split the gubernatorial vote in favor of the Democrats.[53]

It is unclear how much merit these claims had or how they affected election results, but like the charges of bribery and other misconduct, the plausibility of the accusations was enough to intensify doubt. If the charges were true and the leaders campaigned for a party they did not truly support, they not only deceived their followers but purposely used their positions to divide the rank and file for their own personal agendas. Farmers and laborers, then, not only shared common grievances but also organizational divisions and ongoing suspicions. When coupled with the divisions created by differing reform goals, third party or fusion, and racism, such suspicion corroded any remaining foundation for a strong political alliance. Farmer and laborer efforts were simply too decentralized to unite effectively.[54]

"This neglect or overconfidence in our solidarity of unionism has led us into a snare," Ohio official William H. Crawford cautioned while surveying the UMW's precarious condition. "Men have lost confidence in their officials and can not trust one another," he continued. "This is the gigantic evil in our midst."[55] If the union's leadership did not heed the miners' concerns, he and others believed, there would be little need for them or their organizations, regardless of whether they won strikes.

This dysfunction coincided with the already growing tension between UMW national officers and miners west of the Mississippi River after the 1894 suspension. Like most other regions, western states faced wage reductions on resuming work. Their trouble was the result of two distinct causes. First, the depressed coal prices caused mines to increase production in hopes of selling greater volumes to make up for profit loss. For the first time, Iowa mines mined enough coal to compete with Illinois and Missouri mines for the Chicago and railroad markets. At the same time, southern Illinois looked to take a greater portion of the Chicago market as well.[56] Western Pennsylvania miners also moved to benefit from the Chicago market and the overwhelmingly nonunion region forced down wages in competing mines in Ohio, Illinois, and Indiana, regardless of union affiliation.[57]

Second, the competition-fueled reductions were compounded by old problems that intensified with the economic and agricultural crises. Desperate farmers suffering from lower grain prices and western silver miners hurt by the silver legislation all sought relief by mining coal. While some entered the larger shafts as diggers, others used their land to open their own mines. "Every farmer in Bellville who wishes to, can have his own coal mine, and it is not uncommon there to see the 'old man' and his boys digging, and the old woman and girls hoisting the coal with an old gin horse, and thus producing very cheap coal indeed," Illinois union leader James Flynn observed. Such enterprises dug their coal with no overhead and little debt, selling their coal far below the scale. Although individual production was less, collectively, these small-scale ventures produced enough cheap coal to force larger mines to push their wages down to compete. By early 1895, the larger corporations could not drive production costs low enough to compete with the smaller operations.[58] Profits dipped so low that operators in Iowa appealed to the UMW to force the small mines to honor the scale rate.[59]

The UMW did little to address these concerns. Missouri mine worker "Cornfield Sailor" observed that, although his state was loyal to the UMW throughout the 1894 strike, the organization did little to protect them from the competition from union and nonunion miners in neighboring states. When Kansas miners abandoned the UMW and returned to work in 1894, they injured the Missouri miners' strike, which quickly affected neighboring regions. "The reduction that those places [in Iowa] are getting now is only the consequence of former reductions at Bevier [Missouri]," Cornfield Sailor explained. In his mind, the trouble was rooted in the UMW's inability to regulate the mines west of the Mississippi because the organization focused on the mines related to the Chicago market.[60]

As the February 1895 UMW national convention neared, however, UMW president Phil Penna looked to Iowa with newfound interest. With rank-and-file miners pushing for a formal investigation into his role in the 1894 settlement, and the growing threat that the Knights miners would vote to break from the UMW, Penna seized the opportunity to cast the UMW in a positive light. According to Penna, miners in Des Moines, who had recently abandoned the UMW by transferring their NTA 135 charter to the Knights of Labor's Iowa State Assembly, were working below UMW scale rates, forcing all miners to accept the same reductions.[61] Noting that this assembly was under Sovereign's jurisdiction rather than the UMW, Penna challenged Sovereign to "exemplify the ability of the Knights of Labor, to care for the miners' interests" by commanding the Des Moines non-UMW Knights miners to honor the scale "or admit your inability to do so."[62] Such claims, designed to highlight the Knights' weakness, also made light of the problems miners faced. More concerned with the fight between the UMW and Knights than rank-and-file concerns, Penna used the situation to jab at a rival organization instead of trying to help the Iowa miners. Penna's actions reflected his lack of concern for all miners west of the Mississippi. In fact, by the time Penna declared Sovereign unable and unfit to care for the Iowa miners, the remaining UMW miners west of the Mississippi were considering seceding from the UMW to form a western miners' union.[63]

Splinters

By the time they delivered the ultimatum to the miners, the Knights' leaders were locked in similar battles with other dissatisfied groups. The glassworkers had severed ties to the Knights completely by 1895, forming the Glass Bottle Blowers' Association, separate from both the Knights and the AFL, while Daniel De Leon's socialist faction was turned out from the Knights at the General Assembly just one year after the miners.[64]

The UMW fared no better. Despite Penna and the national officers' claims that the Knights' ultimatum would split a unified order, many miners understood that what remained of the UMW was already splintered over the 1894 strike. Those who willed the UMW to survive used the 1895 convention at Columbus, Ohio, to patch wounds, even if it could not heal them entirely. Even miner wife Laurene Gardner, who accused Penna of accepting bribes during the 1894 strike, not only encouraged miners to put aside differences, but endorsed Penna for president.[65] While Penna won the presidency his reputation remained injured and his salary was reduced by three hundred dollars.[66]

The investigation of the 1894 settlement yielded equally muddled results. Labor leader and UMW historian Chris Evans wrote that Adams's accusations "created a feeling of unrest among the delegates, and questions rather hard to explain were propounded on all sides until time for adjournment."[67] ARU member Mark Wild presented allegations that McBride had not only accepted money to end the miners' strike but also gave Wild $600 to end the railroad strike. When questioned, McBride refused to state where he got the $600 he gave to Wild but denied it was paid to him as a bribe or given to Wild as a bribe to end the strike. Off the record, McBride explained the details of the exchange to the investigating committee, which unanimously ruled that "McBride did a very indiscreet thing in having anything to do with that money." The committee then found him innocent of wrongdoing and exonerated McBride and the other officers of the charge of selling out. At the same time, they also unanimously agreed that the officers had "exceeded their authority" in settling the strike.[68]

The UMW miners' decisions regarding the Knights-UMW split were less ambiguous. At a meeting after the UMW convention, NTA 135 miners voted in favor of seceding from the Knights to remain loyal to the UMW. Within weeks, the former Knights miners, along with several other trades assemblies, formed the Independent Order of the Knights of Labor.[69] Led by General Master Workman William Bauchop Wilson, a former UMW organizer and delegate at the New Orleans General Assembly, members of the new order insisted their actions were not a break from Knights principles. Instead, Independent Order members and leaders claimed their decision to form the new order was a break from an organization that had turned away from its founding ideals. Many of the old Knights' objectives continued under the Independent Order. Independent Knights aimed to end wage labor and reform society in a way that would give workers "the full benefit of the product of his toil," and it encouraged workers "to become their own employers" through cooperatives. The only major break from the Knights was over membership. Whereas the Knights of Labor demanded that miners break from the UMW, the Independent Order allowed miners to retain dual membership in the Independent Order's NTA 135 and the UMW.[70] The fact that the new order changed so little indicates the miners' frustration lay with Knights leadership rather than any sort of ideological difference.

The Independent Knights' decision to break from the old order while holding to Knights tradition was a trend that extended beyond NTA 135. Many miners who remained in union ranks after the 1895 convention likewise wished that aspects of the UMW would be remade. Old pushes for "local rule" generated new fervor throughout the districts. Indiana District Eleven delegates at the state convention considered a resolution to leave the UMW and use the ten cents paid in national dues to build a local defense fund.[71] Local Union 296 of Ohio declared to local presses that they were leaving the UMW and encouraged others to follow suit. The plan resonated throughout the state, enough for Ohio UMW leader R. L. Davis to express alarm that the UMW was at a breaking point.[72]

Davis and the other officers had good reason to worry about their ranks breaking apart. As the Independent Order incorporated former Knights into its ranks, its actions were matched by Knights of Labor secretary John Hayes. Recognizing that the Knights organization continued to decline, he "reorganized" the Knights' own NTA 135 and called for the former Knights miners' assemblies to leave the UMW and return to the order. Eleven delegates representing ten assemblies from Ohio and Indiana attended the founding meeting, held in Evansville, Indiana, in June 1895.[73]

UMW officials dismissively reported that one or two locals in their districts turned to the Knights and insisted the new NTA 135 of the Knights of Labor would be short-lived. However, the move had a greater impact on the weakened UMW than the officers implied. Ohio and Indiana were among the most thoroughly organized states. Any gains the reorganized Knights NTA 135 made likely came not from the nonunion masses but from the few who remained within the UMW despite their dissatisfaction. Indiana district secretary John Kennedy knew this to be true. The first three Indiana assemblies to secede to form the Knights of Labor NTA 135 constituted nearly one-quarter of the total locals still paying dues in UMW District Eleven.[74]

Perhaps more tellingly, the Knights NTA 135's decision to appoint A. A. Adams as master workman of the assembly left little doubt that those who rejoined the Knights did so out of an unwillingness to sit under current UMW leadership. By the summer of 1895, Adams was a symbol to many for organizational purity. He became a hero in 1894 when he refused to sign the 1894 settlement and charged UMW national officers of misconduct. His claims to fight union officer corruption were a primary reason the charges of betrayal and overstepping authority were investigated at the 1895 UMW convention.[75] Adams, then, was the ideal leader for miners unhappy with UMW officers or the union structure that, to many, seemed to bypass worker desires and concerns.[76]

The divisions that developed with the reorganization of the Knights NTA 135 had more to do with miners' mistrust of UMW officers than any preference for the Knights' organization, ideology, or goals. By 1895, neither Knights nor the UMW could achieve their goals and the ongoing battles between Knights and UMW leadership were met with little comment from the miners. In most regions, the local assemblies and local unions were more concerned with reviving their dying locals and finding trustworthy leadership than they were with the ongoing union rivalries.[77] In fact, one Pennsylvania assembly under the Independent Order declared that the infighting among the officers in the newspapers was tiresome and urged leaders to organize the miners in whatever organization the miners wished instead of attacking each other.[78]

The Pennsylvania assembly's statement reflected that rank-and-file condemnation for officer actions ran throughout the ranks, even those who remained loyal to the UMW and Independent Order. When the UMW told the miners to accept a new wage reduction in spring 1895, UMW miners in Ohio and Indiana charged that officers had once again sold out the miners and demanded state officers' resignations.[79] Miners in Summit, Indiana, called for the resignation of the national and state officers, prompting UMW president Penna to immediately reject their request, claiming the local was three months behind in dues.[80] If Penna's claim was true, the local had stopped paying dues to the national at the time national officers instructed them to accept the reduction.

Summit had allies. Officers everywhere reported locals suspended for not paying dues.[81] Miner "Next Week" noted that "there are some 32,000 miners [in

Illinois] and not one in ten are organized." This was a far cry from the energetic union of a few months earlier. His call to the workers who had left the union laid bare the reason for their departure. If an officer was guilty "of evil doing" they should "kick him so far that he cannot get back any more." With that, Next Week advised miners to "stick to the order yourself." Clearly the officers, not the strike, had convinced many to leave.[82]

Assertions like Next Week's indicated that many workers believed the atrophy labor organizations experienced in the mid-1890s was at least partially the result of workers' lack of confidence in their leaders. "Had we a Debs," one miner posited, "we might claim nine-tenths of the miners of our country as members."[83] Eugene Debs's proximity to the midwestern coalfields, charisma, and likely his stance in 1894 that harkened back to the generalist principles of the Knights of Labor, made him a hero for workers' justice in many miners' minds.[84] Their cries for "a Moses" who would "lead us out of this wilderness in which we find ourselves" gave way to new non-UMW worker organizations consisting largely of miners frustrated with the UMW.[85] Miners in Ohio formed the Massillon Independent Movement. In Indiana miners became a base for the American Industrial Union, which planned to make Eugene Debs their president while Iowa formed the Iowa Miners' Protective Association that former Missouri UMW mine worker "Cornfield Sailor" hoped Missouri would emulate.[86]

Misgivings over leadership rippled throughout rural laborers' ranks and into the Populist Party. When Independent Order leader Charles Martin wrote to the *Southern Mercury* claiming the Knights of Labor leadership was corrupt, his charges quickly spread beyond organized labor and reached into US politics. Infuriated by Martin's allegations, Knights of Labor master workman James Sovereign penned a reply, not to the *Journal of the Knights of Labor,* but to Jacob Coxey's newspaper, *Sound Money*, denying the claims. Martin immediately wrote a rebuttal to *Sound Money* defending his charges. Sovereign and Knights secretary John Hayes conducted multiple deals with Knights factions (particularly Daniel De Leon and the socialist faction) to gain and keep control of the Knights of Labor. Martin also claimed to have proof that Hayes had a "scheme" to establish "gas machine" franchises in Ohio and used Knights money to pay personal lawyer fees. "Persons who read Populist papers don't need to be told what this means," Martin wrote in his rebuttal. "Bribery and Bonds, Bonds, Bonds!" This was not the behavior of true leaders with the concerns of working people in mind, Martin continued, and, in his opinion, the People's Party was no better. They "have been assisting in furnishing salaries to these hypocritical demagogues, and I have no apologies to make for my warnings to the press." In Martin's mind, the organizations and political parties that claimed to be for the workers needed to be cleaned out. Until then, Martin believed, justice would not be done for the worker.[87]

Given his scathing indictment of the People's Party, it is unlikely that Martin was surprised when the editor of *Sound Money* declined to print his letter on the ground the newspaper wanted to avoid the dispute. "Funny that Mr. Coxey's editor did not think of this before publishing Mr. Sovereign's letter," Martin quipped in an Independent Order of the Knights of Labor circular addressed to "Reform Editors and Ohio Populists." The circular included the letter that *Sound Money* had rejected. In it, Martin recalled the original goal of the Populists to break from old party corruption and noted that now it was time for the Populists to address the problems within their party rather than calling for "harmony at the expense of honor and integrity." Martin wanted no part of such corruption. "Populism existed before Coxeyism, and I will continue as I have in the past, up 'the middle of the road,' exposing rascality inside or outside the party," he concluded.[88]

"Rascality" seemed to be everywhere in the organizations that claimed to be for the worker. The miners may not have known who was most trustworthy, but their years in the coalfields had shown them how easy it was for an individual (whether worker or union leader) to sell out their principles for better stability. This understanding likely lingered in the back of workers' minds when any leader's reputation was called into question. Claims like Martin's played on this suspicion, causing individuals to question every leader of every organization. As a union official, Martin's words had power. He claimed to have exposed the Knights' treachery and then claimed this dishonesty carried over to the Populists. His words could at least cause the members of the Independent Order, who already distrusted the Knights of Labor, to think twice before casting their vote for the People's Party. For the thousands of other workers who were not sure who to believe, Martin's was one more voice to consider, and his claims offered more possibilities of dishonesty to entertain. Perhaps the Knights were not alone in betraying the workers. Perhaps the People's Party was no longer truly for the people. As a result, the splinters that plagued organized labor only further widened fractures within politics as well.

The sheer number of conflicting voices claiming to speak for the common man made it nearly impossible to discern which individuals were trustworthy. Topeka attorney David Overmeyer conveyed a similar assessment to William Jennings Bryan regarding fears of dishonesty within the Democrat Party on the eve of the 1896 Democratic National Convention. He advised Bryan to speak in a way that would dispel confusion. "The friends of the people ... must be plain and outspoken, or they can have no power with the people," he insisted.[89]

If Bryan wished to win the vote of the people, he needed to convince them that he was the most reliable of all the candidates claiming to have the interests of the common man at heart.

Confusion between who was trustworthy and who was a "wolf," then, shattered any unified foundation Gilded Age producer organizations had built. Jaded by years of promises of grand victories that never materialized, by the mid-1890s, many producers had grown weary of the rhetoric that never seemed to result in change.

The membership decline in the miners' union captured this weariness vividly. "At our annual convention in 1891 Secretary Watchorn reported a membership of a fraction over 34,000. Since that time our membership has been on the decline," Indiana District Eleven secretary John Kennedy wrote angrily. Uniting the miners into one grand union was supposed to usher in a new period of success for the miners, but this vision only seemed to slip further away. "We have tried for six years to perfect our organization and we are farther from the goal than we were five years ago."[90] Only 5 percent of Illinois miners were organized and Indiana barely had one-quarter in the union, *UMWJ* editor John Kane declared. "Take Pennsylvania and the same condition of affairs exists, even to a worse degree. Take West Virginia, Tennessee, Kentucky, Virginia and Missouri, yes, even Ohio, and every other state whose relations to each other are such that what affects one influences the other, and they are all in a condition in which the crudest methods of warfare are almost impracticable," he observed. A vision of success meant nothing if the organization did not have the means to carry it out.[91]

The fracture of the miners' movement meant that the UMW was powerless. Numbers were small because the union could not achieve its objectives, but securing these goals would prove nearly impossible until leaders found a way to increase membership. As a result, it was damned no matter what course of action it pursued. This realization left many unionists puzzled over what path to pursue. Kennedy observed that the UMW "would lose some members" if they tried again to work to raise wages. But, he reasoned, "it is equally true if we remain inactive and do nothing we will lose members."[92] Miners in Streator, Illinois, agreed, noting that, instead of uniting across district and state lines, miners were "making a fight by themselves, the same as in olden days before we were brought in such close competition with one another by improved methods of transportation." Such efforts would only end in failure, they acknowledged, but they saw no alternative. While surveying the UMW's failures, the Streator miners claimed that "lack confidence in one another and also in our officers," intensified UMW weaknesses, because, they wrote, "instead of building[,] it keeps us rebuilding."[93]

There was little the union could offer the miners, but "masterly inactivity," or sitting around and "hoping for better times," Linton, Indiana, miner and former union leader "Incog" declared. "Why just think of it, we are all in the habit of speaking of Earlington district (Kentucky) as a blackleg hole and yet those men have not come below 62½ cents a ton and are now getting 76 cents, and a man can put out as many tons of coal there as he can at any mine around Linton."[94] Editors of the *American Federationist* made a similar observation, commenting that the miners believed their best chance at finding work was to "take a cold-blooded business view of the situation" and work for lower wages. "No other trade or calling in America today has the same gloomy outlook for the immediate future as have the bituminous coal miners," the editor continued.[95] The observation proved true at the UMW National Convention in April 1896, where officers sourly noted the union's poor condition of affairs. Over the course of the past year, the UMW's debt had increased to $3,000 while membership remained low; fewer than eight thousand miners paid dues to the order.[96] Too weak to strike, the UMW collected dues and ordered the rank and file to wait until conditions improved. If the miners were going to be masters at inactivity, many believed it would be better if they did so outside the union rather than in it.

If the unions were not active, the miners still were. Under the cover of darkness in the late summer of 1896, several masked men burned down the Old Pittsburg Coal Company's mine in Hymera, Indiana.[97] Prior to this act of arson, the Hymera miners were locked in a dispute not with the company but with the neighboring mines over the size of the screen used to filter the coal.[98] "The lawful screen for this state, or at least the law recognized, is 1¼ inch diamond bar," Indiana District Secretary John Kennedy explained. "The screen at Hymera was $1^{17}/_{56}$ inches between diamond bars, and they were nearly always in trouble for the last couple of years with these men because of their unfair screen."[99] The $^3/_{56}$-inch difference between the two drove down regional coal prices enough to help trigger a 5-cent-per-ton wage reduction in mines throughout the area. Even the formerly thoroughly unionized District Eleven no longer had the power to enforce its regulations.

The other miners in the region walked out on strike when asked to accept the new reduction that summer, but Hymera accepted the terms. Most who worked there were also farmers and saw no reason to fight a reduction in their supplemental income. They continued mining at the newly reduced rate until the fire destroyed everything from the tipple to the shaft. "So far, nobody seems to have any idea who done it," Kennedy wrote, insisting that the "deplorable" arson would do more harm to an already depressed region. Yet even as he condemned the vigilantes' actions, Kennedy wanted some good to come from the event. Namely, he hoped the company would use its insurance money to purchase a new screen compliant with Indiana regulations.[100]

The Old Pittsburg Coal Company did not share Kennedy's vision. The company already experienced financial difficulties before the fire, and, after claiming nearly $50,000 in damages, company executives declared the mine was not worth rebuilding and made plans to leave the region altogether. In the following weeks, the Hymera farmer-miners pleaded with the company not only to remain in Hymera but to rebuild the mine as soon as possible. In exchange, some offered money to help cover the initial building costs while other farmer-miners promised the company six days of work without wages. To everyone's surprise, the company complied, rebuilt the mine, and announced that anyone seeking a spot in the new shaft would first have to give the company six days of free labor. "And that is not the worst of it," Kennedy railed, "this is to be the rule for a year. Fellow miners, any of you that have six days' labor to pay for a job at a mine where they are paying less than scale rates . . . and will promise not to claim any of the rights of citizenship, you might be able to get work at Hymera, Ind." Despite Kennedy's outrage, however, over a hundred men agreed to the company terms.[101]

The desperation that ran throughout the corn and coalfields by the mid-1890s made situations like that in Hymera far too common. Miners in Spring Valley, Illinois, were irate when the city inspector found that the company's scales cheated the miners out of five hundred pounds per ton, which amounted to 25 percent of their pay. The revelation exacerbated an already tense situation. For months, black miners in the region had been working for wages lower than the promised rate and when they decided to accept the cheated weight, other miners in the community looked for a reason to attack the black miners. Tensions escalated further when an unknown black man shot a local Italian man while robbing him. The *Streator Daily Free Press* noted that the incident "gave the Italians a long cherished chance to . . . drive the negroes out of town." Within hours, a mob of "foreigners" led by the region's Italian miners and a second mob of "white" miners emerged. They ransacked the black miners' living quarters, shooting and beating men, women, and children. For nearly two days, black miners and their families hid in the woods as the mobs armed with shotguns scoured the land, "hunting for negroes."[102]

The conditions that caused the Hymera miners to burn down the shaft were the same that caused Spring Valley miners to divide along racial lines. Such actions exposed the forces that caused rural workers to attack each other as much as their employers. By then, the southern Midwest was almost solidly nonunion. Bituminous miners' annual income had declined from $292 in 1894 to $282 just two years later, making their earnings 68 percent of what factory workers earned in 1896.[103]

Faced with a crippled economy, increasing debt, and defunct producer organizations, thousands of producers pinned their hopes for change on the ballot box, but their efforts there were fruitless. Just as they remained divided over which organization or leader to follow, neither farmers nor miners in the South, Midwest, or indeed anywhere could agree on which party or platform would improve their conditions. Meanwhile, ethnic divisions further prevented rural producers from voting together. Even with a fusion ticket in 1896, they failed to unite on a national stage. Instead, miners, like farmers and other rural laborers, split their votes among the parties.[104] Their refusal to vote together, their embrace of vigilantism, and their willingness to work for depreciated terms exemplified what many producers throughout the nation thought: that they were better off looking after their own interests than following an organization or party, even when they accepted worse terms than they desired.

Epilogue

There had never been much reason to visit the tiny coal mining town just outside "Egypt" until December 7, 1930. On that day, the number of people in Mount Olive, Illinois, swelled by four thousand as visitors came to pay respects to one of the miners' greatest champions before she was interred. Mary "Mother" Jones had dedicated much of her life to the miners' unions, first as a volunteer in the late nineteenth century and then as a paid UMW organizer after 1901. "The miner's angel" became famous for her involvement in Colorado and West Virginia strikes, but her heart remained with the Illinois miners. Consequently, at her request, her body was placed with the miners and wives buried at the Union Miners' Cemetery in Mount Olive.[1]

The union cemetery had been created to hold the bodies of three Mount Olive miners killed during an 1898 coal strike in Virden, Illinois, when strikers and their wives waged a gunfight against mine guards. Six miners and five guards were killed.[2] Seen as "murderers" by community leaders, the three miners from Mount Olive were denied burial in the local cemetery. The Virden miners were given a proper burial when the UMW purchased a one-acre tract of land to place their bodies. By the time Jones made her burial request in 1923, the cemetery was a resting place for dozens of mining families, including "General" Alexander Bradley, who marched with Jacob Coxey in 1894 and led a group of "soldier-miners" in an 1898 march on Virden.[3] Jones wished to be part of this legacy. "I hope it will be my consolation when I pass away to feel I sleep under the clay with those brave boys," she wrote, for in her mind, "they are responsible for Illinois being the best organized labor state in America."[4]

In many respects, Jones's assessment of the strength of organized labor was correct. By 1930, the UMW claimed over 160,000 members, a giant compared to where it stood at the close of 1896, with fewer than ten thousand in its ranks.[5] No one could deny that the UMW was crippled in 1896, but changes in both the union and the national economy in the years following gradually improved its strength. The 1894 strike did not secure the miners' demands, but it proved that the UMW could mobilize miners on a national scale. This set the UMW apart from other miners' organizations and gave the union more validity, even if miners mistrusted its leadership.

By late 1896, many of the national leaders whose reputations were stained by the 1894 settlement had moved out from the order. Phil Penna, for example, stepped down as president at the end of his 1896 term. Like other labor leaders of his generation who switched from organizing to positions in government and business, Penna left the union to become superintendent for the coal company he had partially owned while acting as UMW president. Miners' trust for UMW leadership grew only gradually as leaders like Penna left the UMW executive offices.[6]

The shift in UMW leadership coincided with several other changes in the late 1890s. Improved economic conditions allowed farmers once again to turn a profit from their crops. With coal wages remaining low, fewer farmers looked to the mines for their incomes. Meanwhile, UMW leaders decided to mobilize the nation's nonunion miners to strike once again.[7] By then, years of under-cutting, competition, low profits, and endless local strikes made at least some coal operators more willing to consider cooperating with competing mines and the miners' unions to raise the price of coal.[8] Organizations like the UMW and AFL were not stable, but by the late 1890s, their willingness to negotiate with businessmen while reigning in radical elements gave them legitimacy and bargaining power, even if membership numbers remained low.[9]

Mother Jones became directly involved with the miners' organizations just as the UMW came onto the national stage. She had volunteered for the UMW since the end of the 1894 strike, but in 1897 she joined leaders like Eugene Debs, James Sovereign, and Samuel Gompers in a multi-organizational push to mo-bilize the nonunion coalfields. The effort pulled the AFL into cooperation with both the Knights of Labor and socialists, creating for the first time in years an unlikely but forceful labor coalition.[10] Their labors culminated in a somewhat successful 1897 strike led by UMW president Michael Ratchford that increased the average miners' wage, revived the interstate scale agreements, and, in some places, implemented an eight-hour workday. While not an overwhelming success, especially since the West Virginia mines remained staunchly nonunion, the victory, no matter how limited, was welcome after so many years of defeat.[11]

During those months, young Illinois miner John Mitchell gained fame for brokering peaceful negotiations between Illinois miners and operators and for bringing "discipline" to a rank and file accustomed to local strikes, a task previous UMW leaders had attempted with less success. Hailing from the northern Illinois mines, Mitchell understood the local and national problems that affected miners' wages and working conditions and was a firm believer in collective bargaining. The stance won him favor among midwestern coal operators, including coal magnate Charles Devlin of the Atchison, Topeka, and Santa Fe Railroad, but his successes in settling disputes in Illinois also earned him the miners' respect.[12]

Mitchell continued this trend when he unofficially assumed the UMW presidency in 1898. Although he intensified the UMW's centralizing trend, the twenty-eight-year-old labor leader also worked to increase rank-and-file involvement in the order. He granted Illinois miners the right to set their own terms for when they would work and pushed to expand the executive board to include members from all UMW districts who were directly appointed by the rank and file of each district. The change meant that national officers were no longer disconnected from the masses. Mitchell's efforts to include the rank and file complemented his tactics, which allowed the UMW to make strides in negotiating wage agreements with operators, most notably in the 1902 anthracite coal strike.[13] These successes carried into the twentieth century and increased under the leadership of former southern Iowa grain dealer and miner John L. Lewis.[14]

By the time Mother Jones died in 1930, the UMW was one of the strongest labor organizations in the United States. Fewer than six years after Jones was laid to rest, fifty thousand miners returned to the miners' cemetery to dedicate a monument in her honor.[15] Despite the high turnout for the legendary labor leader, however, Illinois miners were still far from unified. Rather, the organized miners of the state were divided between two vying unions. The miners who built and dedicated Jones's monument were members of the Progressive Miners of America (PMA) and its women's auxiliary. Founded in 1932 by southern Illinois union miners dissatisfied with UMW leadership, PMA affiliates claimed that UMW president Lewis had betrayed their interests by entering into an agreement with coal operators, including former UMW president Phil Penna. By then, Penna had risen through the ranks of the coal industry, not only accumulating new holdings and forming new coal companies with other mine owners but also serving as a leader in the Bituminous Operators Association (BOA). By the time he sat at the negotiation table with Lewis, Penna was a BOA spokesperson vehemently opposed to trade unionism and was among those who negotiated the terms that infuriated midwestern miners.[16]

The PMA and UMW spent the next several years engaged in violent battles throughout the southern Illinois coalfields, breaking each other's strikes and attacking each other in legal battles, in newspapers, and in sporadic gunfights.[17] When the PMA erected Jones's monument, twenty new names were listed on the monument with Jones and the 1898 Virden miners. According to the monument's inscription, these nineteen miners and one miner's wife gave their lives in the 1930s PMA mine wars, fighting against both the government and the UMW, for "the cause of clean unionism in America."[18]

Like Jones herself, the memorial testified to the complexities of labor organizing and how divided loyalties and internal divisions are typically understood and remembered. Jones's career as a labor organizer began long before she joined the UMW payroll.[19] As with many other women involved in the labor movement, she held no membership in these early years, which allowed her unofficial efforts to be easily overlooked. Her monument reveals a story also easily forgotten. It was funded and built by union workers who opposed the main labor organization of their industry so bitterly that they were willing to die fighting against it. In honoring those killed fighting the UMW, Jones's monument was anti-UMW propaganda, proof that "organized labor," even in the 1930s, was divided against itself. Even the strongest unions at the height of their strength alienated workers who doubted that labor organizations had workers' interests at heart.[20]

These nuances are often missed when historical actors are lumped into neat categories. Terming rural residents as exclusively "miner" or "farmer" hides the dual occupation tendency that crucially allowed rural families to survive. Casting workers as either union or nonunion likewise obscures a host of laborers who supported some ideas of unionism while simultaneously acting against the union. In the case of the 1930s, "organized labor" consisted of competing organizations, yet this period is often remembered as a time when workers were united. In the Gilded Age, the formation and development of labor organizations like the United Mine Workers often overshadows the challenges these new orders had to overcome. In each case, not looking closely at these divisions runs the risk of oversimplifying our understandings of the people and organizations we study.

Although workers' conditional support for unions is not unique to the late nineteenth century, worker dissatisfaction with labor organizations is particularly vivid in that period. The problems created by an increasingly competitive market required that rural producers pragmatically pursue multiple avenues to make ends meet. Sometimes this meant cobbling together industrial work with farming or investing. It required wives to be not only homemakers but active partners in financial decisions. As companies and unions fought for control of the market, and governments sided with corporations, many workers approached the situation similar to how they lived their lives. They cobbled various views together, siding with whatever entity offered the best opportunity for advancement.

While these decisions were practical for mining families, they were not always understood by union leaders. Neither conditional acceptance nor partial rejection of the union reflected what union organizers desired to see in their rank and file. For organizers dedicated to establishing a place for unions in a rapidly industrializing nation, success depended on centralizing the order and relying on a "disciplined" rank and file that followed orders unwaveringly. To union organizers, the workers who only sometimes followed orders and fell in and out of the union were unconscionable and seemed to threaten the meager success the order had achieved.

Still, as this book shows, such workers were not as nonunion as leadership claimed. The rural workers' livelihoods demanded they continually seize opportunities for personal gain, whether in the form of collective action or through "selling out" their neighbors. Many miners based their decisions to work with the union on their perceptions of whether the union had the ability to address their immediate needs. In 1894 nonunion workers joined with the UMW to stage a national strike. Farmer-miners joined the UMW during winter strikes to have access to union aid, while some black miners such as Richard Davis saw the UMW as a means to achieve greater equality in the workplace and society. Workers, then, had no trouble seeing value in unionism when it fit with their own goals.

At the same time, the multiple roles rural workers maintained also pulled workers away from union goals and agendas as often as they pulled them into the union fold. The need to look after their own income and stability at times placed workers at odds with the orders that claimed to represent their interests. Jimmy Wilson, whose inexperience caused the mine to explode in 1888 Frontenac, Kansas, was not the only worker to get his job because his boss disregarded safety regulations. Those who owned mines or stock in mines thought twice before following union orders to demand higher wages or go on strike. Black and non-English-speaking miners and those who mined west of the Mississippi felt overlooked by the UMW and saw little reason to join an organization that attacked them as incompetent and dishonorable.

Others turned away because they feared that the union or its leadership had stopped looking after the miners' interests. Worker reactions to orders to accept wage reductions instead of striking, the aborted strike in 1891, and the fallout from the 1894 settlement showed that workers thought critically about union orders before following them. These decisions to partially or fully reject the union were not products of indifference for their interests or a lack of faith in collective action, however. Workers' decisions to remain in the union but to withhold dues, break away from one organization but join a rival order, or go on strike despite union orders to work are all instances that demonstrate that workers valued collective action. Their collective decisions in these cases simply ran against union desires.

Looking beyond the union and nonunion categories, then, reveals not only a much more complex picture of rural families' lives, identities, and experiences in the Gilded Age, but also how and why worker organizations formed and failed. As their communities and organizations collectively adapted to the changes taking place in their hometowns and industries, workers adapted their under-standings of capitalism and profit on an individual basis, as well. Appreciation for capitalism was mixed with desire for fairness among Gilded Age miners who were torn between loving their "neighbor" and making a personal profit. This varied identity, which allowed a worker to simultaneously identify as a part of a collective body and as an individual, is at the heart of the workers' decisions to join or reject union orders.

As workers wrestled with balancing their consciences with their budgets, unions like the UMW struggled with balancing worker demands while trying to regulate the national market. Wrestling for control of the national market against major corporations demanded a centralized structure but this structure was also what frequently shattered the rank-and-file allegiance that unions needed to succeed. While they did not always understand why worker's desires did not completely align with the union's, the workers' fluid concepts of union-ism shaped how unions developed. At least part of union success in these early years hinged on union leaders' ability to listen to and accommodate grassroots desires while building a centralized structure capable of securing favorable negotiations with corporations.

This tradition of balancing union agendas with worker desires applies as much to the 1930s coalfields and present-day workers as it does to the workers of the Gilded Age. Union leaders did not always understand, but these workers shared a legacy as individuals whose interests were mixed and conflicting, but not without reason. They were not, as organizers claimed, duped into rejecting the union. They were not fooled into thinking the union did not look after their interests or tricked into voting "against their interests." They were not always good unionists, but they also were not the individualistic actors unwilling to cooperate with one another. Rather, these workers were far more cooperative than organizers recognized. Their concepts of community and collective action simply did not always fit the mold created by the fledgling national labor organizations. Instead, their experiences, needs, and desires bound them together informally in their workplaces, regions, and states. Sometimes these connections pulled them closer to their employers' worldviews than their unions'. Through all of this, their search to improve their livelihoods and protect their autonomy was constant, even if their union membership and union identity were not.

Notes

Abbreviations

ATSF Records	Atchison, Topeka, and Santa Fe Railway Company Records
BLS	Bureau of Labor Statistics (Illinois; Kansas)
BLSI	Bureau of Labor Statistics and Inspection (Missouri)
BLIS	Bureau of Labor and Industrial Statistics (Kansas)
CTJ	*Coal Trade Journal*
EMJ	*Engineering and Mining Journal*
FAMI	Federated Association of Miners and Mine Laborers of Indiana
IMPA	Illinois Miners' Protective Association
JKL	*Journal of the Knights of Labor*
JUL	*Journal of United Labor*
JWH Papers	John W. Hayes Papers
NLT	*National Labor Tribune*
NYT	*New York Times*
TVP Papers	Terence Vincent Powderly Papers
UMWJ	*United Mine Workers' Journal*
WBW Papers	William Bauchop Wilson Papers
WJB Papers	William Jennings Bryan Papers

Introduction

1. Richard Wilson testimony, *Cherokee & Pittsburg Coal & Mining Company v. Amelia Siplet*, 50–90.

2. "Mass Meeting," *Pittsburg (KS) Headlight*, November 15, 1888.

3. Ibid.

4. "The Mine Horror," *Pittsburg (KS) Headlight*, November 15, 1888; "A Mine of Death," *NLT*, November 17, 1888; Ohio Federation of Miners and Mine Laborers Official Report, "Ohio Miners," *NLT*, November 24, 1888; Gorn, *Mother Jones*, 71.

5. "Mass Meeting," *Pittsburg (KS) Headlight*, November 15, 1888.

6. Patrick McBryde, interview excerpts in *UMWJ*, June 22, 1893.

7. Dubofsky, *Industrialism and the American Worker*, 38.

8. Case, "Losing the Middle Ground."

9. "Non-unionist Miner Loquitur," *Punch*, or the *London Charivari*, April 26, 1879; "Economy," to the editor, *UMWJ*, February 25, 1892.

10. Roll, "Faith Powers and Gambling Spirits"; Roll, "Sympathy for the Devil," 15; Minchin, *What Do We Need a Union For?*; Norwood, *Strikebreaking and Intimidation*, 6–7.

11. Miners were paid less for mine run coal because of its impurities. Phil Penna, to the editor, *UMWJ*, May 28, 1891; Roy, *History of the Coal Miners*, 354.

12. Dix, *What's a Coal Miner to Do?*, 5, 189–94; D. Nelson, *Shifting Fortunes*, 9, 15–17; Mitchell, *Carbon Democracy*, 19–22.

13. "An Old Ninety-Sixer," to the editor, *UMWJ*, July 9, 1891 (quotation); Jack Sparrow, letter to editor, *UMWJ*, December 3, 1891; Caldemeyer, "Unfaithful Followers," 115.

14. Weir, *Beyond Labor's Veil*; McMath, *Populist Vanguard*; Gutman, *Work, Culture, and Society*, 79–118; Creech, *Righteous Indignation*; Blum, "By the Sweat of Their Brow"; Van Tine, *Making of the Labor Bureaucrat*, 34–40.

15. "Fair Play," to the editor, *NLT*, July 25, 1891; "Practical Christianity," reprinted from the *Farmer's Tribune* (Des Moines, IA), *NLT*, January 9, 1892; Richard Wilson testimony; Gourevitch, *From Slavery to Cooperative Commonwealth*.

16. "A Miner," to the editor, *UMWJ*, January 4, 1894.

17. "Wigs, the Kid," to the editor, *UMWJ*, January 4, 1894; M. Commesky, to the editor, *UMWJ*, April 23, 1891; Dan McLaughlin, to the editor, *UMJW*, September 24, 1891; "Dhroleen," to the editor, *UMWJ*, October 20, 1892; Groat, *Introduction*, 455–58.

18. P. H. Donnelly, to the editor, *UMWJ*, January 5, 1893.

19. John McBride, to the editor, *UMWJ*, March 9, 1893; John McBride, Speech to the 1893, UMW National Convention, in Evans, *History of United Mine Workers*, 2:180.

20. "Miner," to the editor, *UMWJ*, November 9, 1893 (quotation); William B. Wilson, to the editor, *UMWJ*, July 7, 1898; "Lincoln," to the editor, *NLT*, August 13, 1887; Robert Smith, to the editor, *NLT*, March 3, 1888; "Miner," to the editor, *JUL*, June 23, 1888; J. H. Kennedy, UMW District Eleven Report, *UMWJ*, December 8, 1892.

21. William B. Wilson, to the editor, *UMWJ*, July 7, 1898; "Tramp," to the editor, *UMWJ*, July 27, 1893.

22. R. L. Davis, to the editor, *UMWJ*, March 14, 1895.

23. Phillips-Fein, *Invisible Hands*; E. Fones-Wolf, *Selling Free Enterprise*; N. Lichtenstein, "From Corporatism to Collective Bargaining."

24. Moreton, *To Serve God and Wal-Mart*; Kruse, *One Nation under God*; E. Fones-Wolf and K. Fones-Wolf, *Struggle for the Soul*.

25. Fraser, *Age of Acquiescence*, 292.

26. Destler, *American Radicalism*, 2 (quotation), 7–9, 14–15; Fink, *Workingmen's Democracy*, 112.

27. Hild, *Greenbackers, Knights of Labor, and Populists*; Dubofsky, *Industrialism and the American Worker*, 73–75.

28. McMath, *American Populism*, 42–43; Hild, *Greenbackers, Knights of Labor, and Populists*.

29. Postel, *Populist Vision*, 4, 106 (quotation).

30. Higbie, *Indispensable Outcasts*, 13; Fink, *Workingmen's Democracy*, 9; Goldstene, *Struggle for America's Promise*, 47, 53–54; Gourevitch, *From Slavery to Cooperative Commonwealth*; Leikin, *Practical Utopians*.

31. UMW Circular, *UMWJ*, April 30, 1891 (quotation); Samuel Gompers Address to the 1891 UMW Convention, *NLT*, February 14, 1891.

32. Arnold, *Fueling the Gilded Age*, 10, 165–66; White, *Republic for Which It Stands*, 799; Jensen, *Winning of the Midwest*, 239–40.

33. Laurie, *Artisans into Workers*; Oestreicher, *Solidarity and Fragmentation*; Forbath, *Law*, ix, 31, 135; Voss, *Making of American Exceptionalism*, 228; Form, *Divided We Stand*; Beik, *Miners of Windber*; Letwin, *Challenge of Interracial Unionism*; Gerteis, *Class and the Color Line*; Goldstene, *Struggle for America's Promise*, 49, 203–4.

34. Arnold, *Fueling the Gilded Age*, 10, 169.

35. White, *Railroaded*; White, *Republic for Which It Stands*, 349; Arnold, *Fueling the Gilded Age*; Wolff, *Industrializing the Rockies*; Adams, "Promotion, Competition, Captivity."

36. Higbie, *Indispensable Outcasts*, 6–13, 46.

37. One exception was the Campbell Act enacted in Pennsylvania. This act levied a tax on companies for each nonnaturalized employee. Companies passed this tax on to the workers in the form of a pay deduction. Additional racial and ethnic exploitation is discussed in more detail in chapters 1, 4, and 6; Gutman, *Work, Culture, and Society*, 122; Shackel, *Remembering Lattimer*, 26.

38. George A. Fitch to Willard C. Flagg, March 5, 1878, folder 6, box 1, Flagg Family Collection; Arnold, "Mother Jones"; Armstrong, "Georgia Lumber Laborers," 439; Jensen, *Winning of the Midwest*, 240; Douglas, *Real Wages*, 223, 350, 353; Rees, *Real Wages in Manufacturing*, 74.

39. Jensen, *Winning of the Midwest*, 238–68, esp. 245; Destler, *American Radicalism*, 175–211; Mitchell, *Carbon Democracy*, 19–20; Pierce, *Striking with the Ballot*, 11–14.

40. "Restriction" *UMWJ*, November 21, 1895; J. H. Kennedy, UMW District Eleven Report, *UMWJ*, November 5, 1891.

41. Jameson, "Imperfect Unions"; Susan Levine, "Workers' Wives"; Chateauvert, *Marching Together*; Merithew, "We Were Not Ladies."

42. Brown, "To Catch the Vision of Freedom."

43. Osterud, *Bonds of Community*; Marti, *Women of the Grange*, 7–11, 26; Jeffery, "Women in the Southern Farmers' Alliance," 79; Ayers, *Promise of the New South*, 205–7, 233.

44. Jeffery, "Women in the Southern Farmers' Alliance"; Sen, "Sexual Division of Labor."

45. Kane assumed the editorship in the early 1890s from an unnamed "practical printer" and served as editor until his death in 1897. Thomas W. Davis took his place. Roy, *History of the Coal Miners*, 294.

46. Samuel Simon, to the editor, *NLT*, July 25, 1891; "Miner," to the editor, *NLT*, July 18, 1891; John Donnelly, to the editor, *NLT*, May 30, 1891; Llewellyn, to the editor, *NLT*, May 23, 1891; editorial response to J. H. Kennedy, *UMWJ*, November 12, 1891.

47. This policy quietly changed in late 1894 and early 1895 when UMW leadership was embroiled in scandal and membership declined. Nearly bankrupt, the *Journal* printed fewer pages and carefully selected the letters it would print. "A Compliment," *UMWJ*, July 2, 1891; "Outlook," to the editor, *UMWJ*, June 11, 1891; editorial, "We Were Pleased," *UMWJ*, August 13, 1891; "Keep Off the Grass," to the editor, *UMWJ*, June 28, 1894; Van Tine, *Making of the Labor Bureaucrat*, 104–7.

Chapter 1. Deceived: Producers in a Dishonest World

1. Hedges, *Speeches of Benjamin Harrison*, 255, 257; "The President's Trip," *Humboldt (IA) Republican*, October 9, 1890; "A Coal Palace," *Osage City (KS) Free Press*, January 2, 1890; "Ottumwa's Coal Palace," *Hawarden (IA) Independent*, February 6, 1890; "We See It Announced," *Humeston (IA) New Era*, February 12, 1890; "Iowa's Coal Palace," *Davenport (IA) Daily Republican*, September 17, 1890.

2. McCalley, *On the Warrior Coal Field*, 11–12; "The State of Trade," *CTJ*, February 16, 1887; "Kansas Coal News," *CTJ*, February 16, 1887; "Utah," *EMJ*, February 4, 1893.

3. Green, *The Devil Is Here*, 17; Fraser, *Age of Acquiescence*, 27–29; Adams, "Promotion, Competition, Captivity," 74–95.

4. "Sioux City," *Topeka (KS) State Journal*, April 1, 1890 (quotation); "The Only Corn Palace," *Sioux Valley News*, September 4, 1890; "Leavenworth a Coal Palace," *Leavenworth (KS) Times*, April 3, 1890; "Osage City a Coal Palace," *OFCP*, April 10, 1890; "A Coal Palace," *Pittsburg (KS) Smelter*, reprinted in *Leavenworth (KS) Times*, April 18, 1890; "The Flax Palace," *Des Moines Register*, September 1, 1891.

5. L. A. Quellmalz to Lorenzo D. Lewelling, July 29, 1893, folder 8, box 8, MSC 307944, Lorenzo D. Lewelling Papers.

6. "Christianizing the Upper Masses," *Christian Advocate*, reprinted in *NLT*, November 20, 1886.

7. "A Thinker," to the editor, *UMWJ*, June 28, 1894; "A Mine Workers' Wife," to the editor, *UMWJ*, December 22, 1892.

8. McMath, *Populist Vanguard*; K. Fones-Wolf, *Trade Union Gospel*; Kazin, *Populist Persuasion*; Creech, *Righteous Indignation*; Mirola, *Redeeming Time*.

9. E. Wilder to Aldace F. Walker, November 4, 1896, Aldace Walker to E. Wilder, November 11, 1896, and E. Wilder telegram to Aldace Walker, November 12, 1896, all in file 514, RR 516:10, Cherokee & Pittsburg Coal Company General, Cherokee & Pittsburg Coal Company Records; James M. Devore, to the *Fort Scott (KS) Daily Monitor*, "An Answer to Limb," *Fort Scott (KS) Daily Monitor*, January 26, 1897; James M. Devore,

written statement to the *Fort Scott (KS) Daily Monitor*, "Hill and M'Donald," January 27, 1897; Richard Wilson to Lacodia Labeack, "Hill and M'Donald," *Fort Scott (KS) Daily Monitor*, January 27, 1897; J. D. Hill, written statement to *Fort Scott (KS) Daily Monitor*, "Hill and M'Donald," January 27, 1897 (quotation); "Where Is Judge M'Donald?," *Fort Scott (KS) Daily Monitor*, January 9, 1897.

10. "Charles J. Devlin," Illinois Department of Corrections, *Alton State Penitentiary* and Joliet/Stateville Correctional Center—Index to Registers of Prisoners, record series 423.201, Illinois State Archives, Springfield; "Pioneers in the Western Coal Industry: Charles Devlin," *Fuel*, April 12, 1910; US 1870 Census, Family Search, "Charles Devlin," https://goo.gl/1xaccE (accessed October 23, 2014).

11. Laslett, *Colliers across the Sea*, 128; Phelan, *Divided Loyalties*, 60, 108–9, 227; "Pioneers in the Western Coal Industry: Charles Devlin," *Fuel*, April 12, 1910; Charles J. Devlin to W. K. Gillett, September 33, 1894, RR 132:3, file 1005, Charles J. Devlin Coal Properties in Southern Kansas, ATSF Records; Charles J. Devlin to Joseph P. Whitehead, October 20, 1894, RR 132:3, file 1005, Charles J. Devlin Coal Properties in Southern Kansas, ATSF Records; "Reports from Leading Coal Markets of the West," *Black Diamond*, April 8, 1905.

12. Lloyd, *Strike of Millionaires*, 13–14.

13. P. H. Donnelly, to the editor, *NLT*, September 7, 1889; "Pro Bono Publico," to the editor, *NLT*, September 14, 1889; Charles J. Devlin to Joseph P. Whitehead, October 20, 1894, file 1005, RR 132:3, ATSF Records; Lloyd, *Strike of Millionaires*; "The Philadelphia Record," *NLT*, September 26, 1891; "Mr. Scott's Big Farm," *NYT*, October 20, 1889; "William L. Scott Dead," *NYT*, September 21, 1891; "Mining," *Western Manufacturer*, April 30, 1885.

14. "Western Coal and Coke Notes," *CTJ*, November 7, 1894; "The Marquette Third Vein Coal Co.," *CTJ*, December 19, 1894; "Devlin's New Move," *Osage City (KS) Free Press*, September 17, 1896; "Pioneers in the Western Coal Industry: Charles Devlin," *Fuel*, April 12, 1910; Arnold, *Fueling the Gilded Age*, 37–43; 92–102, 185–220.

15. "The Santa Fe's Troubles," *Chicago Tribune*, December 21, 1888; "Santa Claus," to the editor, *UMWJ*, January 11, 1894; Bryant, *History*; White, *Railroaded*; Arnold, *Fueling the Gilded Age*, 213, 225–27.

16. "Devlin's New Move," *Osage City (KS) Free Press*, September 17, 1896; E. P. Ripley memo to Aldace Walker, November 2, 1896, file 664, RR 122:1, ATSF Records; E. P. Ripley to Victor Morawetz, September 18, 1896, file 1005, RR 132:3, ATSF Records; unsigned memo to E. P. Ripley, December 7, 1896, file 664, RR 122:1, ATSF Records; E. P. Ripley to Aldace Walker, March 30, 1897, file 1005, RR 132:3, ATSF Records; Cerrillos Coal and Iron Company Records, Cerrillos Coal Railroad Company Records, and Cerrillos Coal Mining Company Records, all in files 662–664, RR 122:1, ATSF Records.

17. Summers, *Gilded Age*, 68–70, 80–81; Cronon, *Nature's Metropolis*, 47, 97; White, *Railroaded*, 17–36; Arnold, *Fueling the Gilded Age*,; Fraser, *Age of Acquiescence*, 59–61.

18. "Another Devlin Bank Wreck," *NYT,* June 21, 1905; "Topeka Bank Closed; Made Loans to Devlin," *NYT,* July 4, 1905; "Two More Banks Shut on Account of Devlin," *NYT,* July 6, 1905; "To Act with Cy and Hurley," *Fort Scott (KS) Daily Monitor,* July 15, 1905; "Charles J. Devlin Dead" *NYT,* November 2, 1905, "Illinois," *EMJ,* July 14, 1906; "Thomas v. Woods," in Cook, *American Bankruptcy Reports,* 132–33.

19. "The Strike Is Still On," *Chicago Tribune,* August 17, 1889; Lewis Wabel, "Charles J. Devlin: Coal Mines and Railroads, His Empire" (N.p.: n.p, 1991), Abraham Lincoln Presidential Library; "Pioneers in the Western Coal Industry: Charles Devlin," *Fuel,* April 12, 1910. "Northwestern Coal Co" folder, box 25; "Union Pacific Mining Co., Pittsburgh, PA" folder, box 31; and "East Kentucky Coal, Lumber, and Railroad Co." folder, box 36, all in Levi O. Leonard Railroad Collection.

20. Missouri BLSI, *Sixth Annual Report,* 11; Rajala, "Forest as Factory."

21. Jensen, *Winning of the Midwest,* 239–40; Dix, *What's a Coal Miner to Do?*; Green, *The Devil Is Here,* 26.

22. Missouri BLSI, *Sixth Annual Report,* 11; "Live and Let Live," to the editor, *UMWJ,* October 12, 1893; Illinois BLS, *Statistics of Coal, 1891,* 1.

23. "A Victim," to the editor, *NLT,* October 5, 1889; Phil Penna, to the editor, *UMWJ,* December 10, 1891.

24. Fraser, *Age of Acquiescence,* 59–62.

25. Missouri State Board of Agriculture, *Twenty-Seventh Annual Report,* 62; "San Francisco Coal Supply," *CTJ,* January 5, 1887; "Coal and the Inter-State Act," *CTJ,* January 26.1887; "San Francisco Trade Report," *CTJ,* April 6, 1887; US Department of Agriculture, *Report, 1894,* 481; Destler, "Agricultural Readjustment," 106–7; Fraser, *Age of Acquiescence,* 48–49; Baker, *Journal of the Department of Agriculture,* 190; US Department of Agriculture, *Report, 1893,* 416–17.

26. Missouri State Board of Agriculture, *Twenty-Seventh Annual Report,* 63; US Department of State, *Commercial Relations,* 79, 176; "The World's Wheat Surplus," in US Department of Agriculture, *Report, 1888,* 570–73; "Wheat," in US Department of Agriculture, *Report, 1890,* 298–300.

27. Levy, *Freaks of Fortune,* 231–34; Levy, "Contemplating Delivery."

28. "Statement of Mr. Melvin J. Forbes, Representing the Duluth Board of Trade," in House Committee on Agriculture, *Fictitious Dealings,* 143.

29. "Statement of Mr. Melvin J. Forbes, Representing the Duluth Board of Trade," in House Committee on Agriculture, *Fictitious Dealings,* 138.

30. "Statement of William P. Howard, of St. Louis," in House Committee on Agriculture, *Fictitious Dealings,* 146–47; J. R. Sovereign Address, "Sovereign's Report," *New Orleans Daily Picayune,* November 16, 1894; Fraser, *Age of Acquiescence,* 95–96.

31. "Statement of C. Wood Davis," in House Committee on Agriculture, *Fictitious Dealings,* 6–8.

32. Samuel Anderson, to the editor, *NLT,* September 9, 1887; "A Miner," to the editor, *JKL,* February 5, 1891; "The Centralia Miners," *JKL,* February 2, 1892; Fabian, *Card Sharps and Bucket Shops,* 154; Sanders, *Roots of Reform,* 304–10; Fraser, *Age of Acquiescence,*

95–96; Levy, *Freaks of Fortune*, 241–47; Cowing, *Populists, Plungers, and Progressives*, 3–24, esp. 15.

33. Fink, *Workingmen's Democracy*; Salvatore, *Eugene V. Debs*, 19, 62–64.

34. Montrie, *Making a Living*, 91–112.

35. Kansas BLI, *Ninth Annual Report*, 12–14, 69, 340, 352 (quotation).

36. Ibid., 63, 144, 358; Iowa State Mine Inspectors, *Seventh Biennial Report*, 85 (quotation).

37. "T.F.B.," to the editor, *NLT*, December 24, 1887. "A K. of L.," to the editor, *NLT*, February 19, 1887. For an example from the cigar industry, see Cooper, *Once a Cigar Maker*, 124.

38. Laurie, *Artisans into Workers*; Dix, *Work Relations*, 21–22.

39. E. O. Glidden, "Old Fogy Brickmaking," *Clay-Worker* 19, no. 2 (February 1893): 166; "Brickmaking Machinery," *Brickmaker*, October 15, 1893; "Land O' Flowers," to the editor, *Clay-Worker* 22, no. 5 (November 1894): 455; M. Jay, "Hints for Amateur Clay-Workers. No. 5," *Clay-Worker* 21, no. 1 (January 1894): 22.

40. Illinois BLS, *Statistics of Coal, 1893*, xix, xxxi; "Two Old Miners," to the editor, *UMWJ*, October 21, 1897; Terence Powderly, "The Army of the Unemployed" in McNeill, *Labor Movement*, 580; S. Nelson, *Steel Drivin' Man*, 75, 90–91; Brody, *In Labor's Cause*, 131–32; McShane and Tarr, *Horse in the City*.

41. Dix, *Work Relations*, 31.

42. "Pro Bono Publico," to the editor, *NLT*, June 29, 1889; William Houston, to the editor, *NLT*, November 9, 1889; J. H. Kennedy, UMW District Eleven Report, *UMWJ*, September 8, 1898; Adams, "Promotion, Competition, Captivity," 86; Amsden and Brier, "Coal Miners on Strike."

43. "Bitten," to the editor, *NLT*, June 9, 1888; "Pro Bono Publico," to the editor, *NLT*, Mary 18, 1889; "C.," to the editor, *NLT*, February 22, 1890; J. H. Kennedy, UMW District Eleven Report, *UMWJ*, July 23, 1891; Dix, *Work Relations*, 16; Fishback, *Soft Coal*, 72.

44. "Justice," to the editor, *UMWJ*, December 3, 1891; "A Would-Be Knight," to the editor, *UMWJ*, November 12, 1896 (quotation); "Illiterate," to the editor, *UMWJ*, July 6, 1893; "Captain," to the editor, *UMWJ*, October 4, 1894.

45. "Jumbo," to the editor, *NLT*, August 3, 1889; E. A. Sparls, to the editor, *UMWJ*, January 4, 1894; "A Thinker," to the editor, *UMWJ*, June 28, 1894; Bay, ch. 4, "Us Is Human Flesh," in *White Image*, 117–49.

46. "Semi-Monthly Review," to the editor, *UMWJ*, October 12, 1893.

47. Adam Stewart, to the editor, *NLT*, March 22, 1884; Special Report to the Governor of an Investigation by Commissioner of Labor Statistics and Inspection of the Coal Mine Explosion at Rich Hill, Mo. March 29, 1888, in Missouri BLSI, *Tenth Annual Report*, 9, 16; Illinois BLS, *Fifth Biennial Report*, 350.

48. Missouri BLSI, *Tenth Annual Report*, 50; Rosenow, *Death and Dying*.

49. "T. B. T.," to the editor, *NLT*, May 7, 1887; G. A. Dinsmoor, Jos. McKernan, Frank Kenoyer, demands to Missouri governor Albert Morehouse reprinted in "An Investigation Demanded," *NLT*, April 14, 1888; "Mass Meeting," *Pittsburg (KS) Headlight*,

November 15, 1888; "A. Miner" to the editor, *NLT,* August 25, 1888; P. H. Donnelly, to the editor, *NLT,* October 5, 1889; Samuel Anderson, to the editor, *NLT,* December 21, 1889; "Illinois: Examination for Mine Inspectors at Springfield," *Colliery Engineer* 8, no. 4 (November 1887): 79; "Jack the Ripper," to the editor, *UMWJ,* August 31, 1893.

50. William Gardner, to the editor, *NLT,* November 9, 1893.

51. A. Lichtenstein, *Twice the Work,* 133, 169–71; Fraser, *Age of Acquiescence,* 56–57 (quotations), 139; Kansas BLIS, *Seventh Annual Report,* 54.

52. "Cambrian," to the editor, *NLT,* August 3, 1889. "Justice," to the editor, *UMWJ,* December 3, 1891.

53. Fishback, *Soft Coal.*

54. J. M. Carson, to the editor, *UMWJ,* March 21, 1895; Arnold, *Fueling the Gilded Age,* 114.

55. "Semi-Monthly," to the editor, *UMWJ,* November 9, 1893; R. L. Davis, to the editor, *UMWJ,* December 15, 1892; Illinois BLS, *Statistics of Coal, 1891,* 25–26; "1892–1893 Daily Production at Echols, Ky," folder 1, box 1, McHenry Coal Company Records; Missouri Bureau of the Mines, *Sixth Annual Report,* 159.

56. William Scaife, to the editor, *UMWJ,* December 16, 1897.

57. Jas. A. Connery, to the editor, *NLT,* March 28, 1891; Dan McLaughlan, to the editor, *UMWJ,* May 21, 1891; "What Is It About?," *NLT,* August 15, 1891; J. C. Heenan, to the editor, *NLT,* July 30, 1887; Selwyn Taylor, "General Mining Methods of the Pittsburg Coal Region," *Colliery Engineer* 8, no. 4 (November 1887): 86; Saward, *Coal Trade,* 106.

58. "Snake Eye Saul," to the editor, *UMWJ,* August 10, 1893.

59. "K. of L.," to the editor, NLT, February 5, 1887; Missouri BLSI, *Thirteenth Annual Report,* 9; Montgomery, *Workers' Control in America,* 115; Boris, "Man's Dwelling House," 128.

60. Lee Meriwether report to Governor David R. Francis, in Missouri BLSI, *Eleventh Annual Report,* 48, 51; "K. of L.," to the editor, *NLT,* February 5, 1887.

61. "Johnny Bull," to the editor, *UMWJ,* November 17, 1892; Henry Carter Mulberry letter to Lorenzo Lewelling, February 13, 1894, folder 8, box 3, Lorenzo D. Lewelling Papers; Corbin, *Life, Work, and Rebellion,* 32; Eller, *Miners, Millhands, and Mountaineers,* 188.

62. "Illiterate," to the editor, *UMWJ,* July 6, 1893.

63. Missouri BLSI, *Thirteenth Annual Report,* 9.

64. "J. D.," to the editor, *UMWJ,* May 21, 1891; Missouri BLSI, *Eleventh Annual Report,* 15.

65. Meriwether report, in Missouri BLSI, *Eleventh Annual Report,* 56.

66. S. C. Pearce to Lee Meriwether, in Missouri BLSI, *Eleventh Annual Report,* 22–23.

67. "J. D.," to the editor, *UMWJ,* May 21, 1891.

68. Section 2441–2 in Taylor, *General Statutes of Kansas,* 1:724; "House Bill No. 28" and "Senate Bill No. 40" (Illinois), 661–62, 995, 1076; "The Truck Store," *UMWJ,* May 28, 1891; Will Hall, to the editor, *UMWJ,* April 7, 1892; Kansas BLI, *Ninth Annual Report,* 800–805; Forbath, "Ambiguities of Free Labor," 796–797.

69. "Jim," to the editor, *NLT,* March 30, 1889; Meriwether report, in Missouri BLSI, *Eleventh Annual Report,* 49–51; Meriwether quoted in "The Company Store in Missouri," *NLT,* November 2, 1889.

70. Missouri BLSI, *Eleventh Annual Report,* 18–29; Robert Linn, to the editor, *NLT,* May 12, 1883; "Miner," to the editor, *NLT,* December 14, 1889.

71. "J. D.," to the editor, *UMWJ,* May 21, 1891.

72. "A Well Wisher," to the editor, *NLT,* April 25, 1891; *Samuel G. Clevinger v. The Chicago, Milwaukee & St. Paul Railway Co.,* District Court of Iowa and Woodbury County, March 1888, box 4, folder 23, Charles Almon Dewey Paper; "A Miner," to the editor, *UMWJ,* May 10, 1894.

73. Weir, *Beyond Labor's Veil,* esp. 68–92, 69 (quotation); Montgomery, *Beyond Equality,* 200–204; Gutman, *Work, Culture, and Society,* 105 (quotation); K. Fones-Wolf, *Trade Union Gospel*; Mirola, *Redeeming Time*; Blum, "By the Sweat of Their Brow"; Kazin, *Populist Persuasion,* 50, 169, 260; Kazin, *Godly Hero*; McMath, *Populist Vanguard,* 75–76; Creech, *Righteous Indignation.*

74. Gutman, *Work, Culture, and Society,* 107.

75. P. H. Donnelly, to the editor, *NLT,* April 2, 1887; "Federation," to the editor, *NLT,* January 7, 1888; Aaron Litten, to the editor, *NLT,* March 16, 1889; Henry Evans, to the editor, *NLT,* February 1, 1890; "Trades Unionism," *UMWJ,* May 28, 1891; R. L. Davis, to the editor, *UMWJ,* June 4, 1891.

76. IMPA Report, *NLT,* March 5, 1888; "Federation," to the editor, *NLT,* January 7, 1888; "Fifty Years a Union Miner," to the editor, *NLT,* July 9, 1887; "An Old Timer," to the editor, *NLT,* May 11, 1893.

77. "A Laborer," to the editor, *UMWJ,* June 22, 1893.

78. "Indiana," *CTJ,* March 21, 1888.

79. Goldstene, *Struggle for America's Promise,* 45–67.

80. Sanders, *Roots of Reform,* 42, 53; Foner, *From the Founding,* 165–66; T. J. Roberts, to the editor, *NLT,* January 22, 1887; NFM report, *NLT,* January 29, 1887; Warne, *Coal-Mine Workers,* 57.

81. Minutes of the Joint Convention of Operators and Miners, February 23 and 24, 1886, reel 1, John Mitchell Papers; "Pro Bono Publico," to the editor, *NLT,* March 2, 1889; George Harrison, to the editor, *NLT,* January 1, 1887.

82. Daniel McLaughlin to Terence Powderly, June 9, 1882, reel 4, JWH Papers.

83. NTA 135, Knights of Labor report, *NLT,* August 27, 1887; "Absolute Surrender," *Dixon (IL) Evening Telegraph,* January 12, 1888; Knights of Labor, *Proceedings, 1886,* 42, 265–68; Ware, *Labor Movement,* 213–14.

84. W. T. Lewis, to the editor, *NLT,* February 5, 1887. Foner, *From Colonial Times,* 512.

85. Terence Powderly to John Hayes, March 1, 1888, reel 1, JWH Papers; T. T. O'Malley, to the editor, *NLT,* June 4, 1887; W. T. Lewis, open letter to Terence Powderly," *NLT,* January 12, 1889; "W. T. Lewis Vindicated," editorial, *Ohio State Journal,* reprinted in *NLT,* March 30, 1889; Oestreicher, *Solidarity and Fragmentation*; Voss, *Making of American Exceptionalism*; Weir, *Knights Unhorsed.*

86. Thomas Faulds, to the editor, *NLT,* February 5, 1887; G. W. Dinsmoor, to the editor, *NLT,* February 4, 1888; William Hall, to the editor, *NLT,* March 19, 1887; Chris Campbell, to the editor, *NLT,* March 26, 1887; Frank Campbell to Terence Powderly, January 9, 1884, reel 6, Correspondence of Local Assemblies, 1881–1915, nos. 6514–6974, JWH Papers; James Morrison to Terence Powderly, December 10, 1883, reel 6, JWH Papers.

87. P. H. Donnelly, to the editor, *NLT,* April 2, 1887; "K. of L.," to the editor, *NLT,* February 5, 1887; John Smith, to the editor, *NLT,* February 5, 1887; Evans, *History of United Mine Workers,* 1:224–26; Chris Campbell, to the editor, *NLT,* March 26, 1887; Peter McCall, William Hawthorne, and Thomas Brady, Committee of the Spring Valley, Illinois, IMPA NFM Lodge, report, *NLT,* August 13, 1887; Knights of Labor, *Proceedings, 1886,* 42–44; Knights of Labor, *Proceedings, 1887,* 1699–1701; Van Tine, *Making of the Labor Bureaucrat,* 7; T. J. Roberts, to the editor, *NLT,* February 19, 1887.

88. John Duddey, to the editor, *NLT,* May 21, 1887; Samuel Anderson, to the editor, *NLT,* December 10, 1887; Edward Wilton, to the editor, *NLT,* January 14, 1888.

89. "The Miners' Convention," *Pittsburgh (PA) Post,* December 8, 1888.

90. "Coal Miners Matters," *NLT,* January 5, 1889; Robert Linn, to the editor, *JUL,* January 24, 1889; IMPA Report, "Illinois Miners," *NLT,* July 27, 1889; Ware, *Labor Movement,* 215–21; Roy, *History of the Coal Miners,* 250; Aaron Littin, to the editor, *NLT,* March 16, 1889; Van Tine, *Making of the Labor Bureaucrat,* 7; Spring Valley, Illinois, Lodge 26, "Miners and Mine Laborers Protective Association" of the NPU, in book 1, Knights of Labor IRAD.

91. "Deserted the Knights," *Huntington (IN) Daily Democrat,* December 21, 1888; "Miners Leaving the Knights of Labor," *Chicago Tribune,* December 21, 1888; "Telegraphic Brevities," *Ottawa (KS) Daily Republic,* February 2, 1889;" Amalgamation of Interests," *Indianapolis News,* December 14, 1889.

92. "Coffee," to the editor, *NLT,* April 6, 1889.

93. Aaron Littin, to the editor, *NLT,* March 16, 1889; "Tramp," to the editor, *NLT,* March 16, 1889; "Address of President McBride," *NLT,* January 19, 1889; NPU Indiana District Report, *NLT,* August 24, 1889.

94. "X.," to the editor, *NLT,* February 14, 1895.

Chapter 2. Undermined: Winter Diggers, Union Strikebreakers

1. Illinois BLS, *Fifth Biennial Report,* 332, 358; Parker, *Production of Coal,* 11.

2. Robert Smith, to the editor, *NLT,* February 25, 1888.

3. Robert Smith, to the editor, *NLT,* March 3, 1888.

4. Goodwyn, *Democratic Promise*; Gutman, *Work, Culture, and Society,* 3–78; Gourevitch, *From Slavery to Cooperative Commonwealth,* 5–7; Martin, *Smokestacks in the Hills.*

5. IMPA Report, *NLT,* February 25, 1888.

6. "J.D.C.," to the editor, *JUL,* May 28, 1888; "C.," to the editor, *NLT,* February 22, 1890.

7. US 1870 Census, Family Search, https://familysearch.org/pal:MM9.1.1/M6L3 -BTH (accessed December 18, 2013), Peter Shirkey in household of Henry Mendinhall, Ohio; "United States General Index to Pension Files, 1861–1934," Family Search, "Lydia J Minnis" in entry for Thomas M Minnis, 1888, https://goo.gl/Q9NCrN (accessed 6 February 2015); "Indiana, Marriages, 1811–1959," Family Search, Peter Shirkey and Liddy Minnis, February 12, 1891, https://goo.gl/XstgGN (accessed July 11, 2014); US 1900 Census, Family Search, "Peter Sherkie," https://goo.gl/SQIozc (accessed December 18, 2013).

8. US 1910 Census, Family Search, "Peter Shirkey," https://goo.gl/krENMA (accessed December 18, 2013).

9. Weise, *Grasping at Independence*; Levy, *Freaks of Fortune*, 185, 196–99.

10. US 1900 Census, index and images, Family Search, "Edward Davis," https://goo.gl/hgiwop (accessed October 5, 2013); US 1900 Census, Family Search, "Pete Buss," https://goo.gl/EJbi9t (accessed October 5, 2013); US 1900 Census, Family Search, "Thomas Davis," https://goo.gl/oDlwIU (accessed June 14, 2017); US 1900 Census, Family Search, "Lincoln Guthrie," https://goo.gl/WV3Lwr (accessed June 14, 2017); US 1900 Census, Family Search, "Adair Orin," https://goo.gl/eo4ukP (accessed June 14, 2017);); US 1900 Census, Family Search, "John Tressel," https://goo.gl/lwKIqo (accessed June 14, 2017); US 1900 Census, Family Search, "Eugene Wear," https://goo.gl/bAAwIU (accessed June 14, 2017); US 1900 Census, Family Search, "Barney Guglione," https://goo.gl/wxVayn (accessed June 14, 2017); US 1900 Census, Family Search, "Jacob Klaus," https://goo.gl/VTVP1V (accessed June 14, 2017); US 1900 Census, Family Search, "Wiley Johnson," https://goo.gl/EmIPPt (accessed June 14, 2017); US 1900 Census, Family Search, "John Slater," https://goo.gl/eo4ukP (accessed June 14, 2017); US 1900 Census, Family Search "Julius Heckscher," https://goo.gl/eo4ukP (accessed June 14, 2017); US 1900 Census, Family Search, "John Robertson," https://goo.gl/eo4ukP (accessed June 14, 2017); Missouri BLSI, *Eleventh Annual Report, 1889*, 309.

11. US 1900 Census, Family Search, "Daniel Hornback," https://goo.gl/AfW7Zf (accessed December 18, 2013); US 1880 Census, Family Search, "Daniel Hornback," https://goo.gl/UAGD2w (accessed December 18, 2013).

12. US 1910 Census, Family Search, "Shirly Hornback," https://goo.gl/sE3yM3 (accessed December 18, 2013); "Illinois Deaths and Stillbirths, 1916–1947," Family Search "Shirlie Hornback," https://goo.gl/cxos33 (accessed December 18, 2013).

13. US Department of Agriculture, *Wages of Farm Labor*, 21–26, 32–34.

14. J. G. Greusel, "Making Brick in the Dark," *CW* 22, no. 4 (October 1894): 344; "Brick Making in Canada," *CW* 21, no. 5 (May 1894): 558; D. E. Ryan, to the editor, *CW*, 22:5 (November 1894): 462; Joseph Fairhall, "The Professional Brickmaker, *CW* 19, no. 2 (February 1893): 156; "The Clay-Shingle Works at Ottawa, Ill.," *Brickmaker*, December 1, 1893.

15. Armstrong, "Transformation of Work," 521, 527–28; Armstrong, "Georgia Lumber Laborers," 441–44; Select Committee on Relations with Canada, *Testimony*,

296–97; US Bureau of the Census, "Twelfth Census"; Georgia State Department of Agriculture, *Publications*, 43–46.

16. Illinois BLS, *Fifth Biennial Report*, 357.

17. Kansas BLS, *Third Annual Report*, 264.

18. Montrie, *Making a Living*, 71–90; Missouri BLS, *Eleventh Annual Report*, 341–42; Kansas BLS, *Third Annual Report*, 264.

19. Kansas BLS, *Third Annual Report*, 187.

20. "Coal at Rich Hill, Mo.," *CTJ*, April 27, 1887; "Kansas Coal News," *CTJ*, December 7, 1887; "1896–1905 Production Accounts," folder 1.3, box 1, McHenry Coal Company Records; Missouri BLSI, *Fifteenth Annual Report*, 114; "Bald Head," to the editor, *UMWJ*, January 26, 1893.

21. Missouri BLSI, *Fifteenth Annual Report*, 306–12; Iowa BLS, *Fourth Biennial Report*, 176–77; "Bald Head," to the editor, *UMWJ*, January 26, 1893; "Miner," to the editor, *UMWJ*, August 8, 1894; W. J. Guymon, to the editor, *UMWJ*, December 5, 1895.

22. House of Representatives, *Seventh Annual Report*.

23. Fraser, *Age of Acquiescence*, 56–58.

24. Zanjani, *Mine of Her Own*, 165–66.

25. Account for farmhand John Hiatt, July 1885–September, Account Book 2, 1880–1900, box 2, Clinton S. Campbell Papers; Missouri BLSI, *Eleventh Annual Report*, 51.

26. Goodwyn, *Democratic Promise*, 34–49; Postel, *Populist Vision*, 114–24; Gourevitch, *From Slavery to Cooperative Commonwealth*; Goldstene, *Struggle for America's Promise*, 50.

27. James Cantwell, to the editor, *NLT*, January 12, 1884; "Squib," to the editor, *NLT*, April 9, 1887; Abe Thinkenbinder, to the editor, *UMWJ*, December 21, 1893.

28. "Mendota, Mo.," *NLT*, January 22, 1887; "Avondale," to the editor, *NLT*, April 14, 1888; "Rambler," to the editor, *NLT*, December 3, 1887.

29. Editorial, *Sterling Standard*, December 2, 1886; "Coal at Rich Hill, MO.," *CTJ*, April 27, 1887; "Silver City News," *Malvern Leader*, February 6, 1890; McBride, "Coal Miners," 242; FAMI Report, "Indiana Miners," *NLT*, March 26, 1887; James Boston Jr., to the editor, *NLT*, November 26, 1887; G.W. Dinsmoor, to the editor, *NLT*, February 4, 1888; Editorial, "Harmonious Development of the Industries," *National Economist*, April 6, 1889; T. D. Hinckley, "A Talk to Dakota Farmers," *National Economist*, August 24, 1889; F. G. Blood, "Corrected and Explained," *National Economist*, January 4, 1890. Shifflett, *Coal Towns*, 16, 23; Montrie, *Making a Living*, 71–90.

30. John Neal, to the editor, *UMWJ*, January 5, 1893; "coal butchers" quotation, J. H. Kennedy, UMW District Eleven Report, *UMWJ*, October 20, 1892; "W.H.," to the editor, *JUL*, January 7, 1888; "A Pumpkin-Roller," to the editor, *NLT*, March 1, 1890; Robert Smith, to the editor, *NLT*, March 3, 1888; "Tramp," to the editor, *NLT*, March 16, 1889; "C," to the editor, *JUL*, July 11, 1889.

31. "Kansas Coal News," *CTJ*, March 16, 1887; "O.P.W.," to the editor, *JUL*, October 22, 1887; "St. Louis, MO., Trade Report," *CTJ*, December 7, 1887; "Kansas Coal News," *CTJ*, December 7, 1887; P. H. Donnelly, NPU Southern Illinois District Report, "P. H. Donnelly's Report," *NLT*, March 16, 1889; "Bald Head," to the editor, *UMWJ*, January 26,

1893; "A Former Employe[e] of the Forsythe Company," to the editor, *UMWJ,* October 19, 1893; "Successful Americans," *CTJ,* September 1, 1897.

32. Montgomery, *Workers' Control,* 9–31.

33. "Working Slack," to the editor, *UMWJ,* January 18, 1894; "Fair Play," to the editor, *UMWJ,* December 24, 1891; "Miners and Schools," *NLT,* may 21, 1892.

34. "D.N.P.," to the editor, *NLT,* January 22, 1887; "K of L," to the editor, *NLT,* February 19, 1887; "Amaranth," to the editor, *NLT,* May 21, 1887; Peter McDonald, to the editor, *NLT,* September 15, 1888; Dan McLaughlin, to the editor, *NLT,* April 20, 1889; "Knownothing," to the editor, *UMWJ,* December 7, 1893; McBride, "Coal Miners," 242–43; "The Warner," to the editor, *UMWJ,* October 12, 1893.

35. "K.R.," to the editor, *NLT,* November 8, 1879; "Lincoln," to the editor, *NLT,* August 13, 1887; Editorial, *Sterling (IL) Standard,* December 2, 1886; "Coal at Rich Hill, MO.," *CTJ,* April 27, 1887; "Kansas Coal News," *CTJ,* March 16, 1887; "O.P.W." to the editor, *JUL,* October 22, 1887; "St. Louis, MO., Trade Report," *CTJ,* December 7, 1887; "Kansas Coal News," *CTJ,* December 7, 1887; FAMI Report, *NLT,* January 14, 1888; P. H. Donnelly, NPU Southern Illinois District Report, *NLT,* March 16, 1889.

36. "Mines, Miners and Wages," *CTJ,* April 6, 1887; "Penrod," to the editor, *NLT,* February 5, 1887; "Squib," to the editor, *NLT,* April 9, 1887; T. T. O'Malley, to the editor, *NLT,* July 23, 1887; Dix, *Work Relations,* 5–6.

37. Lewis, *Black Coal Miners,* 39; Foner, *Organized Labor,* 83; Spero and Harris, *Black Worker,* 232–33.

38. "Penrod," to the editor, *NLT,* February 5, 1887; "D.N.P.," to the editor, *NLT,* January 22, 1887.

39. "The Village Brickmaker" and "The Village Brickyard," *CW* 22, no. 6 (December 1894): 537; Jas. J. Flynn, to the editor, *UMWJ,* February 14, 1895; "Burn American Coal—II," *CTJ,* April 18, 1894; "Cornfield Sailor," to the editor, *UMWJ,* February 28, 1895; J. W. Reynolds, to the editor, *UMWJ,* March 21, 1895; J. M. Carson, to the editor, *UMWJ,* March 21, 1895; "Cornfield Sailor," to the editor, *UMWJ,* March 28, 1895; Julius Fromm, to the editor, *UMWJ,* April 25, 1895; "Dan McLaughlin," *NLT,* August 8, 1895.

40. Ware, *Labor Movement,* 321–22; Roll, "Sympathy for the Devil," 13–15; Andrews, *Killing for Coal,* 385; Arnold, *Fueling the Gilded Age,* 20, 25, 130.

41. Postel, *Populist Vision,* 104–8.

42. Case, "Losing the Middle Ground," 54–81; Tuttle, "Some Strikebreakers' Observations."

43. S. Parsons, K. Parsons, Killilae, and Borgers, "Role of Cooperatives"; "Capital and Labor Co-Operating," *Pittsburgh Manufacturer,* reprinted in *CTJ,* July 30, 1884; FAMI Report, "Indiana Miners," *NLT,* October 29, 1887; "The Co-operative Coal Shaft," *Bloomington (IL) Daily Pantagraph,* March 17, 1887; "Mines, Miners and Wages," *CTJ,* April 27, 1887; "The K. of L. Co-Operative Coal Mining Company," *NLT,* November 5, 1887; "The Coal Enterprise," *Humeston (IA) New Era,* April 25, 1888; M. Commesky, to the editor, *UMWJ,* November 19, 1891; "I.N.C.," to the editor, *UMWJ,* August 24, 1893; J. H.

Kennedy, UMW District Eleven Report, *UMWJ*, August 24, 1893; "A Miner's Widow," to the editor," *JKL*, March 8, 1894; "An Old Miner," to the editor, *UMWJ*, June 28, 1894.

44. "Queer Business Methods," *CTJ*, March 2, 1887.

45. "Bad State of Affairs at Spring Valley, Ills.," *Alton (IL) Telegraph*, September 5, 1889; House Committee on Agriculture, *Fictitious Dealings*, 6; Levy, *Freaks of Fortune*, 199, 249–55.

46. "I.N.C.," to the editor, *UMWJ*, September 21, 1893; W. T. Wright, to the editor, *JUL*, June 16, 1888; Knights of Labor General Executive Board Minutes, April 12, 1888, "Mutual Mining Company—Report of Mr. Bailey," reel 13, JWH Papers; Knights of Labor General Executive Board Minutes, June 12, 1888, Afternoon Session, "Mutual Mining Co," reel 13, JWH Papers; Powderly, *Thirty Years of Labor*, 460–64; Ware, *Labor Movement*, 320–33; Sanders, *Roots of Reform*, 38; Phelan, *Grand Master Workman*, 145–46; Leikin, *Practical*, 66–69; Postel, *Equality*, 243–44.

47. George Purcell to William B. Wilson, May 17, 1895, folder 1895, box 1, WBW Papers.

48. Foner, *From the Founding*, 77–78; Leikin, *Practical Utopians*, 70–71.

49. Robert Smith, to the editor, *NLT*, February 25, 1888.

50. "Deist," to the editor, *UMWJ*, May 26, 1898; J. C. Heenan and William Sheffler, to the editor, *UMWJ*, September 1, 1898; Alfred Klang, to the editor, *UMWJ*, June 7, 1894.

51. "Philip H. Penna, Taken by Death," *Linton (IN) Daily Citizen*, January 6, 1939; Dan O'Leary, UMW District Eleven Subdistrict Three Special Convention, "Report," *UMWJ*, April 8, 1897; Indiana Department of Geology and Natural Resources, *Twenty-Ninth Annual Report*, 754.

52. "Mine Postals," *NLT*, May 21, 1887 (quotation); "Mine Postals," *NLT*, June 4, 1887.

53. "Your Committee," IMPA Circular, *NLT*, October 8, 1887; "Notes of the Week," *CTJ*, November 2, 1887.

54. Fabian, *Card Sharps and Bucket Shops*, 153–202; Levy, "Contemplating Delivery."

55. Hochfelder, "Where the Common People," 336; Levy, *Freaks of Fortune*, 222 and 242; Cowing, *Populists, Plungers, and Progressives*.

56. Levy, *Freaks of Fortune*, 242–45.

57. House Committee on Agriculture, *Fictitious Dealings*.

58. Montgomery, *Fall of the House of Labor*, 17; Arnold, *Fueling the Gilded Age*; Gutman, *Power and Culture*, 154–55, 169, 170, 179, 192; Lewis, *Black Coal Miners*, 43; Maitland, *American Slang Dictionary*, sv. "blackleg"; Oxford English Dictionary, sv. "blackleg,"; "W.R.C.," to the editor, *Indiana Farmer*, September 20, 1890; "Col. Hering's Gambling Policy," *Chicago Tribune*, January 27, 1893; Fabian, *Card Sharps and Bucket Shops*, 29, 37, 80.

59. George H. Christman and Elijah Chadwick, to the editor, *NLT* June 1, 1889; "Pro Bono Publico," to the editor, *NLT*, June 1, 1889.

60. "K of L," to the editor, *NLT*, February 19, 1887; IMPA Report, *NLT*, November 26, 1887; James Boston Jr., to the editor, *NLT*, January 7, 1888; "A Miner's Wife," to the editor, *NLT*, February 18, 1888; "D.N.P.," to the editor, *NLT*, January 22, 1887.

61. Margery Jones, to the editor, *UMWJ,* June 25, 1891.

62. "Crows and Hawks," *NLT,* February 8, 1890; "J.D.C.," to the editor, *JUL,* May 28, 1888; "C.," to the editor, *NLT,* February 22, 1890.

63. "Penrod," to the editor, *NLT,* February 5, 1887; "T.B.T.," to the editor, *NLT,* May 7, 1887; K. of L.," to the editor, *NLT,* October 13, 1888; "A Miner," to the editor, *UMWJ,* May 10, 1894.

64. William Houston, to the editor, *NLT,* May 12, 1888.

65. NPU Illinois District Report, *NLT,* June 1, 1889; P. H. Donnelly, to the editor, *NLT,* June 22, 1889.

66. William Houston, to the editor, *NLT,* May 12, 1888.

67. NFM Report, *NLT,* April 2, 1887; IMPA Report, *NLT,* March 5, 1888 (quotation); "Bitten," to the editor, *NLT,* June 9, 1888.

68. Quotation from Matthew 19:19 (King James Version); "Starvation in Indiana," *NLT,* June 22, 1889; Robert Cochrane, to the editor, *UMWJ,* October 8, 1891.

69. David Ross, letter to editor, *NLT,* June 6, 1889; Laurene Gardner, to the editor, *UMWJ,* November 26, 1891; W. D. Ryan, UMW District Twelve Report, *UMWJ,* August 5, 1897; J. H. Kennedy, UMW District Eleven Report, *UMWJ,* September 2, 1897; Postel, *Equality,* 230–31.

70. "Mine Postals," *NLT,* October 29, 1887.

71. "S.," to the editor, *NLT,* August 10, 1893; Adams, "Promotion, Competition, Captivity," 76.

72. "Starvation in Indiana," *NLT,* June 22, 1889.

73. At the time, Devlin owned one-seventh of the company's stock. William Scaife, Illinois District NPU Report, *NLT,* December 7, 1889; "Pro Bono Publico," to the editor, *NLT,* September 14, 1889 (quotation); "Pro Bono Publico," to the editor, *NLT,* May 18, 1889; "Bad State of Affairs at Spring Valley, Ills.," *Alton (IL) Telegraph,* September 5, 1889.

74. "Illinois and Indiana Mining," *NLT,* June 1, 1889; Dan McLaughlin, to the editor, *NLT,* August 3, 1889.

75. John Rowe, to the editor, *NLT,* June 15, 1889.

76. Dan McLaughlin, to the editor, *NLT,* April 20, 1889; John McBride, official circular from National Progressive Union of Miners and Mine Laborers, *NLT,* April 13, 1889.

77. William Monaghan, to the editor, *NLT,* July 6, 1889; Official Missouri NPU order, *NLT,* May 18, 1889 (quotation); Spring Valley, Illinois, Lodge 26 "Miners and Mine Laborers Protective Association" of the NPU, Special Meeting Minutes, May 22, 1889, p. 42, Knights of Labor IRAD; NPU Twelfth District Meeting Minutes, May 1889, p. 37–40, Knights of Labor IRAD; "A Miner," to the editor, *NLT,* June 8, 1889.

78. Dan McLaughlin, to the editor, *NLT,* June 8, 1889; P. H. Donnelly, to the editor, *NLT,* July 6, 1889; William Scaife, Illinois NPU Report, *NLT,* December 7, 1889; "Where Did They Gain?," *Chicago Tribune,* supplement, November 15, 1889.

79. Dan McLaughlin, to the editor, *NLT,* June 8, 1889.

80. William Monaghan, to the editor, *NLT,* July 6, 1889.

81. T. J. Llewellyn, to the editor, *NLT,* July 27, 1889; Dan McLaughlin, to the editor, *NLT,* August 24, 1889; Daniel McNulty, to the editor, *NLT,* June 22, 1889.

82. "Pro Bono Publico," to the editor, *NLT*, July 20, 1889. "Pro Bono Publico," to the editor, *NLT,* June 29, 1889.

83. George Palfreyman, to the editor, *NLT,* July 20, 1889; "W.G.," to the editor, *NLT,* November 2, 1889; William Scaife, NPU Illinois District Report, *NLT,* December 7, 1889; John Rowe, to the editor, *NLT,* June 15, 1889; Robert M. Reed and William Scaife, Official Proceedings of Special Convention of northern Illinois miners, *NLT*, July 6, 1889.

84. "Many Miners Destitute," *Chicago Tribune,* June 25, 1889; C. H. Davis, to the editor, *NLT,* June 29, 1889 (quotation).

85. William Scaife, Illinois NPU Report, *NLT,* December 7, 1889; "Where Did They Gain?" *Chicago Tribune*, supplement, November 15, 1889; "Collapse of the Block-Coal Miners' Strike," *Decatur (IL) Daily Republican,* November 22, 1889.

86. "Anthracite," to the editor, *NLT,* November 23, 1889.

87. Spring Valley, Illinois, Lodge 26, "Miners and Mine Laborers Protective Association" of the NPU, Meeting Minutes, December 21 and November 12, 1889, p. 48–50, Knights of Labor IRAD; William Scaife, Illinois NPU Report, *NLT,* December 7, 1889.

88. John Rowe, to the editor, *NLT,* June 15, 1889.

89. "Pumpkin Smasher," to the editor, *UMWJ*, February 8, 1894.

90. William Houston, to the editor, *NLT,* May 12, 1888.

Chapter 3. "Judases": Union "Betrayal" and the Aborted 1891 Strike

Epigraph. Thomas Faulds to the editor, *NLT,* April 9, 1887.

1. John Mooney, to the editor, *UMWJ,* November 12, 1891; "Strike Among Miners," *Indianapolis News,* November 5, 1891; Joe Dunkerly and T. F. Bolser on behalf of the Clinton, Indiana, miner delegation, *UMWJ,* November 12, 1891; J. H. Kennedy, UMW Indiana-Kentucky District Eleven Report, *UMWJ,* November 12, 1891; Patrick McBryde, to the editor, *UMWJ,* November 26, 1891; "The Indiana Miners," *JKL,* December 17, 1891; US 1900 Census, Family Search, "John Mooney," https://familysearch.org/pal:/ MM9.1.1/MMBJ-Z3L (accessed March 12, 2015).

2. J. H. Kennedy, UMW Indiana-Kentucky District Eleven Report, *UMWJ,* November 12, 1891.

3. John Mooney, to the editor, *UMWJ,* November 12, 1891.

4. Ibid.

5. For a recent example, see Green, *The Devil Is Here.*

6. Oestreicher, *Solidarity and Fragmentation*; Voss, *Making of American Exceptionalism,* 228; D. Nelson, *Shifting Fortunes*; McWilliams, *Idea of Fraternity*, 395; Fink, *Workingmen's Democracy,* 35; Oestreicher, "Terence Powderly," 54.

7. Report of Robert Watchorn, Proceedings of the United Mine Workers 1891 National Convention, *NLT,* February, 14, 1891; Evans, *History of United Mine Workers*, 2:122–24.

8. Phil Penna, to the editor, *UMWJ*, July 23, 1891; "M.F.," to the editor, *UMWJ*, May 7, 1891; Laurene Gardner, to the editor, *UMWJ*, January 7, 1892; "Mike," to the editor, *UMWJ*, February 2, 1892; Thomas Faulds, to the editor, *NLT*, April 9, 1887; T. J. Llewellyn, to the editor, *NLT*, January 23, 1892; M. Commesky, UMW District Eleven Report, *UMWJ*, April 27, 1893; John Mooney, to the editor, *UMWJ*, November 12, 1891.

9. UMW National Executive Board, Official Circular to the miners of the UMW, *UMWJ*, April 30, 1891; "Reasons Given for Deferring the Movement for Eight Hours" [official UMW notice], reprinted in Evans, *History of United Mine Workers*, 2: 122–25.

10. "Down with the Twine Trust," *National Economist*, May 11, 1889; "An experiment has been made," *National Economist*, May 18, 1889; N. B. Ashby, "Alliance Matters in Iowa," *National Economist*, April 27, 1889; "The Situation," *National Economist*, May 11, 1889; N.B. Ashby, "Organization in Iowa," *Humeston (IA) New Era*, June 29, 1889; House Committee on Agriculture, *Fictitious Dealings*, 8.

11. "All Are In the Same Boat," *JKL*, May 21, 1891; Sanders, *Roots of Reform*; Hild, *Greenbackers, Knights of Labor, and Populists.*

12. Garlock, *Guide to the Local Assemblies*; J. D. Thompson, to the editor, *Indiana Farmer*, April 27, 1889; W. C. Latta, to the editor, *Indiana Farmer*, December 28, 1889; Milton Trussler, "Report on the 19th Session of the Indiana State Grange," *Indiana Farmer*, January 11, 1890; Jonathan Shields, to the editor, *Indiana Farmer*, May 17, 1890; Eben Howells, to the editor, *UMWJ*, April 16, 1891; H. G. Strietelmeier, to the editor, *UMWJ*, October 1, 1891; "A New Party is Forming," *NYT*, December 5, 1890; "Alliance Movement," *UMWJ*, April 16, 1891.

13. Report of Proceedings of the Tenth Annual Convention of the American Federation of Labor, 1890, reprinted in American Federation of Labor, *Proceedings, 1889–1892*, 14; Report of Proceedings of the Eleventh Annual Convention of the American Federation of Labor, 1891, reprinted in ibid., 12; Proceedings of the United Mine Workers of America 1891 Convention, *UMWJ*, February 14, 1891.

14. Evans, *History of United Mine Workers*, 2:13–17.

15. Laurene Gardner, to the editor, *UMWJ*, March 31, 1892; Laurene Gardner, to the editor, *UMWJ*, November 26, 1891 ("no mean place"); Laurene Gardner, to the editor, *UMWJ*, December 17, 1891 ("cradle" and "blackleg").

16. Sanders, *Roots of Reform*, 135; Goodwyn, *Democratic Promise*, 245–48.

17. "The Demands of Labor," *NYT*, May 1, 1891; "A Sort of May-Day Fizzle," *NYT*, May 2, 1891; Will Scaife, "The Situation in Illinois," *Trade and Mining Journal*, reprinted in *UMWJ*, June 4, 1891.

18. "Iowa Miners," *UMWJ*, May 7, 1891.

19. "M.F.," to the editor, *UMWJ*, May 7, 1891. "Iowa Miners," *UMWJ*, May 7, 1891.

20. F. J. Llewellyn, to the editor, *NLT*, May 23, 1891; "Miner," to the editor, *NLT*, May 23, 1891; "Miner," to the editor, *NLT*, July 18, 1891; "Shakey," to the editor, *NLT*, June 27, 1891; "Samuel Simon," to the editor, *NLT*, July 25, 1891.

21. "Situation in Illinois," *Trade and Mining Journal,* reprinted in *UMWJ,* June 4, 1891.

22. US 1900 Census, Family Search, "Philip H. Penna," https://goo.gl/oN10SI (accessed February 18, 2012).

23. Phil Penna, to the editor, *NLT,* January 1, 1887; Phil Penna, to the editor, *UMWJ,* August 20, 1891; John Gallagher, to the editor, *UMWJ,* September 24, 1891; "No Kicker," to the editor, *UMWJ,* January 21, 1892.

24. Phil Penna, to the editor, *UMWJ,* July 23, 1891.

25. Phil Penna, to the editor, *UMWJ,* August 27, 1891. M. Commesky, UMW District Eleven Report, *UMWJ,* September 3, 1891; Van Tine, *Making of the Labor Bureaucrat,* 90–103.

26. Girsy McNab, to the editor, *UMWJ,* July 2, 1891; Sinthy Snodgrass, to the editor, *UMWJ* July 2, 1891; R. L. Davis, to the editor, *UMWJ,* July 7, 1892; William B. Wilson, to the editor, *Blossburg (PA) Advertiser,* January 24, 1896; "Zero," to the editor, *UMWJ,* June 10, 1897.

27. Thomas Faulds, to the editor, *NLT,* April 9, 1887; T. J. Llewellyn, to the editor, *NLT,* January 23, 1892; M. Lingenfelter, to the editor, *UMWJ,* June 29, 1899.

28. John Donnelly, to the editor, *NLT,* May 30, 1891; William Blakley, to the editor, *UMWJ,* February 17, 1898.

29. "A Beginner," to the editor, *UMWJ,* July 19, 1894.

30. P. H. Donnelly, to the editor, *NLT,* April 20, 1889; William Scaife, to the editor, *NLT,* February 28, 1891.

31. "Iowa Miners," *UMWJ,* May 7, 1891; P. H. Penna, to the editor, *UMWJ,* July 23, 1891.

32. UMW National Executive Board, Official Circular, *UMWJ,* April 30, 1891.

33. "The Columbus Result," *NLT,* April 26, 1890 (quotations); Robert Watchorn, Official UMW Report, *NLT,* April 26, 1890; J. H. Kennedy, UMW District Eleven Report, *UMWJ,* November 12, 1891.

34. J.H. Kennedy, UMW District Eleven Report, *UMWJ,* May 7, 1891.

35. J.H. Kennedy, UMW District Eleven Report, *UMWJ,* May 14, 1891.

36. F. J. Llewellyn, to the editor, *NLT,* May 23, 1891.

37. "Iowa Miners," *UMWJ,* May 21, 1891; "J. D.," to the editor, *UMWJ,* May 21, 1891; "Spring Valley Miners," *UMWJ,* July 2, 1891; M. J. Goings and Eben. Howells, Official UMW District Twelve Circular, *UMWJ,* July 2, 1891; J. H. Kennedy, UMW District Eleven Report, *UMWJ,* June 4, 1891.

38. T. T. O'Malley, to the editor, *NLT,* May 28, 1887; Oscar Anderson to John Hayes, June 17, 1892, reel 11, JWH Papers.

39. "E.P.," to the editor, *NLT,* February 4, 1888; Thomas Faulds, to the editor, May 19, 1888; FAMI Report, *NLT,* September 7, 1889.

40. W. C. Pearce, to the editor, *UMWJ,* June 4, 1891. R. L. Davis, to the editor, *UMWJ,* June 4, 1891; James H. Eskew, to the editor, *UMWJ,* December 24, 1891. Phil Penna, to the editor, *UMWJ,* July 23, 1891; Arnold, *Fueling the Gilded Age,* 157.

41. Analysis of the Indiana-Kentucky District Eleven dues is only possible because Secretary Kennedy took pains to report every cent he received each week. No other organizer reported dues as consistently during this period.

42. These dues comparisons are taken from a compilation of Kennedy's weekly reports on UMW Indiana-Kentucky District Eleven's status and finances printed in each issue of the UMW's official organ. For 1890 and early 1891, the reports are found on the UMW page of the *National Labor Tribune*. After April 1891, they were printed in the *UMWJ*, most frequently under the heading "District Eleven" or "Indiana Miners."

43. William Bauchop Wilson, to the editor, *UMWJ*, September 24, 1891; John Gallagher, to the editor, *UMWJ*, September 24, 1891.

44. William Houston, to the editor, *NLT*, January 11, 1890; Samuel Anderson, to the editor, *NLT*, August 8, 1891.

45. Samuel Anderson, to the editor, *NLT*, August 8, 1891; "Indiana Miners Give In," *NLT*, January 2, 1892.

46. "Official Notice, [To the Members of the United Mine Workers of America, July 2, 1891]," reprinted in Evans, *History of United Mine Workers*, 2:141–43.

47. Samuel Anderson, to the editor, *NLT*, August 8, 1891.

48. Ibid.

49. John Mooney, to the editor, *UMWJ*, September 3, 1891.

50. Patrick McBryde, to the editor, *UMWJ*, November 12, 1891.

51. John Mooney, to the editor, *UMWJ*, November 12, 1891.

52. J. H. Kennedy, UMW District Eleven report, *UMWJ*, November 12, 1891; "Ten Thousand Miners Quit Work," *NYT*, October 2, 1891.

53. "Strike Among Miners," *Indianapolis News*, November 5, 1891; Joe Dunkerly and T. F. Bolser on behalf of the Clinton, Indiana, miner delegation, *UMWJ*, November 12, 1891; John Mooney, to the editor, *UMWJ*, November 12, 1891; J. H. Kennedy, UMW District Eleven Report, *UMWJ*, November 12, 1891; Patrick McBryde, to the editor, *UMWJ*, November 26, 1891; "The Indiana Miners," *JKL*, December 17, 1891.

54. US 1900 Census, Family Search, "John H. Kennedy," https://familysearch.org/pal:/MM9.1.1/M99X-1H3 (accessed March 12, 2015).

55. "Biographies of the National Executive Board," *UMWJ*, March 10, 1898.

56. Ibid.

57. Ibid.

58. J. H. Kennedy, UMW District Eleven report, *UMWJ*, November 12, 1891; "C.C.," to the editor, *NLT*, January 14, 1888; "M.F.," to the editor, *UMWJ*, May 7, 1891; Phil Penna, to the editor, *UMWJ*, July 23, 1891; "Farmers' Alliance," to the editor, *UMWJ*, December 17, 1891.

59. "Summit Miner," to the editor, *UMWJ*, December 24, 1891; P. H. Penna, to the editor, *UMWJ*, December 17, 1891.

60. J. H. Kennedy, UMW District Eleven Report, *UMWJ*, December 24, 1891; James H. Eskew, to the editor, *UMWJ*, December 24, 1891; Laurene Gardner, to the editor, *UMWJ*, January 7, 1892.

61. "Mike," to the editor, *UMWJ*, December 31, 1891.

62. Laurene Gardner, to the editor, *UMWJ*, December 31, 1891.

63. Postel, *Populist Vision*, 142.

64. J. H. Kennedy, UMW District Eleven Report, *UMWJ*, December 31, 1891.

65. M. Commesky, to the editor, *UMWJ,* December 31, 1891.

66. P. H. Penna, to the editor, *UMWJ,* January 14, 1892.

67. "Farmers' Alliance," to the editor, *UMWJ,* December 17, 1891; R. L. Davis, to the editor, *UMWJ,* December 24, 1891; M. J. Goings, to the editor, *UMWJ,* December 3, 1891; "Faithful," to the editor, *UMWJ,* December 10, 1891.

68. "The Audience Was Absent," *Bloomington (IL) Daily Pantagraph,* January 13, 1892; editorial, "The annual convention," *UMWJ,* January 14, 1892; Report of the UWM District Twelve Convention, *UMWJ,* January 21, 1892.

69. "Napoleon," to the editor, *UMWJ,* January 21, 1892.

70. Laurene Gardner, to the editor, *UMWJ,* January 7, 1892.

71. J. H. Kennedy, UMW District Eleven Report, *UMWJ,* December 31, 1891; Laurene Gardner, to the editor, *UMWJ,* January 28, 1892.

72. J. H. Kennedy, UMW, District Eleven Report, *UMWJ,* March 31, 1892; J. H. Kennedy, UMW District Eleven Report, *UMWJ,* April 7, 1892.

73. Laurene Gardner, to the editor, *UMWJ,* January 7, 1892; "Cambrian," to the editor, *NLT,* August 3, 1889; Samuel Anderson, to the editor, *UMWJ,* August 8, 1891; J. H. Kennedy, UMW District Eleven Report, *UMWJ,* August 13, 1891; "Mike," to the editor, *UMWJ,* February 4, 1892; "Argus," to the editor, *UMWJ,* March 3, 1892; John E. Griffiths, to the editor, *UMWJ,* March 3, 1892.

74. John A. Templeton, to the editor, *UMWJ,* January 21, 1892.

75. P. H. Penna, to the editor, *UMWJ,* May 28, 1891; Laurene Gardner, to the editor, *UMWJ,* February 18, 1892; "Dogtown," to the editor, *UMWJ,* March 10, 1892; "Friend," to the editor, *UMWJ,* March 9, 1893; "Articles of Association," 97.

76. "Dogtown," to the editor, *UMWJ,* March 10, 1892.

77. "Agreement, Pennsylvania Company, Operating Indianapolis and Vincennes Railroad, and Dugger and Neal Coal Company," in Church, *Corporate History,* 690–91.

78. John E. Griffiths, to the editor, *UMWJ,* March 3, 1892; T. J. Llewellyn, to the editor, *NLT,* February 20, 1892; P. H. Penna, to the editor, *UMWJ,* August 20, 1891.

79. P. H. Penna, to the editor, *UMWJ,* May 28, 1891; T. J. Llewellyn, to the editor, *NLT,* January 23, 1892; Sinthy Snodgrass, to the editor, *UMWJ,* March 3, 1892; T. J. Llewellyn, to the editor, *NLT,* January 23, 1892; J. H. Kennedy, UMW District Eleven Report, *UMWJ,* June 30, 1892; J. H. Kennedy, UMW District Eleven Report, *UMWJ,* March 3, 1892.

80. Laurene Gardner, to the editor, *UMWJ,* February 18, 1892.

81. "Old Timer," to the editor, *NLT,* June 22, 1893 (quotation); IMPA Report, *NLT,* January 1, 1887; "Old Timer No. 2," to the editor, *NLT,* April 26, 1894; J. H. Kennedy, "Indiana Block Coal Affairs," in Evans, *History of United Mine Workers,* 2:203.

82. "Economy," to the editor, *UMWJ,* February 25, 1892; Laurene Gardner, to the editor, *UMWJ,* March 10, 1892; "Dogtown," to the editor, *UMWJ,* March 10, 1892.

83. Will Hall, to the editor, *UMWJ,* April 7, 1892; M. J. Guymon, to the editor, *UMWJ,* January 5, 1893.

84. M. J. O'Neil, to the editor, *NLT,* March 19, 1892; Arnold, *Fueling the Gilded Age,* 161.

85. "Mind Your Own Business," to the editor, *NLT,* June 15, 1893; "A Miner," to the editor, *NLT,* July 27, 1893; "Albion," to the editor, *NLT,* August 3, 1893; John A. Cairns, to the editor, *NLT,* August 10, 1893.

86. P. McBryde, "A Suggestion," *UMWJ,* July 6, 1893; Dan Lennon, to the editor, *UMWJ,* July 13, 1893; M. Commesky, to the editor, *UMWJ,* July 20, 1893; "Tramp," to the editor, *UMWJ,* July 27, 1893.

87. Hild, *Greenbackers, Knights of Labor, and Populists,* 178; Fox, *United We Stand,* 44.

88. Editorial, "A delegate meeting," *UMWJ,* October 26, 1893; "Tramp," to the editor, *UMWJ,* July 27, 1893; Fox, *United We Stand,* 47.

89. "Blackbird," to the editor, *UMWJ,* August 3, 1893.

90. Ibid. (quotation); "Blackbird," to the editor, *UMWJ,* June 8, 1893.

91. Willey, *Whither are We Drifting,* 541. Margery Jones, to the editor, *UMWJ,* July 16, 1891.

92. "Farmers' Alliance," to the editor, *UMWJ,* December 17, 1891; "Good Will," to the editor, *UMWJ,* February 4, 1892; L. V. Deloche, to the editor, *UMWJ,* December 1, 1892.

93. "Knights of Labor," *NLT,* November 26, 1892; L. V. Deloche, to the editor, *UMWJ,* December 1, 1892; J. H. Ritter, to the editor, *UMWJ,* December 8, 1892; Laurene Gardner, to the editor, *UMWJ,* December 15, 1892; "The Alliance," *JKL,* December 1, 1892; Goodwyn, *Democratic Promise,* 245–49.

94. "A Fool Leader," *JKL,* May 14, 1891; AFL Circular and Knights' response to it, in "Gompers Cannot Tell the Truth," *JKL,* May 28, 1891; "A Mendacious Circular," *JKL,* June 11, 1891.

95. "A Disgusting Spectacle," *UMWJ,* June 18, 1891.

96. John Kane, to the editor, *UMWJ,* July 30, 1891; "Chris Evans Denies," *UMWJ,* July 30, 1891; P. H. Penna, to the editor, *UMWJ,* December 31, 1891.

97. These charges were later dismissed as unfounded. Powderly, "Report of the General Master Workman," in Knights of Labor, *Proceedings, 1892,* 8; "K. of L. Propositions," *Report of Proceedings of the Twelfth Annual Convention of the American Federation of Labor, 1892,* reprinted in American Federation of Labor, *Proceedings, 1889–1892,* 17; John McBride to Terence Powderly, January 11, 1893, reprinted in *UMWJ,* April 13, 1893; Terence Powderly to John McBride, February 9, 1893, reprinted in *UMWJ,* April 13, 1893; John McBride, Official Address to the 1893 National Convention of the United Mine Workers of America, "McBride's Address," *UMWJ,* April 13, 1894; "Report of William B. Wilson Delegate from National Trade Assembly, No. 135 to the New Orleans Session of the General Assembly of the Knights of Labor, November 1894," folder 1894, box 1, WBW Papers; Arnold, *Fueling the Gilded Age,* 159–60.

98. L. V. Deloche, to the editor, *UMWJ,* December 1, 1892.

99. "United Mine Workers," *NLT,* February 13, 1892.

100. "United Mine Workers," *NLT,* February 20, 1892.

101. T. T. O'Malley, to the editor, *English Labor Tribune,* reprinted in *NLT,* April 2, 1892.

102. William Scaife, to the editor, *UMWJ,* January 7, 1892.

103. John McBride, to the editor, *UMWJ,* March 9, 1893; Fox, *United We Stand,* 43–45.

Chapter 4. Outsiders: Race and the Exclusive Politics of an Inclusive Union, 1892–1894

1. "Willing Hands," to the editor, *UMWJ*, March 31, 1892; "Willing Hands," to the editor, *UMWJ*, April 14, 1892.

2. "Willing Hands," to the editor, *UMWJ*, June 2, 1892; "Willing Hands," to the editor, *UMWJ*, March 24, 1892.

3. "Willing Hands," to the editor, *UMWJ*, May 5, 1892; J. H. Jackson, to the editor, *UMWJ*, August 11, 1892; R. L. Davis, to the editor, *UMWJ*, December 23, 1897; Gutman, *Work, Culture, and Society*, 131; Postel, *Equality*, 259–60.

4. Laurene Gardner, to the editor, *UMWJ*, May 5, 1892; Laurene Gardner, to the editor, *UMWJ*, August 16, 1894.

5. Blight, *Race and Reunion*.

6. Laurene Gardner, to the editor, *UMWJ*, February 18, 1892.

7. J. H. Kennedy, UMW District Eleven Report, *UMWJ*, January 19, 1893; Laurene Gardner, to the editor, *UMWJ*, November 17, 1892; "Argus," to the editor, *UMWJ*, March 3, 1892.

8. Gutman, *Work, Culture, and Society*, 121–208; Hill, "Myth-Making as Labor History"; Painter, "New Labor History"; Brier, "In Defense of Gutman."

9. Mink, *Old Labor and New Immigrants*; Barrett, *Work and Community*; Letwin, *Challenge of Interracial Unionism*; Hild, *Greenbackers, Knights of Labor, and Populists*; Gerteis, *Class and the Color Line*; Goldstene, *Struggle for America's Promise*, 49, 203–4.

10. Laurene Gardner, to the editor, *UMWJ*, October 22, 1891.

11. Waldron, "Lynch-law Must Go!"

12. Fox, *United We Stand*, 38; Gutman, *Work, Culture, and Society*, 131; "A Miner," to the editor, *UMWJ*, June 18, 1891; Margery Jones, to the editor, *UMWJ*, June 25, 1891; J. H. Kennedy, UMW District Eleven Report, *UMWJ*, December 10, 1896.

13. F. B. McGregor, to the editor, *UMWJ*, July 19, 1894; Harris, *Harder We Run*, 19–23.

14. "Observer," to the editor, *UMWJ*, October 20, 1892.

15. Ibid.; editorial response to "Observer," *UMWJ*, October 20, 1892.

16. Marti, *Women of the Grange*, 7–11, 26; Jeffery, "Women in the Southern Farmers' Alliance," 79; Merlinda Sisins, letter to the editor, *JKL*, August 7, 1890.

17. Leonora M. Barry, "Thrift Among the Miners," *JUL*, November 8, 1888; Gorn, *Mother Jones*, 60–86.

18. Phil Penna, to the editor, *UMWJ*, May 28, 1891; Richard L. Davis, to the editor, *UMWJ*, February 25, 1892; Sinthy Snodgrass, to the editor, *UMWJ*, March 3, 1892; Laurene Gardner, to the editor, *UMWJ*, October 13, 1892; J. H. Kennedy, UMWA District Eleven Report, *UMWJ*, May 4, 1893; Laurene Gardner, to the editor, *UMWJ*, October 22, 1891; "Miner's Wife," to the editor, *UMWJ*, January 28, 1892; "Willing Hands," to the editor, *UMWJ*, June 2, 1892; S. C. Burdette, to the editor, *UMWJ*, July 30, 1891; Girsy McNab, to the editor, *UMWJ*, August 13, 1891; "Women Take a Hand," *Mystic Breeze*, reprinted in *UMWJ*, June 4, 1891; "A Cowardly Murder," *UMWJ*, August 2, 1894; "Striking Miners," *Evansville (IL) Courier*, May 13, 1894.

19. Laurene Gardner to the editor, *UMWJ*, March 31, 1892.

20. Eugene Merrell, to the editor, *UMWJ*, December 10, 1896.

21. "Justice vs. Right," letter to editor, *NLT*, June 28, 1884; "Willing Hands," letter to the editor, *UMWJ*, September 15, 1892; "Negroes," *UMWJ*, July 27, 1893; W. H. Foster, to the editor, *UMWJ*, June 8, 1893.

22. Blackmon, *Slavery by Another Name*, 95–98; Albert Pridgen, "How Turpentine and Rosins are Made in Dixieland," *Paint, Oil and Drug Review*, June 14, 1911, 39; A. Lichtenstein, *Twice the Work*, 20; Harris, *Harder We Run*, 19–20; LeFlouria, *Chained in Silence*.

23. Shapiro, *New South Rebellion*; W. J. Kelso, to the editor, *UMWJ*, July 5, 1894; John Lamb, to the editor, *UMWJ*, January 11, 1894.

24. "A Would-Be Knight," to the editor, *UMWJ*, November 12, 1896.

25. Louis Ludlow, "To Import Workmen Against the Law," *EC*, June 22, 1899; "Sympathizer," to the editor, *NLT*, December 8, 1888; "A. Miner," to the editor, *NLT*, August 8, 1888; "Women Take a Hand," *UMWJ*, June 4, 1891; "Negroes," *UMWJ*, July 27, 1893; J. H. Kennedy, UMW District Eleven Report, *UMWJ*, July 23, 1896; J. H. Kennedy, UMW District Eleven Report, *UMWJ*, August 31, 1899.

26. W. J. Smith, to the editor, *UMWJ*, September 21, 1899; "Observer," to the editor, *NLT*, May 11, 1889; "Tramp," to the editor, *NLT*, March 16, 1889.

27. Doppen, *Richard L. Davis*; Gutman, *Work, Culture, and Society*, 121–208; Hill, "Myth-Making as Labor History"; Painter, "New Labor History"; Brier, "In Defense of Gutman."

28. R.L. Davis, to the editor, *UMWJ*, August 4, 1892.

29. F. H. Jackson, to the editor, *UMWJ*, August 11, 1892.

30. Keiser, "Black Strikebreakers and Racism."

31. Harris, *Harder We Run*, 20–23.

32. Dan McLaughlin, to the editor, *UMWJ*, July 23, 1891.

33. Gutman, *Work, Culture, and Society*, 123.

34. Arnesen, "Specter of the Black Strikebreaker"; Whatley, "African-American Strikebreaking": 529; Keiser, "Black Strikebreakers and Racism," 315; Dan McLaughlin, to the editor, *UMWJ*, July 23, 1891.

35. Letwin, *Challenge of Interracial Unionism*, 5.

36. Harris, *Harder We Run*, 41–42.

37. "Pro Bono Publico," to the editor, *NLT*, January 18, 1890.

38. Official Proceedings of the UMW Columbus Convention, *NLT*, February 21, 1891; John Young, to the editor, *NLT*, February 2, 1889; W. H. Foster, to the editor, *UMWJ*, June 8, 1893; "Willing Hands," to the editor, *UMWJ*, March 24, 1892; Norwood, *Strikebreaking and Intimidation*.

39. F. B. McGregor, to the editor, *UMWJ*, July 19, 1894.

40. Ayers, *Promise of the New South*, 258; Harris, *Harder We Run*, 41.

41. F. B. McGregor, to the editor, *UMWJ*, July 19, 1894; Foner, *History of the Labor Movement*, 2:66–69, 2:348–53; Gerteis, *Class and the Color Line*; Hild, *Greenbackers, Knights of*

Labor, and Populists; Hild, "Organizing across the Color Line"; Ward, "Specter of Black Labor," 12–13, 319.

42. R. L. Davis, to the editor, *UMWJ*, August 11, 1892.

43. T. H. Rollins, to the editor, *UMWJ*, March 11, 1897; R. L. Davis, to the editor, *UMWJ*, December 24, 1891.

44. Postel, *Populist Vision*; Roll, *Spirit of Rebellion*; Postel, *Equality*, 256–57.

45. "Willing Hands," to the editor, *UMWJ*, April 14, 1892.

46. "Willing Hands," to the editor, *UMWJ*, March 31, 1892; "Willing Hands," to the editor, *UMWJ*, May 5, 1892; Willing Hands," to the editor, *UMWJ*, June 2, 1892; "Willing Hands," to the editor, *UMWJ*, April 28, 1892; "Willing Hands," to the editor, *UMWJ*, June 2, 1892. "Willing Hands," to the editor, *UMWJ*, April 28, 1892.

47. "Resolution No. 133" and "Resolution No. 6 on Convict Contract Labor," in American Federation of Labor, *Proceedings, Thirteenth Annual*, 45, 49; Evans, *History of the United Mine Workers*, 140, 369; Knights of Labor, *Proceedings, 1887*, 1736.

48. "Mike," to the editor, *UMWJ*, June 9, 1892.

49. R. L. Davis, to the editor, *UMWJ*, June 9, 1892; Gutman, *Work, Culture, and Society*, 121–208.

50. "Willing Hands," to the editor, *UMWJ*, June 16, 1892.

51. R. L. Davis, to the editor, *UMWJ*, December 24, 1891.

52. "The Miners and Their Cause," *NLT*, June 29, 1889.

53. Laurene Gardner, to the editor, *UMWJ*, August 4, 1892; Kansas BLIS, *First Annual Report*, 103–9.

54. Shackel, *Remembering Lattimer*, 20–24; Low, "Maintaining Whiteness"; Smedley, "Race."

55. J. H. Kennedy, UMW District Eleven Report, "District Eleven," *UMWJ*, August 6, 1891; Kansas BLIS, *Sixth Annual Report*, 124–33.

56. Miners routinely used these phrases when discussing immigration. Sullivan and Clay County [Indiana] Citizens, Official Preamble and Resolutions, *UMWJ*, November 19, 1891; Mary Jane Beanblossom, to the editor, *UMWJ*, December 3, 1891; "Freedom," to the editor, *UMWJ*, December 29, 1892; J. H. Kennedy, UMW District Eleven Report, *UMWJ*, November 26, 1891.

57. "A Miner," to the editor, *UMWJ*, June 18, 1891; "Ike," to the editor, *UMWJ*, November 2, 1893.

58. J. H. Kennedy, UMW District Eleven Report, *UMWJ*, August 6, 1891; J. C. Heenan, District Thirteen NPU Report, *NLT*, June 16, 1889; "Screenings," *CTJ*, July 29, 1891; "Screenings," *CTJ*, September 16, 1891; "Good Will," to the editor, *UMWJ*, February 4, 1892; W. J. Guymon, to the editor, *UMWJ*, December 21, 1893; "Strike News of the Past Week," *CTJ*, May 16, 1894; "Broadax," to the editor, *UMWJ*, August 25, 1898; Warne, *Slav Invasion*, 80.

59. "Riots of Coke Drawers," *Harper's Weekly*, January 30, 1886.

60. Laurene Gardner, to the editor, *UMWJ*, August 4, 1892; Kansas BLIS, *First Annual Report*, 103–9 (quotation 109).

61. Charles Fisher testimony, *Cherokee & Pittsburg Coal & Mining Company v. Amelia Siplet*, 195–96, 209–10.

62. Ibid., 196–97.

63. Ibid., 196–98; Richard Wilson testimony, 67, 75, 76, 90; Vincent Gladis testimony, 47; Robert Craig testimony, 321, all in *Cherokee & Pittsburg Coal & Mining Company v. Amelia Siplet*.

64. Fisher testimony, 198, 204; 200–201; 201, 202, 204.

65. Keppen, *Industries of Russia*, 53–70, esp. 68; Select Committee of the House of Representatives, *Testimony*, 214; Board of Trade, *Journal*, 144–48; "Items of Interest," *CTJ*, February 4, 1885; Lamb, "Coal Mining in France,"; Warne, *Slav Invasion*; Postel, *Equality*, 231–32.

66. Haseltine, *Seventeenth Annual Report*, 7; "The Miners and Their Cause," *NLT*, June 29, 1889; Missouri BLSI, *Fifteenth Annual Report*, 47–48; Illinois BLS, *Statistics of Coal, 1893*, 119; Iowa BLS, *Fifth Biennial Report*, 13–29.

67. "Why the Number of English-speaking Miners Is Decreasing," *Colliery Engineer* 11, no. 7 (February 1891): 157.

68. "The Miners and Their Cause," *NLT*, June 29, 1889.

69. "A Delving Serf," to the editor, *NLT*, February 14, 1891; "Mining Bees," *Earlington (KY) Bee*, May 26, 1892; "The Examination of Miners," *Collier Engineer* 14, no. 8 (March 1893).

70. "A Delving Serf," to the editor, *NLT*, February 14, 1891; "The Examination of Miners," *Collier Engineer* 14, no. 8 (March 1893); "Skeletons in Industrial Legislation," *Age of Steel*, March 1893, 10.

71. Laurene Gardner, to the editor, *UMWJ*, August 4, 1892.

72. Sullivan and Clay County [Indiana] Citizens, Official Preamble and Resolutions, *UMWJ*, November 19, 1891.

73. Shackel, *Remembering Lattimer*, 20–24; Mink, *Old Labor and New Immigrants*; Kazin, *Barons of Labor*.

74. Lewis, *Welsh Americans*, 201, 231–32, 238; Shackel, *Remembering Lattimer*, 26.

75. John Hayes to Charles Holm, February 18, 1892, reel 11, JWH Papers; Gust. Granguist to John Hayes, September 7, 1891, reel 11, JWH Papers.

76. Oscar Anderson to John Hayes, June 17, 1892, reel 11, JWH Papers.

77. Gust Dahlstrom to John Hayes, July 4, 1891, reel 11, JWH Papers.

78. Louis Goaziou, to the editor, *NLT*, March 14, 1895; Arnold, *Fueling the Gilded Age*, 160, 181.

79. Phil Penna, to the editor, *UMWJ*, August 20, 1891.

80. "Union," to the editor, *UMWJ*, August 22, 1895; John Young, to the editor, *NLT*, February 2, 1889; Laurene Gardner, to the editor, *UMWJ*, August 4, 1892; T. J. Llewelyn, to the editor, *NLT*, January 23, 1892; "Johnny Bull," to the editor, *UMWJ*, November 17, 1892; Arthur Connery, to the editor, *UMWJ*, February 24, 1898.

81. "Tramp," to the editor, *NLT*, March 16, 1889; "Crows and Hawks," *NLT*, February 8, 1890 (quotation); John Neal, to the editor, *UMWJ*, January 5, 1893; "Bald Head," to

the editor, *UMWJ*, January 26, 1893; "A Former Employee of the Forsythe Company," to the editor, *UMWJ*, October 19, 1893; "Successful Americans," *CTJ*, September 1, 1897; P. H. Donnelly, to the editor, *NLT*, March 16, 1889; "Our Latest Mails," *NLT*, March 26, 1876.

82. *Cherokee & Pittsburg Coal & Mining Company vs. Amelia Siplet*; Kansas BLIS, *First Annual Report*, 40–70.

83. "Old Timer," to the editor, *NLT*, November 9, 1893.

84. "A. Miner," to the editor, *NLT*, August 25, 1888.

85. J. H. Kennedy, UMW Indiana District Report, *UMWJ*, October 20, 1892; T. J. Llewellyn, to the editor, *NLT*, January 23, 1892; "Indiana Miners," FAMI Report, *NLT*, January 14, 1888.

86. J. H. Kennedy, UMW Indiana District Report, *UMWJ*, December 8, 1892.

87. "Old Timer," to the editor, *NLT*, November 9, 1893.

88. John Neal, to the editor, *UMWJ*, January 5, 1893; T. J. Llewellyn, to the editor, *NLT*, January 23, 1892; Laurene Gardner, to the editor, *UMWJ*, February 9, 1893.

89. "Crows and Hawks," *NLT*, February 8, 1890.

90. John McBride, Speech to the 1893, UMW National Convention, reprinted in Evans, *History of the United Mine Workers*, 2:180.

91. T. J. Llewellyn, to the editor, *NLT*, January 23, 1892; M. Commesky, to the editor, UMW District Eleven Report, *UMWJ*, December 24, 1891.

92. "Salamander," to the editor, *UMWJ*, January 12, 1893; "Tow Row," to the editor, *UMWJ*, January 19, 1893; Laurene Gardner, to the editor, *UMWJ*, January 26, 1893 (quotation); "Crows and Hawks," *NLT*, February 8, 1890; "A Pumpkin-Roller," to the editor, *NLT*, March 1, 1890; "Salamander," to the editor, *UMWJ*, December 22, 1892; Laurene Gardner, to the editor, *UMWJ*, January 12, 1893.

Chapter 5. Unsettled: Nonunion Mobilization and the 1894 Strike

1. "Sunshine," to the editor, *UMWJ*, May 3, 1894; "Calamity," to the editor, *UMWJ*, June 7, 1894. J. H. Adams, to the editor, *UMWJ*, May 10, 1894; Julius Fromm, UMW Iowa District Thirteen Convention Report, *UMWJ*, June 14, 1894.

2. W. S. Moke, to the editor, *UMWJ*, June 7, 1894.

3. "Miner," to the editor, *NLT*, May 10, 1894.

4. White, *Republic for Which It Stands*, 769–773.

5. Laurene Gardner, to the editor, *UMWJ*, April 19, 1894; Alfred Broad, to the editor, *UMWJ*, August 30, 1894; Brecher, *Strike!*, 82; Stromquist, "Crisis of 1894," 186, 197.

6. Laurie, *Artisans into Workers*; Amsden and Brier, "Coal Miners on Strike"; White, *Railroaded*; Arnold, *Fueling the Gilded Age*, 164–76.

7. Voss, *Making of American Exceptionalism*, 4; Weir, *Beyond Labor's Veil*, 12; Ware, *Labor Movement*, 213–14.

8. Evans, *History of Labor Movement*, 1:139–40; Ware, *Labor Movement*, 215–21.

9. Evans, *History of Labor Movement*, 1:403–10.

10. Dubofsky, *Industrialization and the American Worker*, 88–89; Greene, *Pure and Simple Politics*, 26–47, 73.

11. Evans, *History of Labor Movement*, 1:405.

12. Van Tine, *Making of the Labor Bureaucrats*, 37–40, 115; Arnold, *Fueling the Gilded Age*, 110, 182.

13. "Vice President Penna Talks," *UMWJ*, June 21, 1894; Fox, *United We Stand*, 45–47.

14. Pierce, "Populist President," 8; McBride, "Coal Miners," 242–43.

15. Commons, *Nationalisation*, 363–64; Doppen, *Richard L. Davis*, 51–53.

16. Postel, *Populist Vision*, 20, 213; Brody, *In Labor's Cause*, 131–74.

17. John McBride, to the editor, *UMWJ*, March 9, 1893; "Convention of Ohio Miners," *Gloversville (NY) Daily Leader*, June 15, 1894; Roy, *History of the Coal Miners*, 249–55.

18. T. Howells, to the editor, *UMWJ*, August 9, 1894; Stromquist, "Crisis of 1894," 186–87.

19. John Kane, to the editor, *UMWJ*, July 30, 1891; P. H. Penna, to the editor, *UMWJ*, December 31, 1891.

20. See ch. 3 of this book.

21. John McBride to Terence Powderly, January 11, 1893, reprinted in *UMWJ*, April 13, 1893; Terence Powderly to John McBride, February 9, 1893, reprinted in *UMWJ*, April 13, 1893; "Report of William B. Wilson Delegate from National Trade Assembly, No. 135 to the New Orleans Session of the General Assembly of the Knights of Labor, November 1894," folder 1894, box 1, WBW Papers.

22. Because the officers of the UMW held the same respective offices in NTA 135 and in the NPU, strife lay with the separate pulls of the Knights of Labor and the AFL rather than divisions between NTA 135 and the NPU. John Kane, to the editor, *UMWJ*, July 30, 1891.

23. Terence Powderly, "Report of the General Master Workman," in Knights of Labor, *Proceedings, 1892*, 8; John McBride to Terence Powderly, January 11, 1893, reprinted in *UMWJ*, April 13, 1893; Terence Powderly to John McBride, February 9, 1893, reprinted in *UMWJ*, April 13, 1893; "Report of William B. Wilson Delegate from National Trade Assembly, No. 135 to the New Orleans Session of the General Assembly of the Knights of Labor, November 1894," folder 1894, box 1, WBW Papers; Weir, *Knights Unhorsed*; Phelan, *Grand Master Workman*, 253–59; Ware, *Labor Movement*, 364–70; Falzone, "Terence V. Powderly," 336.

24. Knights of Labor, *Proceedings, 1893*, 4, 35–66; "Powderly Now Strikes Back," *NYT*, June 15, 1894; For details of the coup and the politics behind it, see Phelan, *Grand Master Workman*, 253–56; Weir, *Knights Unhorsed*, 173–74; Falzone, "Terence V. Powderly," 336–41; Powderly, *Path I Trod*, 365–67; Phelan, "Warp of Fancy."

25. Terence Powderly to Patrick McBryde, November 3, 1894, reel 59, TVP Papers; Stromquist, "Crisis of 1894," 186–87.

26. "Blackbird," to the editor, *UMWJ*, May 17, 1894; "Proposition," *UMWJ*, November

19, 1891; William T. Morris, to the editor, *UMWJ*, August 16, 1894; D. H. Sullivan, to the editor, *UMWJ*, August 22, 1895.

27. John Rowe, to the editor, *NLT*, July 13, 1889; "Shorter Hours," to the editor, *NLT*, August 10, 1889; "J.D.," to the editor, *NLT*, August 24, 1889; "Bob," to the editor, *NLT*, August 24, 1889.

28. Because miners were paid by the ton rather than by the amount of time spent in the mines, the restriction skilled workers exercised in other industries seldom applied to coal producers. For details on restriction success, see Montgomery, *Workers' Control in America*, 9–31.

29. George A. Denison, "Suspension of Work in the Coal Mines," reprinted in *NLT*, January 1, 1887.

30. "Proceedings of the 1894 Convention of the United Mine Workers of America," *UMWJ*, April 19, 1894; John McBride, UMW Official Circular, "Official Bulletin No. 1," *UMWJ*, May 3, 1894; Altgeld, *Live Questions*, 762; Jensen, *Winning of the Midwest*, 249.

31. Amsden and Brier, "Coal Miners on Strike"; Merithew and Barrett, "We Are All Brothers"; Arnold, *Fueling the Gilded Age*, 164–76.

32. Hild, *Greenbackers, Knights of Labor, and Populists*, 176; Arnold, *Fueling the Gilded Age*, 162–66; Foner, *From the Founding*, 217–18, 235–36, 248; "Irish American," to the editor, *UMWJ*, March 15, 1894; "A Miner's Widow," to the editor, *JKL*, March 8, 1894; W.L., to the editor, *UMWJ*, May 10, 1894; "A Miner," to the editor, *UMWJ*, May 10, 1894.

33. Missouri BLSI, *Sixteenth Annual Report*, 523; Hall, *Sympathetic Strikes*, 70; Walter S. Scott, to the editor, *UMWJ*, April 12, 1894; T. B. McGregor, to the editor, *UMWJ*, April 12, 1894.

34. "A Miner," to the editor, *UMWJ*, May 10, 1894.

35. Hild, *Greenbackers, Knights of Labor, and Populists*; McMath, *Populist Vanguard*; Sanders, *Roots of Reform*; Postel, *Populist Vision*; Alexander, *Coxey's Army*; Destler, *American Radicalism*, 175–77.

36. "General News Notes," *UMWJ*, March 22, 1894; "Coxey's March," *NLT*, April 5, 1894; "Incog," to the editor, *UMWJ*, May 10, 1894; "Sorehead," to the editor, *UMWJ*, May 10, 1894; T. J. Llewellyn, to the editor, *NLT*, May 24, 1894; "Junius," to the editor, *UMWJ*, June 14, 1894; Alexander, *Coxey's Army*; Pierce, "Populist President," 12–14.

37. "A Miner," to the editor, *UMWJ*, April 12, 1894 (quotation); "Sorehead," to the editor, *UMWJ*, May 10, 1894; "Addressed by Peffer," *Lawrence (KS) Daily Journal*, September 19, 1894; J. B. Bach, Ch'm, and Charles Bell, to the editor, *UMWJ*, May 17, 1894; Postel, *Populist Vision*; Alexander, *Coxey's Army*; Caldemeyer, "Unfaithful Followers," 118–19.

38. W. L., to the editor, *UMWJ*, May 10, 1894.

39. John Mooney, to the editor, *UMWJ*, May 10, 1894; F. W. Koehler, to the editor, *UMWJ*, June 14, 1894; "Proceedings of the 1894 Convention of the United Mine Workers of America," *UMWJ*, April 19, 1894; J. H. Kennedy, UMW Indiana District Report, *UMWJ*, April 26, 1894; "Old Timer No. 2," to the editor, *NLT*, April 26, 1894; "Blind Robin," to the editor, *UMWJ*, April 26, 1894; "C.T.," to the editor, *NLT*, April 26, 1894.

40. Steeples and Whitten, *Democracy in Desperation*; Foner, *From the Founding*, 265–70; Stromquist, "Crisis of 1894," 189.

41. Warne, *Coal-Mine Workers*, 213–14; Postel, *Populist Vision*, 211.

42. Andrew Roy claimed the number of strikers did not exceed 100,000. Frank Julian Warne, however, claimed that 125,000 walked out on strike on April 21 and increased to 180,000. Maier Fox confirmed Warne's estimate in his own work. Official UMW Report, "The Suspension," *NLT,* April 26, 1894; William P. Bensinger, William Fredrick, and Martin Robinson, to the editor on behalf of Vincennes miners, *UMWJ,* May 17, 1894; "M'Bride is Well Satisfied," *NYT,* April 23, 1894; "Strike of Coal Miners Extending," *NYT,* April 24, 1894; Roy, *History of the Coal Miners,* 305; Warne, *Coal-Mine Workers,* 213–14; Fox, *United We Stand,* 45.

43. J. Carter, to the editor, *UMWJ,* May 10, 1894; J. H. Adams, to the editor, *UMWJ,* May 10, 1894; John McBride, UMW Official Circular, "Official Bulletin No. 1," *UMWJ,* May 3, 1894; "Sunshine," to the editor, *UMWJ,* May 3, 1894; "Hopeful," to the editor, *UMWJ,* May 10, 1894; "Sorehead," to the editor, *UMWJ,* May 10, 1894; "Incog," to the editor, *UMWJ,* May 10, 894; "Iowa," to the editor, *UMWJ,* May 10, 1894; W. J. Guymon, UMW Illinois District Report, *UMWJ,* May 31, 1894; "The Miners' Great Strike," *JKL,* May 10, 1894; Executive Committee, report on behalf of the New Mexico miners, "New Mexico," *UMWJ,* May 17, 1894.

44. John McBride, "Very Latest," *UMWJ,* May 10, 1894.

45. J. H. Kennedy, UMW Indiana District Report, *UMWJ,* May, 10, 1894; J. B. Bach and Charles Bell, to the editor, *UMWJ,* May 17, 1894; "Blackbird," to the editor, *UMWJ,* May 17, 1894.

46. John McBride, UMW Official Circular, "Official Bulletin No. 1," *UMWJ,* May 3, 1894; "The Wives of Miners," *Evansville (IL) Courier,* May 13, 1894; Philip Veal, to the editor, *UMWJ,* June 28, 1894; James Bagnall, to the editor, *UMWJ,* June 28, 1894; "Miner," to the editor, *UMWJ,* May 31, 1894; "Blackbird," to the editor, *UMWJ,* May 24, 1894.

47. Despite Veal's claim, the Kansas miners did not secede from the UMW. Rather, they kept their charters and disregarded the order, prompting Missouri miners to declare them out of their district at the Missouri-Kansas District Convention that summer. Philip Veal, to the editor, *UMWJ,* June 28, 1894; James Bagnal, to the editor, *UMWJ,* June 28, 1894.

48. Philip Veal, to the editor, *UMWJ,* June 28, 1894; James Bagnall, to the editor, *UMWJ,* June 28, 1894; "After the Kansas Miners," *Springfield (MO) Republican,* May 18, 1894; "The Missouri Miners," *Pittsburg (KS) Daily Headlight,* May 22, 1894; "The Strikers Back Down," *Independence (KS) Daily Reporter,* May 26, 1894;

49. J. H. Kennedy, UMW Indiana District Report, *UMWJ,* May 24, 1894.

50. John G. Williams to Claude Matthews, May 30, 1894, folder 1, S931, Claude Matthews Papers; "Strike News of the Past Week," *CTJ,* June 6, 1894. Shelburn, Indiana, miners committee to Claude Matthews, June 8, 1894; John G. Leming to Claude Matthews, June 1, 1894; Morgan Ringo to Claude Matthews, June 1, 1894, all in folder

1, S931, Claude Matthews Papers. "They May Arbitrate," *DIO*, May 28, 1894; "The Miners' Strike," *Indianapolis News*, June 1, 1894; "Junius," to the editor, *UMWJ*, June 14, 1894; J. H. Kennedy, UMW Indiana District Report, *UMWJ*, June 14, 1894; "Examine All Trains," *Bloomington (IL) Daily Pantagraph*, May 28, 1894; "Prevented by Women," *Evansville (IL) Courier*, June 2, 1894; Stromquist, "Crisis of 1894," 190–91.

51. UMW Special Convention Report, "The Convention," *UMWJ*, May 17, 1894; Peter Lauer Jr., to the editor, *NLT*, July 5, 1894.

52. "St. Louis," *CTJ*, May 16, 1894; "Kansas City," *CTJ*, May 16, 1894; "Strike News of the Past Week," *CTJ*, June 6, 1894; "Strike News of the Past Week," *CTJ*, June 13, 1894; "Secretary McBryde," *UMWJ*, June 21, 1891.

53. Proceedings of the "National Convention at Cleveland, Ohio," in Evans, *History of United Mine Workers*, 2:335–50; John McBride, Official UMW Bulletin No. 7, "Bulletin No. 7," *UMWJ*, June 14, 1894; Laurie, *Artisans into Workers*, 13; Van Tine, *Making of the Labor Bureaucrat*, 47; Michels, *Political Parties*; Stabile, *Activist Unionism*, 136–39.

54. Terence Powderly to Patrick McBryde, June 14, 1894, reel 59, TVP Papers; John McBride, P. H. Penna, Patrick McBryde, Cameron Miller, John Fahy, Joseph Dunkerly, and John A. Cairns, Official UMW Circular, "Bulletin No. 7," *UMWJ*, June 14, 1894.

55. "Incog," to the editor, *UMWJ*, July 12, 1894.

56. Alfred Broad, to the editor, *UMWJ*, August 30, 1894; "F.Y.T.," to the editor, *UMWJ*, June 21, 1894; Eddie Ocheltree, to the editor, *UMWJ*, June 21, 1894; "P.D.B.," to the editor, *UMWJ*, June 14, 1894; J. Fromm, to the editor, *UMWJ*, June 14, 1894.

57. W. J. Winterbottom, to the editor, *UMWJ*, June 28, 1894; Phil Penna, to the editor, *UMWJ*, July 5, 1894; "Miner," to the editor, *UMWJ*, January 24, 1895; "The Union is at Stake," *Chicago Daily Tribune*, June 14, 1894.

58. "Coal Miner," letter to the editor, *NLT*, July 26, 1894 (quotation); "Short Creek," to the editor, *UMWJ*, June 21, 1894.

59. "Shorter Hours," to the editor, *NLT*, August 10, 1889; "J.D.," to the editor, *NLT*, August 24, 1889; "Bob," to the editor, *NLT*, August 24, 1889; Montgomery, *Workers' Control in America*, 9–31; Gutman, "Work, Culture, and Society," 3–78.

60. "Convention at Pittsburg To-day," *Gloversville (NY) Daily Leader*, June 15, 1894.

61. Not all Ohio miners agreed. Knights of Labor local assembly 164 rejected Ohio district president A. A. Adams's call for a special convention, believing his refusal to sign the scale was treason. W. Findley, Thomas Miller, and Thomas Kennedy, Committee, Official Resolutions Passed by Chapman Assembly No. 164 K. of L., "Resolutions," *UMWJ*, July 5, 1894; "Hot," *UMWJ*, June 21, 1894; Committee, Official Resolutions, "Dissatisfied Ohio Miners," *NLT*, June 21, 1894.

62. "Justice," to the editor, *UMWJ*, July 5, 1894.

63. Although the convention was for the entire Missouri-Kansas District, nearly all delegates were from Missouri since most of Kansas had left the UMW. During the convention, delegates also decided they would have no further interaction with the Kansas miners. T. B. McGregor and George H. Chapman, UMW Missouri-Kansas District Fourteen Special Convention Report, *UMWJ*, June 28, 1894.

64. J. A. Crawford and W. J. Guymon, UMW District Twelve Special Convention Official Report," *UMWJ*, June 28, 1894; Committee, Report of Resolutions, "Mass Meeting," *UMWJ*, June 28, 1894; "An Old Miner," to the editor, *UMWJ*, June 28, 1894; "Keep Off the Grass," to the editor, *UMWJ*, June 28, 1894.

65. Van Tine, *Making of the Labor Bureaucrat*, 80–81.

66. "New Moses Is Found," *Chicago Tribune*, June 15, 1894 (quotation); "The Outlook Very Gloomy," *Scranton (PA) Tribune*, June 15, 1894; "President M'Bride Talks," *ST*, June 16, 1894.

67. J. H. Kennedy, UMW Indiana District Report of the Special Convention of District Eleven, *UMWJ*, June 21, 1894.

68. W. J. Winterbottom, to the editor, *UMWJ*, June 28, 1894.

69. J. H. Kennedy, UMW District Eleven Report of the Second Special Convention of District Eleven, *UMWJ*, June 28, 1894; "Incog," to the editor, *UMWJ*, July 12, 1894; Joseph Dunkerly, to the editor, *UMWJ*, October 4, 1894.

70. Samuel Anderson, to the editor, *UMWJ*, September 13, 1894.

71. Not all miners in the block district agreed with the decision. Four locals opted to remain in District Eleven. "J. H. Kennedy, UMW District Eleven Report, *UMWJ*, August 30, 1894; "Clay Co, Ind.," *UMWJ*, September 6, 1894; Samuel Anderson, to the editor, *UMWJ*, September 13, 1894; Laurene Gardner, to the editor, *UMWJ*, September 27, 1894; Le[e] Erwin, to the editor, *UMWJ*, September 27, 1894; Sam Anderson, to the editor, *UMWJ*, October 4, 1894; "A.F.C.," to the editor, *UMWJ*, January 31, 1895.

72. "Caught in Coxyland," *Scranton (PA) Tribune*, June 15, 1894; "The Strike at Chicago About Over," *Scranton (PA) Tribune*, July 12, 1894; "It Is Simply an Appeal," *Scranton (PA) Tribune*, July 12, 1894 (quotation).

73. M. J. O'Neil, to the editor, *NLT*, June 28, 1894; Jensen, *Winning of the Midwest*, 247, 249.

74. It is not clear whether Crawford ever responded. Over one month later, Tid wrote of rumors that Crawford was sick, but also noted that the state president regularly gave speeches at political gatherings and had not visited the miners. "Miner," to the editor, *UMWJ*, August 2, 1894 (quotations); "Tid," to the editor, *UMWJ*, September 20, 1894.

75. T. Howells, to the editor, *UMWJ*, August 9, 1894; William T. Morris, to the editor, *UMWJ*, August 16, 1894; James O'Connor, to the editor, *UMWJ*, August 16, 1894; Samuel Anderson, to the editor, *UMWJ*, September 13, 1894; "Hibernia," to the editor, *UMWJ*, September 27, 1894; Laurene Gardner, to the editor, *UMWJ*, September 27, 1894.

76. "The Evil Results of the Strike," *CTJ*, May 16, 1894; "Strike News of the Past Week," *CTJ*, June 6, 1894; "Strike News of the Past Week," *CTJ*, June 6, 1894; "Strike News of the Past Week," *CTJ*, June 13, 1894; W. M. Goodnes to Governor Lorenzo Lewelling, July 4, 1894, Lorenzo D. Lewelling Papers; William Tanner to Governor Lorenzo Lewelling, July 9, 1894, Lorenzo D. Lewelling Papers; Jensen, *Winning of the Midwest*, 243.

77. W. J. Reynolds, to the editor, *UMWJ*, July 19, 1894; "Peace," to the editor, *UMWJ*, July 19, 1894; T. Howells, to the editor, *UMWJ*, August 9, 1894; W. J. Guymon, to the

editor, *UMWJ*, January 17, 1895 (date listed incorrectly as January 10 on the first page of this issue); "Big Foot," to the editor, *UMWJ*, January 17, 1895.

Chapter 6. Wolves: Fractured Unions in the Gilded Age, 1894–1896

Epigraph. William Scaife to the editor, *UMWJ*, December 9, 1897.

1. "The Convention Shuts out Miners," *New Orleans Daily Picayune*, November 20, 1894 (quotation); Hugh Cavanaugh, interview with the *Cincinnati Enquirer,* November 22, 1894; "The Delegates of N.T.A. 135," *UMWJ*, November 29, 1894.

2. "Knights of Labor Re-Elect Leaders," *New Orleans Daily Picayune,* November 21, 1894.

3. "Knights of Labor," *Hutchinson (KS) News,* November 13, 1894.

4. Weir, *Knights Unhorsed*, 161–78; Craig Phelan, *Grand Master Workman*; "Knights of Labor," *Hutchinson (KS) News*, November 13, 1894; Knights of Labor, *Proceedings, 1894*, 44–54.

5. Knights of Labor, *Proceedings, 1894*, 131; "A Pittsburg Plaint," *New Orleans Daily Picayune,* November 16, 1894; "The Convention Shuts Out Miners," *New Orleans Daily Picayune*, November 20, 1894; "Knights of Labor Re-Elect Leaders," *New Orleans Daily Picayune*, November 21, 1894; General Executive Board of the Independent Order of the Knights of Labor, "Address to the Independent Order of Knights of Labor," Official Circular to IOKL Locals, in Independent Order of the Knights of Labor, *Official Handbook*, n.p.

6. Weir, *Knights Unhorsed*; Phelan, *Grand Master Workman*; Greene, *Pure and Simple Politics*; Ware, *Labor Movement*, 364–70.

7. Oestreicher, *Solidarity and Fragmentation*; Voss, *Making of American Exceptionalism*; Phelan, *Grand Master Workman*; Weir, *Beyond Labor's Veil*.

8. "President John McBride," *NLT,* December 27, 1894.

9. "Old Miner," to the editor, *NLT,* May 10, 1894.

10. "One of the Frauds," to the editor, *UMWJ*, September 27, 1894.

11. Le[e] Erwin, to the editor, *UMWJ*, September 27, 1894.

12. Sam Anderson to the editor, *UMWJ*, September 13, 1894; "Tid," letter to the editor, *UMWJ*, September 20, 1894; P. H. Penna, to the editor in reply to Lee Erwin, *UMWJ*, September 27, 1894.

13. Evans, *History of United Mine Workers*, 2:45, 2:236–39, 2:296–99; only Secretary-Treasurer W. C. Pearce was reelected. A.C.H., "Ohio Coal Notes," *CTJ,* April 11, 1894; "President A. A. Adams," *Iron Trade Review,* June 28, 1894; Kleppner, *Cross of Culture*, 247.

14. Over 7,200 votes were cast between candidates Adams, Nugent, James Prithard, and M. F. Moran. W. C. Pearce, "Report of the Regular Annual Convention of [Ohio] District Six," *UMWJ*, April 12, 1894.

15. "The Union is at Stake," *Chicago Daily Tribune,* June 14, 1894; A.C.H., "Ohio Coal Notes," *CTJ,* June 20, 1894; "President A. A. Adams," *Iron Trade Review,* June 28, 1894.

16. "Coal Miners' Sensation!" *JKL*, January 10, 1895.

17. Fox, *United We Stand*, 47; "A Miner," to the editor, *UMWJ*, August 9, 1894.

18. Laurene Gardner, to the editor, *UMWJ*, July 12, 1894; A.C.H., "Ohio Coal Notes," *CTJ*, June 20, 1894; "Alpha and Omega," to the editor, *UMWJ*, June 28, 1894; Phil Penna, to the editor, *UMWJ*, July 5, 1894; Phil Penna to A. A. Adams, open letter printed in *UMWJ*, January 17, 1895; "Phil Penna," to the editor, *UMWJ*, January 17, 1895.

19. "Incog," to the editor, *UMWJ*, July 12, 1894. "A Miner's Wife," to the editor, *UMWJ*, July 19, 1894.

20. "A Miner," to the editor, *UMWJ*, July 5, 1894.

21. "The forcible exit," *NYT*, May 21, 1894 (quotation); "Talk of Expelling Powderly," *NYT*, January 6, 1894; "Why T. V. Powderly Resigned," *NYT*, January 18, 1894.

22. Phelan, *Grand Master Workman*, 248–49; "Powderly's Plain Talk," *Wilkes-Barre (PA) Record*, June 15, 1894 (quotation); "For Powderly in the Knights," *Scranton (PA) Tribune*, January 18, 1894; "Powderly Quietly Expelled," *NYT*, May 20, 1894; "Powderly Now Strikes Back," *NYT*, June 15, 1894.

23. "Mr. Martin Arrested," *Scranton (PA) Tribune*, May 24, 1894 (quotation); "Powderly Now Strikes Back," *NYT*, June 15, 1894.

24. Terence Powderly to E. J. Lynch, December 7, 1894, reel 59, TVP Papers.

25. Terence Powderly to Anson Bigelow, Peter Breen, Hugh Cavanaugh, D. F. Lawlor, Robert McConnell, J. J. Riefgraber, A. W. Wright, W. C. W. Wine, F. Vincent, James L. Michels, J. R. Buchanan, D. A. Carey, Bernard Feeney, Wm. Hubbell, L. Hoechatetter, E. L. Jordan, Thomas Lacombe, George J. Kilt, B. J. Lee, Charles R. Martin, F. H. Mauer, Patrick McBryde, Michael O'Keefe, P. H. Quinn, W. Shuntliff, Edward J. Lynch, William E. Taaife, John H. Murray, John P. Eberhardt, James P. Archibald, and Tom O'Reilly, October 28, 1894, reel 59, TVP Papers.

26. Terence Powderly to Patrick McBryde, November 3, 1894, reel 59, TVP Papers; "Report of William B. Wilson Delegate from National Trade Assembly, No. 135 to the New Orleans Session of the General Assembly of the Knights of Labor, November 1894," folder 1894, box 1, WBW Papers.

27. Knights of Labor, *Proceedings, 1894*, 131; "The K. of L. Convention," *JKL*, November 29, 1894; "A Pittsburg Plaint," *New Orleans Daily Picayune*, November 16, 1894; "The Convention Shuts Out Miners," *New Orleans Daily Picayune*, November 20, 1894; "Knights of Labor Re-Elect Leaders," *New Orleans Daily Picayune*, November 21, 1894; General Executive Board of the Independent Order of the Knights of Labor, "Address to the Independent Order of Knights of Labor," Official Circular to all IOKL Locals, in Independent Order of the Knights of Labor, *Official Handbook*, n.p.; Phelan, *Grand Master Workman*, 257; Weir, *Knights Unhorsed*, 177.

28. Terence Powderly to Tom O'Reilley, December 2, 1894, reel 59, TVP Papers.

29. John W. Hayes to the assemblies of District 10, NTA 135 of the Knights of Labor, February 23, 1895, folder 1895, box 1, WBW Papers; *United*, 48.

30. NTA 135 Official Circular, *UMWJ*, January 17, 1895.

31. J. H. Kennedy, UMW District Eleven Report, January 3, 1895; Fox, *United We Stand*, 49.

32. "Gompers Goes Out," *Topeka Daily Capital*, December 18, 1894; "President John McBride," *NLT*, December 27, 1894; Postel, *Populist Vision*, 208–9; Pierce, "Populist President," 18–19; Pierce, *Striking with the Ballot*, 147, 178; Greene, *Pure and Simple Politics*, 62–64; Destler, *American Radicalism*, 169–74.

33. Greene, *Pure and Simple Politics*, 64.

34. "Coal Miners' Sensation!," *JKL*, January 10, 1895; A. A. Adams to Phil Penna, open letter reprinted in "Adams's Answer," *UMWJ*, January 24, 1895.

35. "Coal Miners' Sensation!," *JKL*, January 10, 1895.

36. The Glass Bottle Blowers' Association formally joined the AFL in 1899. Flannery, *Glass House Boys*, 113–14; McCabe, *Standard Rate*, 156–57.

37. Sanders, *Roots of Reform*, 41–42; Phelan, "Warp of Fancy."

38. George Richards, to the editor, *JKL*, January 10, 1895; editor reply to William H. Crawford, *JKL*, January 10, 1895.

39. "Founded on Principles," *JKL*, January 3, 1895; "What Are They To Do? Coal Miners Starving While Being Used," *JKL*, January 10, 1895; "The Dispute," *UMWJ*, January 10, 1895; NTA 135 Official Circular, "Official Circular," *UMWJ*, January 17, 1895; A. A. Adams to Phil Penna, open letter reprinted in "Adams's Answer," *UMWJ*, January 24, 1895; "McBryde and the Bonds," *JKL*, May 2, 1895; Phelan, *Grand Master Workman*, 257; Sanders, *Roots of Reform*, 83–85; Van Tine, *Making of the Labor Bureaucrat*, 110.

40. Sim Cooper, to the editor, *UMWJ*, January 31, 1895 (quotation); "Young American," to the editor, *UMWJ*, February 14, 1895; David Mason, to the editor, *UMWJ*, January 24, 1895; A. A. Adams to Phil Penna, open letter reprinted in "Adams's Answer," *UMWJ*, January 24, 1895; Phil Penna to A. A. Adams, open letter printed in "Penna to Adams," *UMWJ*, January 31, 1895; "A Looker On," to the editor, *UMWJ*, February 7, 1895; R. L. Davis, to the editor, *UMWJ*, March 14, 1895; "Incog," to the editor, *UMWJ*, May 2, 1895.

41. Sim Cooper, to the editor, *UMWJ*, January 31, 1895.

42. David Mason, to the editor, *UMWJ*, January 24, 1895 (quotation); "A Looker On," to the editor, *UMWJ*, February 7, 1895; J. H. Kennedy, UMW District Eleven Report, *UMWJ*, February 7, 1895; Laurene Gardner, to the editor *UMWJ*, November 8, 1894; F. P. Harkins, to the editor, *UMWJ*, November 22, 1894; Julius Fromm, to the editor, *UMWJ*, June 20, 1895.

43. T. T., to the editor, *NLT*, January 17, 1895 (quotations); Philip Veal, to the editor, *UMWJ*, January 31, 1895; T. T., to the editor, *NLT*, January 17, 1895; William H. Crawford, to the editor, *UMWJ*, January 24, 1895; "Wm. H. Crawford," *UMWJ*, January 24, 1895; Sim Cooper, to the editor, *UMWJ*, January 31, 1895; "Old Miner," to the editor, *NLT*, February 7, 1895.

44. T. T., to the editor, *NLT*, January 17, 1895.

45. At times, however, funds were too low for officers to draw their full salaries. M. J. Goings, to the editor, *UMWJ*, October 12, 1893; UMW District 14 Auditor's Report, *UMWJ*, October 11, 1894; Ware, *Labor Movement*, 375; Falzone, *Terence V. Powderly*, 171.

46. "Next Week," to the editor, *UMWJ*, December 13, 1894.

47. T. T. O'Malley, to the editor, *NLT*, March 7, 1895. Louis Goaziou, to the editor, *NLT*, March 14, 1895.

48. Charles E. Starr, Zoath Hammond, L. M. Redfern, Official Resolutions of LU No. 394, Murray City, Ohio, *UMWJ*, January 24, 1895; "Old Timer No. 2," to the editor, *NLT*, March 22, 1894; "Old Miner," to the editor, *NLT*, February 7, 1895; "V.," to the editor, *NLT*, February 7, 1895; "Incog," to the editor, *UMWJ*, February 14, 1895; Samuel Anderson, to the editor, *NLT*, February 14, 1895; Laurene Gardner, to the editor, *UMWJ*, February 14, 1895; Proceedings of the Sixth Annual Convention of the United Mine Workers of America, 1895, *UMWJ*, February 21, 1895; "An Old Miner," to the editor, *NLT*, March 14, 1895; Ware, *Labor Movement*, 371–73.

49. "Old Timer No. 2," to the editor, *NLT*, November 22, 1894.

50. "The General Lieb Meeting," *Decatur (IL) Herald*, November 2, 1894; Daniel Needham, address at the National Farmers' Congress, "Cause of Low Price of Wheat and of the Depletion of the United States Treasury," *Indiana Farmer*, November 3, 1894.

51. "The Coming Election," *Decatur (IL) Herald*, November 2, 1894; "The Outlook Outside of Cook County," *Chicago Daily Tribune*, November 3, 1894; "Open Defiance to Lewelling," *Leavenworth (KS) Times*, August 7, 1894; Joseph Ouvbier, "Under Which Flag?," *JKL*, August 29, 1895; McMath, *American Populism*.

52. Powderly claimed to not endorse any candidate. McLaurin, *Knights of Labor*, 179; Webb, *Two-Party Politics*, 112; McMath, *Populist Vanguard*, 143–44; Hild, *Greenbackers, Knights of Labor, and Populists*, 174; "Hang Me for a Traitor," *Topeka (KS) Populist*, November 26, 1892.

53. Terence Powderly to John McBryde [*sic*], September 5, 1894, reel 59, TVP Papers (quotation); Powderly, *Path I Trod*, 294.

54. "Governor Altgeld," *UMWJ*, November 15, 1894; "Briedenthal Gives Up Kansas," *NYT*, November 8, 1894; "The Future," *Kinsley (KS) Graphic*, November 23, 1894; "The Farmers Talk," *Leavenworth (KS) Times*, August 7, 1894; Ostler, *Prairie Populism*.

55. Wm. H. Crawford, to the editor, *UMWJ*, March 21, 1895.

56. "Miner," to the editor, *UMWJ*, January 24, 1895; J. H. Kennedy, UMW District Eleven Report, *UMWJ*, May 2, 1895; "President Penna Talks," *UMWJ*, May 2, 1895.

57. "Pittsburgh," *CTJ*, September 16, 1896; "Wages Question in Pittsburgh, Pa.," *CTJ*, September 30, 1896.

58. Jas. J. Flynn, to the editor, *UMWJ*, February 14, 1895; "Burn American Coal—II," *CTJ*, April 18, 1894; "Cornfield Sailor," to the editor, *UMWJ*, February 28, 1895; J. W. Reynolds, to the editor, *UMWJ*, March 21, 1895; J. M. Carson, to the editor, *UMWJ*, March 21, 1895; "Cornfield Sailor," to the editor, *UMWJ*, March 28, 1895; Julius Fromm, to the editor, *UMWJ*, April 25, 1895; "Dan McLaughlin," *NLT*, August 8, 1895.

59. Proceedings of the Sixth Annual Convention of the United Mine Workers of America, 1895, *UMWJ*, February 21, 1895; "Max," to the editor, *UMWJ*, May 2, 1895.

60. "Cornfield Sailor," to the editor, *UMWJ*, May 16, 1895.

61. The complexities of the mining payment system make it impossible to compare miners' wages from mine to mine in any meaningful way.

62. P. H. Penna to James Sovereign, printed in *UMWJ*, January 24, 1895.

63. Philip Veal, to the editor, *UMWJ*, January 31, 1895; W.L., to the editor, *UMWJ*, January 24, 1895; Joseph Whiteman, to the editor, *UMWJ*, January 17, 1895; C. Triesney, to the editor, *UMWJ*, January 3, 1895; E. J. Harris, to the editor, *UMWJ*, November 1, 1894; "Cornfield Sailor," to the editor, *UMWJ*, May 16, 1895; H. Marling, Joseph Perry, John Woodrough, H. W. Walters, Auditing Committee, UMW Missouri-Kansas District Fourteen Official Auditor's Report from December 31, 1894 to May 7, 1895, *UMWJ*, May 23, 1895; G. H. Hewitt, to the editor, *UMWJ*, August 22, 1895.

64. Flannery, *Glass House Boys,* 113–14; McCabe, *Standard Rate,* 156–57; Sanders, *Roots of Reform,* 55.

65. Laurene Gardner, to the editor, *UMWJ*, February 14, 1895.

66. Proceedings of the Sixth Annual Convention of the United Mine Workers of America, 1895, *UMWJ*, February 21, 1895; "Wild Bombarding," *Pittsburgh (PA) Press,* February 14, 1895; Goldstene, *Struggle for America's Promise,* 118; Fox, *United We Stand,* 48.

67. Evans, *History of the United Mine Workers,* 2:366.

68. Chris Evans later wrote that McBride claimed that he had given Wild the money to "compensate him in more of a charitable way," but he refused to disclose the identity of the party that donated the funds. Proceedings of the Sixth Annual Convention of the United Mine Workers of America, 1895, *UMWJ*, February 21, 1895; "Wild Bombarding," *Pittsburgh (PA) Press,* February 14, 1895; "The Miners Endorse Wild," *JKL,* June 6, 1895; Evans, *History of United Mine Workers,* 2:368; Fox, *United We Stand,* 48.

69. Independent Order of the Knights of Labor, Constitution, 1895 (microfiche), Main Library, University of Georgia; "Why the I.O.K. of L.?," ca. 1895 (microfiche), Main Library, University of Georgia; Fox, *United We Stand,* 49.

70. Michael J. Bishop, Report of the General Worthy Foreman, in Knights of Labor, *Proceedings, 1895,* 9; Alice Tregaskis, to the editor, *JKL,* August 15, 1895; William B. Wilson, Independent Order of the Knights of Labor Circular, "I.O.K. of L. Matters," December 5, 1895, folder 1895, box 1, WBW Papers (quotations).

71. J. H. Kennedy, "Proceedings of the UMW District Eleven Convention, 1895," *UMWJ*, March 21, 1895.

72. R. L. Davis, to the editor, *UMWJ*, March 14, 1895.

73. W. G. Gray to John Hayes, March 11, 1895, reel 5, JWH Papers; "Miners' N.T.A. Reorganized," *JKL,* June 27, 1895; J. H. Kennedy, UMW District Eleven Report, *UMWJ*, June, 27, 1895; Charles R. Martin, to the editor, *UMWJ*, July 4, 1895; T. T. O'Malley, to the editor, *UMWJ*, July 25, 1895; Constitution of the Miners and Mine Laborers National Trade Assembly No. 135, printed in *JKL,* October 31, 1895; Report of the General Executive Board, Knights of Labor, *Proceedings, 1895,* 29.

74. This assessment is based on J. H. Kennedy's district dues reports from May 1895 to the time of the secession announcement on June 27, 1895; William Klusmeier, to the editor, *JKL,* August 1, 1895; William R. May, to the editor, *JKL,* October 31, 1895.

75. A. A. Adams to Phil Penna, open letter reprinted in "Adams's Answer," *UMWJ*, January 24, 1895; Phil Penna to A. A. Adams, open letter printed in "Penna to Adams," *UMWJ*, January 31, 1895; Henry Shires, John Spriggs, R. D. Austin, T. R. Jones, M. P. Curran, Committee, Official Resolutions of Subdistrict 2, District 6, UMW, *UMWJ*, March 21, 1895; "Vice President Penna Talks," *UMWJ*, June 21, 1894; Eddie Ocheltree, to the editor, *UMWJ*, June 21, 1894; Laurene Gardner, to the editor, *UMWJ*, July 12, 1894; "F.J.H.," to the editor, *UMWJ*, July 26, 1894; "A Would-Be Knight," to the editor, *UMWJ*, November 12, 1896.

76. J. H. Kennedy, UMW District Eleven Report, *UMWJ*, June 27, 1895; T. T. O'Malley, to the editor, *UMWJ*, July 25, 1895; "Populist," to the editor, *UMWJ*, September 5, 1895.

77. "Irish Jack and Close Observer," to the editor, *UMWJ*, May 2, 1895; A. F. C., to the editor, *UMWJ*, April 18, 1895.

78. "Local Assembly I. O. K. of L. of Barnsboro, PA," Official Resolutions, *UMWJ*, April 18, 1895.

79. Geo. Whitehead, to the editor, *NLT*, May 30, 1895; "J. B. Donnelly," to the editor, *UMWJ*, August 15, 1895; Alfred Broad, to the editor, *UMWJ*, July 18, 1895; D. E. Jones, to the editor, *UMWJ*, July 18, 1895 ("sold out"); J. H. Kennedy, Report of UMW District Eleven Special Convention, August 8, 1895; J. A. Crawford, to the editor, *UMWJ*, February 6, 1896; Julius Fromm, to the editor, *UMWJ*, February 6, 1896.

80. Summit Miners, Official Resolutions of Summit, Indiana, Local Union 31, *UMWJ*, August 8, 1895; Phil Penna, to the editor, *UMWJ*, August 8, 1895; I. N. Cassady, to the editor, *UMWJ*, August 15, 1895; "Union," to the editor, *UMWJ*, August 22, 1895; D.C. (name illegible), to the editor, "Opposed to a New Organization," *NLT*, August 29, 1895; J. H. Kennedy, UMW District Eleven Report, *UMWJ*, August 29, 1895; J. H. Kennedy, UMW District Eleven Report, *UMWJ*, September 5, 1895; editorial, "For several weeks," *UMWJ*, November 21, 1895.

81. W. J. Winterbottom, to the editor, *UMWJ*, October 25, 1894; W. J. Guymon, to the editor, *UMWJ*, January 17, 1895; "Whirlwind," to the editor, *UMWJ*, September 27, 1894; E. J. Harris, to the editor, *UMWJ*, November 1, 1894; "A. F. C.," to the editor, *UMWJ*, January 31, 1895; "Populist," to the editor, *UMWJ*, September 5, 1895; "W. J. Guymon," *UMWJ*, November 7, 1895; Patrick McBryde, "Important Notice," *UMWJ*, November 21, 1895; J. H. Kennedy, UMW District Eleven Report, *UMWJ*, March 26, 1896; Fox, *United We Stand*, 47–49.

82. "Next Week," to the editor, *UMWJ*, December 20, 1894; "Miner," to the editor, *UMWJ*, January 17, 1895; Fox, *United We Stand*, 49.

83. "Incog," to the editor, *UMWJ*, December 5, 1895.

84. Stromquist, "The Crisis of 1894," 190; White, *Republic for Which It Stands*, 780.

85. Editorial, "For several weeks," *UMWJ*, November 21, 1895 (quotation); "Incog," to the editor, *UMWJ*, November 14, 1895.

86. "A Battle On," *St. Louis (MO) Post Dispatch*, May 25, 1894; D. H. Sullivan, to the editor, *UMWJ*, August 22, 1895; Michael Ratchford, to the editor, *UMWJ*, March 13,

1896; G. W. Purcell, to the editor, *UMWJ,* August 29, 1895; D.C. (name illegible), to the editor, "Opposed to a New Organization," *NLT,* August 29, 1895; "Cornfield Sailor," to the editor, *UMWJ,* November 28, 1895; D. E. Jones, to the editor, *UMWJ,* July 18, 1895.

87. Charles Martin circular, "Hear Both Sides, Then Judge," January 1896, folder 1896, box 1, WBW Papers.

88. Ibid.

89. David Overmeyer to William Jennings Bryan, February 29, 1896, folder 1896 Jan–Feb, box 3, WJB Papers.

90. J. H. Kennedy, UMW District Eleven Report, *UMWJ,* December 12, 1895.

91. Editorial, "For several weeks," *UMWJ,* November 21, 1895; R. L. Davis, to the editor, *UMWJ,* December 5, 1895; W. J. Guymon, to the editor, *UMWJ,* December 5, 1895.

92. J. H. Kennedy, UMW District Eleven Report, *UMWJ,* November 28, 1895.

93. Secretary of Progress Assembly No. 963, I.O.K. of L. Report of Resolutions, "Local Assembly," *UMWJ,* November 19, 1896.

94. "Incog," to the editor, *UMWJ,* November 21, 1895; "Vigo Kicker," to the editor, *UMWJ,* November 7, 1895; "Scot," to the editor, *UMWJ,* December 5, 1895; L. W. Hubbell to William Jennings Bryan, May 11, 1895, folder 1895 May 2–15, box 3, WJB Papers.

95. "The Coal Miners," *American Federalist,* June 1895. The piece was likely written by John McBride, who was editor of the *American Federationist* during his term as AFL President; however, due to severe illness during most of his term, McBride often relied on others to fulfill his duties.

96. "[Proceedings of the] Seventh Annual Convention," in Evans, *History of United Mine Workers,* 2:413–15.

97. "Indiana Labor Commission Report of the Settlement of the Coal Miners' Strike at Star City and Hymera, Sullivan, Indiana, November 30, 1897," folder 4, box 37, James A. Mount Papers.

98. "General News," *Indianapolis News,* June 8, 1896; "Notes from the Mines," *Indianapolis News,* June 10, 1896; "Apply the Torch," *Logansport (IN) Pharos-Tribune,* July 31, 1896.

99. J. H. Kennedy, UMWA District Eleven Report, *UMWJ,* August 6, 1896.

100. "Western Coal and Coke Notes," *CTJ,* July 1, 1896; "The State of Trade," and "Notes of the Week," *CTJ,* August 5, 1896; J. H. Kennedy, UMWA District Eleven Report, *UMWJ,* August 6, 1896; "The State of Trade," *CTJ,* September 30, 1896.

101. J.H. Kennedy, UMWA District Eleven Report, *UMWJ,* February 18, 1897 (quotations); "Notes of the Week," *CTJ,* August 12, 1896; "Hymera Mines Change Owners," *Indianapolis News,* October 14, 1896; "Striking for Arrearages in Pay," *Indianapolis News,* April 16, 1897; "Mining Outlook in Sullivan County," *Indianapolis News,* May 17, 1897; "Indiana Miners," *Elwood (IN) Daily Record,* July 7, 1897; "Indiana Labor Commission Report of the Settlement of the Coal Miners' Strike at Star City and Hymera, Sullivan, Indiana, November 30, 1897," folder 4, box 37, James A. Mount Papers.

102. "Old Miner," to the editor, *NLT,* August 8, 1895; "They Shot to Kill," *Streator (IL) Daily Free Press,* August 5, 1895; "Mobs at the Mines," *NLT,* August 8, 1895 ("hunting for negroes"); "Two Mobs in a Riot," *Chicago Daily Tribune,* August 5, 1895; "Rioters to be Tried," *Daily Inter Ocean,* August 17, 1895; Waldron, "Lynch-Law Must Go!," 50–77.

103. Jensen, *Winning of the Midwest,* 240; Douglas, *Real Wages,* 223, 350, 353.

104. Pierce, *Striking with the Ballot;* Jensen, *Winning of the Midwest,* 244–46, 258–61; Hild, *Greenbackers, Knights of Labor, and Populists.*

Epilogue

1. "Mother Jones Eulogized," *NYT,* December 8, 1930; "Mother Jones Buried," *NYT,* December 9, 1930.

2. Five guards also died in the gunfight. Phelan, *Divided Loyalties,* 43; "Our Illustrations," *UMWJ,* November 3, 1898; George Bagwill, to the editor, *UMWJ,* November 10, 1898; "Mt. Olive's Dead," *Decatur (IL) Daily Review,* October 15, 1898; "Monuments Dedicated," *Decatur (IL) Herald,* December 2, 1899.

3. "Are Ready for a Fight," *Decatur (IL) Herald,* October 8, 1898; Fliege, *Tales and Trails,* 140–43; Keiser, "Union Miners' Cemetery."

4. Mary Harris Jones, "Special Request to the Miners of Mt. Olive, Illinois," November 12, 1923, Mt. Olive Public Library, Mt. Olive, Illinois; "Conduct Memorial," *Edwardsville (IL) Intelligencer,* October 12, 1921.

5. Walsh, "United Mine Workers of America," 193.

6. "Notes of the Week," *CTJ,* October 7, 1896; "A Would-Be Knight," to the editor, *UMWJ,* November 12, 1896; Dan O'Leary, UMW District Eleven Subdistrict Three Special Convention, *UMWJ,* April 8, 1897; P. H. Penna, to the editor, *UMWJ,* April 22, 1897; "Indiana Coal Operators' Association," *Black Diamond,* July 15, 1905; Fox, *United We Stand,* 47–48; Van Tine, *Making of the Labor Bureaucrat.*

7. Although corn prices decreased, wheat prices increased significantly. States Department of Agriculture, Division of Statistics "Circular No. 6: Cereal Crops of 1896," in Hyde, *Publications;* Davis, "Annual Index"; John Barron, to the editor, *UMWJ,* May 6, 1897.

8. Fox, *United We Stand,* 50–51.

9. Laurie, *Artisans into Workers;* Arnold, *Fueling the Gilded Age.*

10. Samuel Gompers objected to the joint effort, but UMW president Ratchford ignored his requests. Fox, *United We Stand,* 52.

11. The Miners' Great Struggle," *American Federationist,* August 1897; "Miners' Victory Encourages All Workers," *American Federationist,* October 1897; William Scaife, to the editor, *UMWJ,* December 9, 1897; Roy, *History of the Coal Miners,* 324.

12. Phelan, *Divided Loyalties,* 36–42 ("discipline" quotation, 38), 60, 108–9, 227; Green, *The Devil Is Here,* esp. 36–54.

13. Fox, *United We Stand,* 118; McGerr, *Fierce Discontent,* 118–22; Foner, *History of the Labor Movement,* 2:345; Green, *The Devil Is Here,* esp. 36–54.

14. Walsh, "United Mine Workers of America," 193; Singer, "Something of a Man," 105, 119; Dubofsky and Van Tine, *John L. Lewis*; Fox, *United We Stand*, 54.

15. "Laud 'Mother' Jones as Lemke Hits Lewis," *NYT*, October 12, 1936.

16. "Indiana Coal Operators' Association," *Black Diamond*, July 15, 1905; "Trade News by the Telegraph," *CTJ*, June 23, 1915; "Bituminous Operators in Annual Convention," *CTJ*, May 31, 1922; Dubofsky and Van Tine, *John L. Lewis*, 66–68.

17. "Illinois Coal War Flares at Hearing," *NYT*, August 12, 1933; "Coal Miner Slain in Illinois March," *NYT*, October 20, 1933; "88,500 Out in Midwest," *NYT*, September 24, 1935; "21 Illinois Miners Held in Bombings," *NYT*, December 11, 1936; Kopald, *Rebellion in Labor Unions*, 33, 69–70; Singer, "Something of a Man," 108, 110–13, 118–19 (quotation 110).

18. Mary Harris "Mother" Jones Monument Plaque, Union Miners' Cemetery, Mt. Olive, Illinois.

19. "Women Lead the Miners," *CDT*, September 23, 1900.

20. Keiser, "Union Miners' Cemetery."

Bibliography

Manuscript Collections and Other Archival Materials

Atchison, Topeka, and Santa Fe Railway Company Records. Kansas State Historical Society, Topeka.

Bryan, William Jennings. Papers. Library of Congress, Washington D.C.

Campbell, Clinton S. Papers. Abraham Lincoln Presidential Library, Springfield, Illinois.

Cherokee & Pittsburg Coal & Mining Company v. Amelia Siplet, as the Administratrix of Alexis Siplet, deceased. Case No. 10702 Supreme Court of the State of Kansas, 1896. Kansas State Historical Society, Topeka.

Cherokee & Pittsburg Coal Company Records. Atchison, Topeka, and Santa Fe Railway Company Records. Kansas State Historical Society, Topeka.

Cerrillos Coal and Iron Company Records. Atchison, Topeka, and Santa Fe Railway Company Records. Kansas State Historical Society, Topeka.

Cerrillos Coal Railroad Company Records. Atchison, Topeka, and Santa Fe Railway Company Records. Kansas State Historical Society, Topeka.

Cerrillos Coal Mining Company Records. Atchison, Topeka, and Santa Fe Railway Company Records. Kansas State Historical Society, Topeka.

Dewey, Charles Almon. Papers, MSC103. University of Iowa Special Collections, Iowa City.

Flagg Family Collection. University of Illinois Special Collections, Champaign.

Hayes, John W. Papers, 1880–1921. Glen Rock, NJ: Microfilming Corp. of America, 1974. Microfilm.

Knights of Labor IRAD. LA 8617 Minutes Book 1, Illinois Regional Archives Depository, Normal.

Lewelling, Lorenzo D. Papers. Kansas State Historical Society, Topeka.

Leonard, Levi O. Railroad Collection. MSC 159, University of Iowa Special Collections, Iowa City.

Matthews, Claude. Papers. Indiana State Library, Indianapolis.

McHenry Coal Company Records. MSS 29. Western Kentucky University Special Collections, Bowling Green.

Mitchell, John Papers, 1885–1919. Glen Rock, NJ: Microfilming Corp. of America, 1974. Microfilm.

Mount, James A. Papers. Indiana State Archives, Indianapolis.

Mt. Carmel Coal Company Records. Kansas State Historical Society, Topeka.

National Progressive Union. Miners and Mine Laborers Protective Association Lodge 26, Spring Valley, Illinois Records. In Knights of Labor LA 8617 Minutes Book 1, Illinois Regional Archives Depository, Normal.

Powderly, Terence Vincent Papers, 1864–1937. Glen Rock, NJ: Microfilming Corp. of America, 1975. Microfilm.

Wilson, William Bauchop Papers. Collection 1588. Historical Society of Pennsylvania, Philadelphia.

Newspapers and Periodicals

Alton (IL) Telegraph
Age of Steel, St. Louis, MO
American Federationist, Washington, DC
Black Diamond, Chicago
Bloomington (IL) [Daily] Pantagraph
Blossburg (PA) Advertiser
Brickmaker, Chicago
Chicago [Daily] Tribune
Cincinnati Enquirer
Coal Trade Journal, New York
Clay-Worker, Indianapolis
Christian Advocate, New York
Colliery Engineer, Scranton, PA
Huntington (IN) Daily Democrat
Daily Inter Ocean, Chicago
Davenport (IA) Daily Republican
Decatur (IL) Daily Republican
Decatur (IL) Daily Review
Decatur (IL) Herald
Dixon (IL) Evening Telegraph
Earlington (KY) Bee

Edwardsville (IL) Intelligencer
Elwood (IN) Daily Record
Engineering and Mining Journal, New York
Evansville (IN) Courier
Farmer's Tribune, Des Moines, IA
Fort Scott (KS) Daily Monitor
Fuel, Chicago
Gloversville (NY) Daily Leader
Harper's Weekly, New York
Humboldt (IA) Republican
Hutchinson (KS) News
Hawarden (IA) Independent
Humeston (IA) New Era
Independence (KS) Daily Reporter
Indiana Farmer, Indianapolis
Indianapolis News
Iron Trade Review, Cleveland, OH
Journal of the Knights of Labor, Philadelphia, PA
Journal of United Labor, Philadelphia, PA
Kinsley (KS) Graphic
Leavenworth (KS) Times
Linton (IN) Daily Citizen
Logansport (IN) Pharos-Tribune
Malvern (IA) Leader
National Economist, Washington, DC
National Labor Tribune, Pittsburgh, PA
New Orleans Daily Picayune
New York Times
Osage City (KS) Free Press
Ottawa (KS) Daily Republic
Paint, Oil and Drug Review, Chicago
Pittsburg (KS) [Daily] Headlight
Pittsburgh (PA) Press
Pittsburgh (PA) Post
Punch, or the London Charivari, London, England
Scranton (PA) Tribune
Sioux Valley News, Correctionville, IA
Sterling (IL) Standard
Streator (IL) Daily Free Press
St. Louis (MO) Post Dispatch
Topeka (KS) Daily Capital
Topeka (KS) Populist

Topeka (KS) State Journal
Trade and Mining Journal, Joliet, IL
United Mine Workers' Journal, Columbus, OH, and Indianapolis
Western Manufacturer, Chicago
Wilkes-Barre (PA) Record

Other Sources

Adams, Sean Patrick. "Promotion, Competition, Captivity: The Political Economy of Coal." *Journal of Policy History* 18, no. 1 (2006): 74–95.
Alexander, Benjamin F. *Coxey's Army: Popular Protest in the Gilded Age.* Baltimore, MD: Johns Hopkins University Press, 2015.
Altgeld, John. *Live Questions.* Chicago: George S. Bowen and Son, 1899.
American Federation of Labor. *Proceedings of the American Federation of Labor, 1889–1892.* Bloomington, IL: Pantagraph Printing and Stationary, 1906.
———. *Report of Proceedings of the Thirteenth Annual American Federation of Labor.* New York: Concord Co-Operative Printing, 1894.
Amsden, Jon, and Stephen Brier. "Coal Miners on Strike: The Transformation of Strike Demands and the Formation of a National Union." *Journal of Interdisciplinary History* 7, no. 4 (spring 1977): 583–616.
Andrews, Thomas G. *Killing for Coal: America's Deadliest Labor War.* Cambridge, MA: Harvard University Press, 2008.
Armstrong, Thomas F. "Georgia Lumber Laborers, 1880–1917: The Social Implications of Work." *Georgia Historical Quarterly* 67, no. 4 (winter 1983): 435–50.
———. "The Transformation of Work: Turpentine Workers in Costal Georgia, 1865–1901." *Labor History* 25, no. 4 (1984): 518–32.
Arnesen, Eric. "Specter of the Black Strikebreaker: Race, Employment, and Labor Activism in the Industrial Era." *Labor History* 44, no. 3 (2003): 319–35.
Arnold, Andrew B. *Fueling the Gilded Age: Railroads, Miners, and Disorder in Pennsylvania Coal Country.* New York: New York University Press, 2014.
———. "Mother Jones and the Panics of 1873 and 1893." *Pennsylvania Legacies* 11, no. 1 (May 2011): 18–23.
"Articles of Association." In *Annual Reports of the Officers of State of the State of Indiana.* Indianapolis: Wm. B. Burford, Contractor for State Printing and Binding, 1893.
Ayers, Edward. *The Promise of the New South: Life after Reconstruction.* New York: Oxford University Press, 1992.
Barrett, James. *Work and Community in the Jungle: Chicago's Packinghouse Workers, 1894–1892.* Urbana: University of Illinois Press, 1987.
Bay, Mia. *The White Image in the Black Mind: African-American Ideas about White People, 1830–1925.* New York: Oxford University Press, 2000.
Beik, Mildred Allen. *The Miners of Windber: The Struggles of New Immigrants for Unionization, 1890s–1910.* University Park: Pennsylvania State University Press, 1996.

Blackmon, Douglas. *Slavery by Another Name: The Re-enslavement of Black Americans from the Civil War to World War II*. New York: Doubleday, 2008.

Blight, David W. *Race and Reunion: The Civil War in American Memory*. Cambridge, MA: Belknap Press of Harvard University Press, 2001.

Blum, Edward J. "'By the Sweat of Your Brow': The Knights of Labor, the Book of Genesis, and the Christian Spirit of the Gilded Age." *Labor* 11, no. 2 (spring 2014): 29–34.

Board of Trade [Great Britain]. *Journal of Tariff and Trade Notices and Miscellaneous Commercial Information*, vol. 13, *July–December 1892*. London: Eyre and Spottiswoode, 1893.

Boris, Eileen. "'A Man's Dwelling House Is His Castle': Tenement House Cigarmaking and the Judicial Imperative." In *Work Engendered: Toward a New History of American Labor*, edited by Ava Baron, 114–91. Ithaca, NY: Cornell University Press, 1991.

Brecher, Jeremy. *Strike!* Revised, expanded, updated ed. Oakland, CA: PM Press, 2014.

Brier, Stephen. "In Defense of Gutman: The Union's Case." *International Journal of Politics, Culture and Society* 2, no. 3 (spring 1989): 382–95.

Brody, David. *Labor's Cause: Main Themes on the History of the American Worker*. New York: Oxford University Press, 1993.

Brown, Elsa Barkley. "To Catch the Vision of Freedom: Reconstructing Southern Women's Political History, 1865–1880." In *African-American Women and the Vote, 1837–1965*, edited by Ann D. Cordon and Bettye Collier-Thomas, 66–99. Amherst: University of Massachusetts Press, 1997.

Bryant, Keith L., Jr. *History of the Atchison, Topeka and Santa Fe Railway*. New York: Macmillan, 1974.

Caldemeyer, Dana M. "Unfaithful Followers: Rethinking Southern Nonunionism in the Late Nineteenth Century." In *Reconsidering Southern Labor History: Race, Class, and Power*, edited by Matthew Hild and Keri Leigh Merritt, 112–25. Gainesville: University Press of Florida, 2018.

Case, Theresa Ann. "Losing the Middle Ground: Strikebreakers and Labor Protest on the Southwestern Railroads." In *Rethinking U.S. Labor History: Essays on the Working-Class Experience, 1756–2009*, edited by Donna T. Haverty-Stacke and Daniel J. Walkowitz, 54–81. New York: Continuum, 2010.

Chateauvert, Melinda. *Marching Together: Women of the Brotherhood of Sleeping Car Porters*. Urbana: University of Illinois Press, 1998.

Church, S. H. *Corporate History of the Pennsylvania Lines, West of Pittsburgh....* Series B, vol. 2. Baltimore, MD: Friedenwald, 1900.

Commons, John Rogers, et al. *Nationalisation (1860–1877)*. Vol. 2 of *History of Labour in the United States:* New York: Macmillan, 1918.

Cook, John T, ed. *American Bankruptcy Reports Annotated Reporting the Bankruptcy Decisions and Opinions in the United States of the Federal Courts, State Courts and Referees in Bankruptcy*. Vol. 23. Albany, NY: Matthew Bender, 1910.

Cooper, Patricia A. *Once a Cigar Maker: Men, Women, and Work Culture in American Cigar Factories, 1900–1919*. Urbana: University of Illinois Press, 1987.

Corbin, David A. *Life, Work, and Rebellion in the Coal Fields: The Southern West Virginia Miners, 1880–1922.* Urbana: University of Illinois Press, 1981.

Cowing, Cedric B. *Populists, Plungers, and Progressives: A Social History of Stock and Commodity Speculation, 1890–1936.* Princeton, NJ: Princeton University Press, 1965.

Creech, Joe. *Righteous Indignation: Religion and the Populist Revolution.* Urbana: University of Illinois Press, 2006.

Cronon, William. *Nature's Metropolis: Chicago and the Great West.* New York: W. W. Norton, 1991.

Davis, Joseph H. "An Annual Index of U.S. Industrial Production, 1790–1915." *Quarterly Journal of Economics* 119, no. 4 (November 2004): 1177–1215.

Destler, Chester McArthur. "Agricultural Readjustment and Agrarian Unrest in Illinois, 1880–1896." *Agricultural History* 21, no. 2 (April 1947): 104–16.

———. *American Radicalism, 1865–1901, Essays and Documents.* New York: Octagon Books, 1963.

Dix, Keith. *What's a Coal Miner to Do? The Mechanization of Coal Mining.* Pittsburgh: University of Pittsburgh Press, 1988.

———. *Work Relations in the Coal Industry: The Hand-Loading Era, 1880–1930.* Morgantown, WV: Institute for Labor Studies, Division of Social and Economic Development, Center for Extension and Continuing Education, West Virginia University, 1977.

Doppen, Frans H. *Richard L. Davis and the Color Line in Ohio Coal: A Hocking Valley Mine Labor Organizer, 1862–1900.* Jefferson, NC: McFarland, 2016.

Douglas, Paul. *Real Wages in the United States: 1890–1926.* Boston: Houghton Mifflin, 1930.

Dubofsky, Melvyn. *Industrialism and the American Worker, 1865–1920.* 2nd ed. Arlington Heights, IL: Harlan Davidson, 1985.

Dubofsky, Melvyn, and Warren Van Tine. *John L. Lewis: A Biography.* New York: Quadrangle, 1977.

Eller, Ronald D. *Miners, Millhands, and Mountaineers: Industrialization of the Appalachian South, 1880–1930.* Knoxville: University of Tennessee Press, 1982.

Evans, Chris. *History of United Mine Workers of America.* 2 vols. Indianapolis: N.p., 1918?–20.

Fabian, Ann. *Card Sharps and Bucket Shops: Gambling in Late Nineteenth Century America.* New York: Routledge, 1999.

Falzone, Vincent J. "Terence V. Powderly: Mayor and Labor Leader, 1849–1893." PhD diss., University of Maryland, 1970.

———. *Terence V. Powderly: Middle Class Reformer.* Washington, DC: University Press of America, 1978.

Fink, Leon. *Workingmen's Democracy: The Knights of Labor and American Politics.* Urbana: University of Illinois Press, 1983.

Fishback, Price V. *Soft Coal, Hard Choices: The Economic Welfare of Bituminous Coal Miners, 1890–1930.* New York: Oxford University Press, 1992.

Flannery, James L. *The Glass House Boys of Pittsburgh: Law, Technology, and Child Labor.* Pittsburgh, PA: University of Pittsburgh Press, 2009.

Fliege, Stu. *Tales and Trails of Illinois.* Urbana: University of Illinois Press, 2002.

Foner, Philip S. *From Colonial Times to the Founding of the American Federation of Labor.* Vol. 1 of *History of the Labor Movement.* New York: International, 1947, 1998.

———. *From the Founding of the A. F. L. to the Emergence of American Imperialism.* Vol. 2 of *History of the Labor Movement.* New York: International, 1955, 1995.

———. *Organized Labor and the Black Worker, 1619–1973.* New York: Praeger, 1974.

Fones-Wolf, Elizabeth. *Selling Free Enterprise: The Business Assault on Labor and Liberalism, 1945–60.* Urbana: University of Illinois Press, 1994.

Fones-Wolf, Elizabeth, and Kenneth Fones-Wolf. *Struggle for the Soul of the Postwar South: White Evangelical Protestants and Operation Dixie.* Urbana: University of Illinois Press, 2015.

Fones-Wolf, Kenneth. *Trade Union Gospel: Christianity and Labor in Industrial Philadelphia.* Philadelphia: Temple University Press, 1989.

Forbath, William E. "The Ambiguities of Free Labor: Labor and the Law in the Gilded Age." *Wisconsin Law Review* 4 (July 1985): 767–817.

———. *Law and the Shaping of the American Labor Movement.* Cambridge, MA: Harvard University Press, 1991.

Fox, Maier B. *United We Stand: The United Mine Workers of America, 1890–1990.* Washington, DC: United Mine Workers of America, 1990.

Fraser, Steve. *Age of Acquiescence: The Life and Death of American Resistance to Organized Wealth and Power.* New York: Little, Brown, 2015.

Form, William. *Divided We Stand: Working-Class Stratification in America.* Urbana: University of Chicago Press, 1985.

Garlock, Jonathan. *Guide to the Local Assemblies of the Knights of Labor.* Westport, CT: Greenwood Press, 1982.

Georgia State Department of Agriculture. *Publications of the Georgia State Department of Agriculture for the Year 1882.* Vol. 8. Atlanta: Jas. P. Harrison, 1883.

Gerteis, Joseph. *Class and the Color Line: Interracial Class Coalition in the Knights of Labor and the Populist Movement.* Durham, NC: Duke University Press, 2007.

Goldstene, Claire. *Struggle for America's Promise: Equal Opportunity and the Dawn of Corporate Capital.* Jackson: University Press of Mississippi, 2014.

Goodwyn, Lawrence. *Democratic Promise: The Populist Moment in America.* New York: Oxford University Press, 1976.

Gorn, Elliott J. *Mother Jones: The Most Dangerous Woman in America.* New York: Hill and Wang, 2001.

Gourevitch, Alex. *From Slavery to Cooperative Commonwealth: Labor and Republican Liberty in the Nineteenth Century.* New York: Cambridge University Press, 2015.

Green, James R. *The Devil Is Here in These Hills: West Virginia's Coal Miners and Their Battle for Freedom.* New York: Atlantic Monthly Press, 2015.

Greene, Julie. *Pure and Simple Politics: The American Federation of Labor and Political Activism, 1881–1917.* New York: Cambridge University Press, 1998.

Groat, George Gorham. *An Introduction to the Study of Organized Labor in America.* New York: MacMillan, 1916.

Gutman, Herbert G. *Power and Culture: Essays on the American Working Class*. Edited by Ira Berlin. New York: Pantheon Books, 1987.

———. *Work, Culture, and Society in Industrializing America: Essays in American Working-Class and Social History*. New York: Vintage Books, 1977.

Hall, Frederick Smith. *Sympathetic Strikes and Sympathetic Lockouts*. New York: Columbia University, 1898.

Harris, William H. *The Harder We Run: Black Workers since the Civil War*. New York: Oxford University Press, 1982.

Haseltine, Robert M. *Seventeenth Annual Report of the Chief Inspector of Mines of Ohio for the Year 1891*. Columbus, OH: Westbote Co., State Printers, 1892.

Hedges, Charles. *Speeches of Benjamin Harrison, Twenty-Third President of the United States*. New York: United States Book Company, 1892.

Higbie, Frank Tobias. *Indispensable Outcasts: Hobo Workers and Community in the American Midwest, 1880–1930*. Urbana: University of Illinois Press, 2003.

Hild, Matthew. *Greenbackers, Knights of Labor, and Populists: Farmer-Labor Insurgency in the Late-Nineteenth-Century South*. Athens: University of Georgia Press, 2007.

———. "Organizing across the Color Line: The Knights of Labor and Black Recruitment Efforts in Small-Town Georgia." *Georgia Historical Quarterly* 81, no. 2 (summer 1997): 287–310.

Hill, Herbert. "Myth-Making as Labor History: Herbert Gutman and the United Mine Workers of America." *International Journal of Politics, Culture, and Society* 2, no. 2 (winter 1988): 132–200.

Hochfelder, David. "'Where the Common People Could Speculate': The Ticker, Bucket Shops, and the Origins of Popular Participation in Financial Markets, 1880–1920." *Journal of American History* 93, no. 2 (September 2006): 335–58.

"House Bill No. 28" and "Senate Bill No. 40." *Journal of the House of Representatives of the Thirty-Seventh General Assembly of the State of Illinois*. Springfield, IL: H. W. Rokker, State Printer and Binder, 1891, 661–62, 995, 1076.

House Committee on Agriculture. *Fictitious Dealings in Agricultural Products: Hearings on H. R. 392, 2699, and 3870*. 52nd Con. 3rd sess. Washington, DC: Government Printing Office, 1892.

House of Representatives. 52nd Congress, 1st Session. *Seventh Annual Report of the Commissioner of Labor, 1891*. Vol. 2. Washington, DC: Government Printing Office, 1892.

Hyde, John. *Publications of the Division of Statistics of the U.S. Department of Agriculture, Reports Nos. 145 to 149, Circulars Nos. 5 to 7, 1897*. Washington, DC: Government Printing Office, 1897.

Illinois Bureau of Labor Statistics. *Fifth Biennial Report of the Bureau of Labor Statistics of Illinois, 1888*. Springfield: Springfield Printing. 1888.

———. *Statistics of Coal in Illinois, 1891: Ninth Annual Report*. Springfield, IL: H. W. Rokker, 1891.

———. *Statistics of Coal in Illinois, 1893: Twelfth Annual Report*. Springfield, IL: H. W. Rokker, 1894.

Independent Order of the Knights of Labor. *Official Handbook of the Independent Order of the Knights of Labor*. N.p.: n.p, 1896.

Indiana Department of Geology and Natural Resources. *Twenty-Ninth Annual Report*. Indianapolis: W. F. Buford, 1905.

Iowa Bureau of Labor Statistics. *Fifth Biennial Report of the Bureau of Labor Statistics for the State of Iowa 1892–93*. Des Moines, IA: G. H. Ragsdale, 1893.

———. *Fourth Biennial Report of the Bureau of Labor Statistics for the State of Iowa 1890–91*. Des Moines, IA: G. H. Ragsdale, 1891.

Iowa State Mine Inspectors. *Seventh Biennial Report, 1895*. Des Moines, IA: F. R. Conway, State Printer, 1895.

Jameson, Elizabeth. "Imperfect Unions: Class and Gender in Cripple Creek." In *Class, Sex, and the Woman Worker*, edited by Milton Cantor and Bruce Laurie, 166–202. Westport, CT: Greenwood, 1977.

Jeffery, Julie Roy. "Women in the Southern Farmers' Alliance: A Reconsideration of the Role and Status of Women in the Late Nineteenth-Century South." *Feminist Studies* 3, no. 1/2 (fall 1975): 72–91.

Jensen, Richard. *The Winning of the Midwest: Social and Political Conflict, 1888–1896*. Chicago: University of Chicago Press, 1971.

Kansas Bureau of Labor and Industrial Statistics. *First Annual Report of the Bureau of Labor and Industrial Statistics*. Topeka: Kansas Publishing House, T. D. Thatcher, 1886.

———. *Seventh Annual Report of the Bureau of Labor and Industrial Statistics, 1892*. Topeka, KS: Press of the Hamilton Printing Co., 1892.

———. *Sixth Annual Report of the Bureau of Labor and Industrial Statistics, 1891*. Topeka, KS: Clifford C. Baker, 1891.

Kansas Bureau of Labor and Industry. *Ninth Annual Report of the Bureau of Labor and Industry of Kansas, 1893*. Topeka, KS: Press of the Hamilton Printing Co., Edwin H. Snow, 1894.

Kansas Bureau of Labor Statistics. *Third Annual Report of the Bureau of Labor, 1888*. Topeka: Kansas Publishing House: Clifford C. Baker, 1888.

Kazin, Michael. *Barons of Labor: The San Francisco Building Trades and Union Power in the Progressive Era*. Urbana: University of Illinois Press, 1987.

———. *A Godly Hero: The Life of William Jennings Bryan*. New York: Knopf, 2006.

———. *The Populist Persuasion: An American History*. Ithaca, NY: Cornell University Press, 1998.

Keiser, John H. "Black Strikebreakers and Racism in Illinois, 1865–1900." *Journal of the Illinois State Historical Society* 65, no. 3 (1972): 313–26.

———. "The Union Miners' Cemetery at Mt. Olive: A Spirit-Thread of Labor History." *Journal of the Illinois State Historical Society* 62, no. 3 (autumn 1969): 229–66.

Kleppner, Paul. *The Cross of Culture: A Social Analysis of Midwestern Politics, 1850–1900*. New York: Free Press, 1970.

Knights of Labor. *Record of the Proceedings of the General Assembly of the Knights of Labor, Eighteenth Regular Session, 1894*. Terence Powderly Papers, Microfilm.

———. *Record of Proceedings of the General Assembly of the Knights of Labor, Eleventh Regular Session, 1887*. Terence Powderly Papers, Microfilm.

———. *Record of the Proceedings of the General Assembly of the Knights of Labor, Nineteenth Regular Session of the [Knights of Labor] General Assembly, 1895*. Terence Powderly Papers, Microfilm.

———. *Record of the Proceedings of the General Assembly of the Knights of Labor, Seventeenth Regular Session, 1893*. Terence Powderly Papers, Microfilm.

———. *Record of the Proceedings of the General Assembly of the Knights of Labor, Sixteenth Regular Session, 1892*. Terence Powderly Papers, Microfilm.

———. *Record of Proceedings of the General Assembly of the Knights of Labor, Tenth Session, 1886*. Terence Powderly Papers, Microfilm.

Keppen, A. *The Industries of Russia: Mining and Metallurgy with a Set of Mining Maps*. Translated by John Martin Crawford. St. Petersburg, Russia: Mining Department Ministry of Crown Domains, 1893.

Kopald, Sylvia. *Rebellion in Labor Unions*. New York: Boni and Liveright, 1924.

Kruse, Kevin M. *One Nation under God: How Corporate America Invented Christian America*. New York: Basic Books, 2015.

Lamb, George J. "Coal Mining in France, 1873–1895." *Journal of Economic History* 37, no. 1 (March 1977): 255–57.

Laslett, John. *Colliers across the Sea: A Comparative Study of Class Formation in Scotland and the American Midwest, 1830–1924*. Urbana: University of Illinois Press, 2000.

Laurie, Bruce. *Artisans into Workers: Labor in Nineteenth Century America*. New York: Hill and Wang, 1989.

LeFlouria, Talitha. *Chained in Silence: Black Women and Convict Labor in the New South*. Chapel Hill: University of North Carolina Press, 2015.

Leikin, Steve. *The Practical Utopians: American Workers and the Cooperative Movement in the Gilded Age*. Detroit: Wayne State University Press, 2005.

Letwin, Daniel. *The Challenge of Interracial Unionism: Alabama Coal Miners, 1878–1921*. Chapel Hill: University of North Carolina Press, 1998.

Levine, Susan. "Workers' Wives: Gender, Class and Consumerism in the 1920s United States." *Gender and History* 3, no. 1 (spring 1991): 45–64.

Levy, Jonathan Ira. "Contemplating Delivery: Futures Trading and the Problem of Commodity Exchange in the United States, 1875–1905." *American Historical Review* 111, no. 2 (April 2006): 307–55.

———. *Freaks of Fortune: The Emerging World of Capitalism and Risk in America*. Cambridge, MA: Harvard University Press, 2012.

Lewis, Ronald L. *Black Coal Miners in America: Race, Class and Community Conflict 1780–1980*. Lexington: University Press of Kentucky, 1987.

———. *The Welsh Americans: A History of Assimilation in the Coalfields*. Chapel Hill: University of North Carolina Press, 2008.

Lichtenstein, Alex. *Twice the Work of Free Labor: The Political Economy of Convict Labor in the New South*. New York: Verso, 1996.

Lichtenstein, Nelson. "From Corporatism to Collective Bargaining: Organized Labor and the Eclipse of Social Democracy in the Postwar Era." In *The Rise and Fall of the New Deal Order*, edited by Steve Fraser and Gary Gerstle, 122–54. Princeton, NJ: Princeton University Press, 1989.

Lloyd, Henry Demarest. *A Strike of Millionaires Against Miners or The Story of Spring Valley: An Open Letter to the Millionaires.* 2d ed. Chicago: Belford-Clarke, 1890.

Low, Setha. "Maintaining Whiteness: The Fear of Others and Niceness." *Transforming Anthropology* 17, no. 2 (2009): 79–92.

Maitland, James. *The American Slang Dictionary.* Chicago: R. J. Kittredge, 1891.

Marti, Donald. *Women of the Grange: Mutuality and Sisterhood in Rural America, 1866–1920.* Westport, CT: Greenwood, 1991.

Martin, Lou. *Smokestacks in the Hills: Rural Industrial Workers in West Virginia.* Urbana: University of Illinois Press, 2015.

McBride, John. "Coal Miners." In *The Labor Movement: The Problem of To-Day*, edited by George E. McNeill, 241–67. Boston: A. M. Bridgman; New York: M. W. Hazen Co., 1887.

McCabe, David Aloysius. *The Standard Rate in American Trade Unions.* Baltimore, MD: Johns Hopkins University Press, 1912.

McCalley, Henry. *On the Warrior Coal Field.* Montgomery, AL: Barrett, 1886.

McGerr, Michael. *A Fierce Discontent: The Rise and Fall of the Progressive Movement in America.* New York: Oxford University Press, 2003.

McLaurin, Melton Alonza. *The Knights of Labor in the South.* Westport, CT: Greenwood, 1978.

McMath, Robert C., Jr. *American Populism: A Social History, 1877–1898.* New York: Hill and Wang, 1993.

———. *Populist Vanguard: A History of the Southern Farmers' Alliance.* New York: Norton, 1977; first published 1975.

McShane, Clay, and Joel Tarr. *The Horse in the City: Living Machines in the Nineteenth Century.* Baltimore, MD: Johns Hopkins University Press, 2007.

McWilliams, Wilson Carey. *The Idea of Fraternity in America.* Berkeley: University of California Press, 1973.

Merithew, Caroline Waldron. "'We Were Not Ladies': Gender, Class, and a Women's Auxiliary's Battle for Mining Unionism." *Journal of Women's History* 18, no. 2 (summer 2006): 63–94.

Merithew, Caroline Waldron, and James R. Barrett. "'We Are All Brothers in the Face of Starvation': Forging an Interethnic Working Class Movement in the 1894 Bituminous Coal Strike." *Mid-America* 83, no. 2 (summer 2001): 121–54.

Michels, Robert. *Political Parties: A Sociological Study of the Oligarchical Tendencies of Modern Democracy.* Translated by Eden and Cedar Paul. New York: Hearst's International Library, 1915.

Minchin, Timothy J. *What Do We Need a Union For? The TWUA in the South, 1945–1955.* Chapel Hill: University of North Carolina Press, 1997.

Mink, Gwendolyn. *Old Labor and New Immigrants in American Political Development: Union, Party, and State, 1875–1920*. Ithaca, NY: Cornell University Press, 1986.

Mirola, William. *Redeeming Time: Protestantism and Chicago's Eight-Hour Movement, 1866–1912*. Urbana: University of Illinois Press, 2015.

Missouri Bureau of Labor Statistics and Inspection. *Eleventh Annual Report, 1889*. Jefferson City, MO: Tribune Printers and State Binders, 1889.

——. *Fifteenth Annual Report of the Bureau of Labor Statistics and Inspection of the State of Missouri, 1893*. Jefferson City, MO: Tribune Printing, 1893.

——. *Sixteenth Annual Report, 1894*. Jefferson City, MO: Tribune Printing, 1894.

——. *Tenth Annual Report of the Bureau of Labor Statistics of the State of Missouri . . ., 1888*. Jefferson City, MO: Tribune Printing Company, 1889.

——. *Thirteenth Annual Report of the Bureau of Labor Statistics of the State of Missouri Being for the Year Ending November 5, 1891*. Jefferson City, MO: Tribune Printing Company, State Printers and Binders, 1891.

Missouri Bureau of the Mines. *Sixth Annual Report of the State Mine Inspector of the State of Missouri*. Jefferson City, MO: Tribune Printing, 1892.

Missouri State Board of Agriculture. *Twenty-Seventh Annual Report of the Missouri State Board of Agriculture for the Year 1894*. Jefferson City, MO: Tribune Printing, 1895.

Mitchell, Timothy. *Carbon Democracy: Political Power in the Age of Oil*. New York: Verso, 2011.

Montgomery, David. *Beyond Equality: Labor and the Radical Republicans, 1862–1872*. New York: Vintage Books, 1967.

——. *Fall of the House of Labor: The Workplace, the State, and American Labor Activism, 1865–1925*. New York: Cambridge University Press, 1987.

——. *Workers' Control in America: Studies in the History of Work, Technology, and Labor Struggles*. New York: Cambridge University Press, 1979.

Montrie, Chad. *Making a Living: Work and Environment in the United States*. Chapel Hill: University of North Carolina Press, 2008.

Moreton, Bethany. *To Serve God and Wal-Mart: The Making of Christian Free Enterprise*. Cambridge, MA: Harvard University Press, 2009.

Nelson, Daniel. *Shifting Fortunes: The Rise and Decline of American Labor, from the 1820s to the Present*. Chicago: Ivan R. Dee, 1997.

Nelson, Scott Reynolds. *Steel Drivin' Man: John Henry, the Untold Story of an American Legend*. New York: Oxford University Press, 2006.

Norwood, Stephen H. *Strikebreaking and Intimidation: Mercenaries and Masculinity in Twentieth Century America*. Chapel Hill: University of North Carolina Press, 2002.

Oestreicher, Richard Jules. *Solidarity and Fragmentation: Working People and Class Consciousness in Detroit, 1875–1900*. Urbana: University of Illinois Press, 1986.

——. "Terence Powderly, The Knights of Labor, and Artisanal Republicanism." In *Labor Leaders in America*, edited by Melvyn Dubofsky and Warren Van Tine, 30–61. Urbana: University of Illinois Press, 1987.

Osterud, Nancy G. *Bonds of Community: The Lives of Farm Women in Nineteenth-Century New York*. Ithaca, NY: Cornell University Press, 1991.

Ostler, Jeffrey. *Prairie Populism: The Fate of Agrarian Radicalism in Kansas, Nebraska, and Iowa.* Lawrence: University Press of Kansas, 1993.

Painter, Nell Irvin. "The New Labor History and the Historical Moment." *International Journal of Politics, Culture and Society* 2, no. 3 (spring 1989): 367–70.

Parker, Edward Wheeler. *The Production of Coal in 1894.* Washington, DC: Government Printing Office, 1895.

Parsons, Stanley B., Karen Toombs Parsons, Walter Killilae, and Beverly Borgers. "The Role of Cooperatives in the Development of the Movement Culture of Populism." *Journal of American History* 69, no. 4 (March 1983): 866–85.

Phelan, Craig. *Divided Loyalties: The Public and Private Life of Labor Leader John Mitchell.* Albany: State University Press of New York, 1994.

———. *Grand Master Workman: Terence Powderly and the Knights of Labor.* Westport, CT: Greenwood, 2000.

———. "The Warp of Fancy: The Knights of Labor and the Home Club Takeover Myth." *Labor History* 40, no. 3 (August 1999): 283–99.

Pierce, Michael. "The Populist President of the American Federation of Labor: The Career of John McBride, 1880–1895." *Labor History* 41, no. 1 (February 2000): 5–24.

———. *Striking with the Ballot: Ohio Labor and the Populist Party.* DeKalb: Northern Illinois University Press, 2010.

Phillips-Fein, Kim. *Invisible Hands: The Making of the Conservative Movement from the New Deal to Reagan.* New York: W. W. Norton, 2009.

Postel, Charles. *Equality: An American Dilemma, 1866–1896.* New York: Farrar, Straus and Giroux, 2019.

———. *The Populist Vision.* New York: Oxford University Press, 2007.

Powderly, Terence V. "Army of the Unemployed." In *The Labor Movement: The Problem of To-Day,* edited by George E. McNeill, 575–84. Boston: A. M. Bridgman; New York: M. W. Hazen Co., 1887.

———. *The Path I Trod: The Autobiography of Terence V. Powderly.* Edited by Harry J. Carman, Henry David, and Paul N. Guthrie. New York: AMS Press, 1968; first published 1940.

———. *Thirty Years of Labor, 1859–1889.* Columbus, OH: Excelsior Publishing House, 1889.

Rajala, Richard A. "The Forest as Factory: Technological Change and Worker Control in the West Coast Logging Industry, 1880–1930." *Labour/Le Travail* 32 (fall 1993): 73–104.

Rees, Albert. *Real Wages in Manufacturing: 1890–1914.* Princeton, NJ: Princeton University Press, 1961.

Roll, Jarod. "Faith Powers and Gambling Spirits in Late Gilded Age Metal Mining." In *The Pew and the Picket Line: Christianity and the American Working Class,* edited by Christopher Cantwell, Heath Carter, and Janine Giordano Drake, 74–95. Urbana: University of Illinois Press, 2016.

———. *Spirit of Rebellion: Labor and Religion in the New Cotton South.* Urbana: University of Illinois Press, 2010.

———. "Sympathy for the Devil: Missouri's Notorious Strikebreaking Metal Miners, 1896–1910." *Labor History* 11, no. 4 (winter 2014): 11–37.

Rosenow, Michael K. *Death and Dying in the Working Class, 1865–1920*. Urbana: University of Illinois Press, 2015.

Roy, Andrew. *A History of the Coal Miners of the United States, from the Development of the Mines to the Close of the Anthracite Strike of 1902, Including a Brief Sketch of Early British Miners*. Columbus, OH: Press of J. L. Trauger Print Co., 1906.

Salvatore, Nick. *Eugene V. Debs: Citizen and Socialist*. Urbana: University of Illinois Press, 1982.

Sanders, Elizabeth. *Roots of Reform: Farmers, Workers, and the American State, 1877–1917*. Chicago: University of Chicago Press, 1999.

Saward, Frederick E. *The Coal Trade: A Compendium of Valuable Information Relative to Coal Production, Prices, Transportation, Etc., at Home and Abroad* . . . N.p.: n.p, 1891.

Select Committee of the House of Representatives. *Testimony Taken by the Select Committee of the House of Representatives to Inquire into the Alleged Violation of the Laws Prohibiting the Importation of Contract Laborers, Paupers, and Convicts*, 50th Cong., 1st sess., Mis. Doc. No. 572. Washington, DC: Government Printing Office, 1888.

Select Committee on Relations with Canada. *Testimony Taken by the Select Committee on Relations with Canada, United States Senate*. 51st Cong., 1st sess. Washington, DC: Government Printing Office, 1890.

Sen, Gita. "The Sexual Division of Labor and the Working-Class Family: Towards a Conceptual Synthesis of Class Relations and the Subordination of Women." *Review of Radical Political Economics* 12, no. 2 (July 1980): 76–86.

Shackel, Paul A. *Remembering Lattimer: Labor, Migration, and Race in Pennsylvania Anthracite Country*. Urbana: University of Illinois Press, 2018.

Shapiro, Karin A. *A New South Rebellion: The Battle against Convict Labor in the Tennessee Coalfields, 1871–1896*. Chapel Hill: University of North Carolina Press, 1998.

Shifflett, Crandall A. *Coal Towns: Life, Work, and Culture in Company Towns of Southern Appalachia, 1880–1960*. Knoxville: University of Tennessee Press, 1991.

Singer, Alan J. "'Something of a Man': John L. Lewis, the UMWA, and the CIO, 1919–1943." In *The United Mine Workers of America: A Model of Industrial Solidarity?*, edited by John Laslett, 104–50. University Park: Pennsylvania State University Press, 1996.

Smedley, Audrey. "'Race' and the Construction of Human Identity." *American Anthropologist* 100, no. 3 (1998): 690–702.

Spero, Sterling D., and Abram L. Harris. *The Black Worker: The Negro and the Labor Movement*. New York: Athenaeum, 1968.

Stabile, Donald. *Activist Unionism: The Institutional Economics of Solomon Barkin*. Armonk, NY: M. E. Sharpe, 1993.

Steeples, Douglas, and David O. Whitten. *Democracy in Desperation: The Depression of 1893*. Westport, CT: Greenwood, 1998.

Stromquist, Shelton. "The Crisis of 1894 and the Legacies of Producerism." In *The Pullman Strike and the Crisis of the 1890s: Essays on Labor and Politics*, edited by Richard

Schneirov, Shelton Stromquist, and Nick Salvatore, 179–203. Urbana: University of Illinois Press, 1999.

Summers, Mark Wahlgren. *The Gilded Age: Or, The Hazard of New Functions.* Upper Saddle River, NJ: Prentice Hall, 1997.

Taylor, Irwin. *General Statues of Kansas 1889.* Vol. 1. Topeka, KS: George W. Krane. 1889.

Tuttle, William M. "Some Strikebreakers' Observations of Industrial Warfare." *Labor History* 7, no. 2 (spring 1966): 193–96.

US Bureau of the Census. United States Census, 1870. Accessed through FamilySearch.org.

——. United States Census, 1880. Accessed through FamilySearch.org.

——. United States Census, 1900. Accessed through FamilySearch.org.

——. United States Census, 1910. Accessed through FamilySearch.org.

——. "Twelfth Census of the United States Census Bulletin No. 203: The Logging Industry." June 24, 1902.

US Department of Agriculture. *Report of the Commissioner of Agriculture, 1887.* Washington, DC: Government Printing Office, 1888.

——. *Report of the Secretary of Agriculture, 1890.* Washington, DC: Government Printing Office, 1890.

——. *Report of the Secretary of Agriculture, 1892.* Washington, DC: Government Printing Office, 1893.

——. *Wages of Farm Labor in the United States: Results of Nine Statistical Investigations, from 1866 to 1892, with Extensive Inquiries Concerning Wages from 1840 to 1865.* Washington, DC: Government Printing Office, 1892.

US Department of State. *Commercial Relations of the United States with Foreign Countries During the Years 1890–1891.* Washington, DC: Government Printing Office, 1892.

Van Tine, Warren. *The Making of the Labor Bureaucrat: Union Leadership in the United States, 1870–1920.* Amherst: University of Massachusetts Press, 1973.

Voss, Kim. *The Making of American Exceptionalism: The Knights of Labor and Class Formation in the Nineteenth Century.* Ithaca, NY: Cornell University Press, 1993.

Waldron, Caroline A. "'Lynch-Law Must Go!': Race, Citizenship, and the Other in an American Coal Mining Town." *Journal of American Ethnic History* 20, no. 1 (fall 2000): 50–77.

Walsh, William J. "The United Mine Workers of America as an Economic and Social Force in the Anthracite Territory." PhD diss., Catholic University of America, 1931.

Ward, Alonzo M. "The Specter of Black Labor: African American Workers in Illinois before the Great Migration, 1847–1910." PhD diss., University of Illinois Urbana-Champaign, 2017.

Ware, Norman J. *The Labor Movement in the United States, 1860–1895.* New York: D. Appleton, 1929.

Warne, Frank Julian. *The Coal-Mine Workers: A Study in Labor Organization.* New York: Longmans, Green, 1905.

——. *The Slav Invasion and the Mine Workers: A Study in Immigration.* Philadelphia, PA: J. B. Lippincott, 1904.

Webb, Samuel. *Two-Party Politics in the One-Party South: Alabama's Hill Country, 1874–1820.* Tuscaloosa: University of Alabama Press, 1997.

Weir, Robert. *Beyond Labor's Veil: The Culture of the Knights of Labor.* University Park: Pennsylvania State University Press, 1996.

——. *Knights Unhorsed: Internal Conflict in a Gilded Age Social Movement.* Detroit: Wayne State University Press, 2000.

Weise, Robert S. *Grasping at Independence: Debt, Male Authority, and Mineral Rights in Appalachia 1850–1915.* Knoxville: University of Tennessee Press, 2001.

Whatley, Warren C. "African-American Strikebreaking from the Civil War to the New Deal." *Social Science History* 17, no. 4 (winter 1993): 525–58.

White, Richard. *Railroaded: The Transcontinentals and the Making of Modern America.* New York: W. W. Norton, 2011.

——. *The Republic for Which It Stands: The United States during Reconstruction and the Gilded Age.* New York: Oxford University Press, 2017.

Willey, Freeman Otis. *Whither are We Drifting as a Nation.* St. Louis: Geo. C. Hackstaff, 1882.

Wolff, David A. *Industrializing the Rockies: Growth, Competition, and Turmoil in the Coalfields of Colorado and Wyoming, 1868–1914.* Boulder: University Press of Colorado, 2003.

Zanjani, Sally. *A Mine of Her Own: Women Prospectors in the American West, 1850–1950.* Lincoln: University of Nebraska Press, 1997.

Index

Republican Party, 150–51
rival unions, 86–87, 103–4. *See also* Independent Order of the Knights of Labor; Nickel Knights
Roll, Jarod, 4
"run of mine" coal. *See* mine run coal

"scabs." *See* strikebreaking
Scaife, William, 33, 63–64, 73–74, 90, 139
scale rates, 59, 61, 64, 79–80, 122, 126–27, 131. *See also* wage variations
Scott, William L., 25, 26, 61
screened coal, 33, 126
screens, 33, 53, 101, 159–60
scrip, 34–35, 50–51, 142
seasonal labor, 5, 12, 15, 46–49
slack, 33, 35
small-scale investing, 46, 54–58, 167
social Darwinism, 106
socialists, 145–46, 153, 156, 164
Sovereign, James, 126, 136, 140, 144–45, 152–53, 156–57, 164
Spring Valley (IL), 24, 40, 61, 64, 160
strike aid, 71, 74, 78–85, 112, 116, 125, 167
strikebreaking, 4–5, 43–45, 55, 58, 60–61, 100–103, 115–17, 130–31. *See also* "blackleg"
strikes, 4, 43, 45, 56, 60–61, 94, 103, 112, 117, 146–47, 153, 159, 163–65; cancelled strike (1891), 70–73; Illinois/Indiana winter strike (1889), 61–65, 75, 102; Indiana fall/winter strike (1891), 79–82; local strikes (1894), 133–34, 136, 152; nationwide suspension (1894), 119–20, 129–31, 140–42, 149

Tennessee, 48, 100, 105, 158
tons of coal. *See* coal weight; wage variations
"turns" in mines, 51–54, 114, 127
turpentine industry, 32, 48, 99, 101

United Mine Workers' Journal: policy on letter publications, 15–16

United Mine Workers of America: and the AFL, 88–89, 140, 146; and African-Americans, 93–97, 99–106; and the canceled national strike (1891), 70, 72–73, 76; centralization of union structure, 11, 68–70, 71, 78–79, 82, 84, 90–91, 120–21, 123–25, 127, 132–34, 136–37, 155; defense fund, 78–9, 84–85, 149; dues payments, 68–69, 76–78, 81–83, 89, 112–13, 115–16, 125–26, 149, 154–55, 159; and farmers, 114–17, 127, 130–31; and fights with the Knights of Labor, 89, 125–26, 147–49, 152–53, 157; formation, 68, 89, 71; and the Knights of Labor New Orleans General Assembly (1894), 139–40, 145–47, 149; and local strikes, 67–69, 74, 79–83, 90, 134–35; and the nationwide bituminous coal strike (1894), 119, 122, 126, 128–32, 136, 138; and the nationwide bituminous coal strike settlement (1894), 131, 141–43, 153; and non-native, English-speaking immigrants, 106–13; and separation from the Knights of Labor, 153–54
United States Department of Agriculture, 48

Virginia, 130
voluntarism, 88, 158
Voss, Kim, 11

"wage slavery," 10
wage variations, 13, 32–35, 49–52, 54, 61, 64, 122, 159–60
Watchorn, Robert, 158
Weise, Robert, 46
West Virginia, 25, 48, 105, 130, 158, 163, 165
White, Richard, 11–12
Willey, Freeman Otis, 87
Willing Hands, 93–96, 103–5, 118
Wilson, Jimmy, 1, 3, 5, 9, 19, 167
Wilson, William Bauchop, 8, 56, 154
workplace conditions, 1–2, 29–31, 33–34; deaths, 32, 100, 115

DANA M. CALDEMEYER is an assistant professor of history at South Georgia State College.

THE WORKING CLASS IN AMERICAN HISTORY

Worker City, Company Town: Iron and Cotton-Worker Protest in Troy and Cohoes, New York, 1855–84 *Daniel J. Walkowitz*

Life, Work, and Rebellion in the Coal Fields: The Southern West Virginia Miners, 1880–1922 *David Alan Corbin*

Women and American Socialism, 1870–1920 *Mari Jo Buhle*

Lives of Their Own: Blacks, Italians, and Poles in Pittsburgh, 1900–1960 *John Bodnar, Roger Simon, and Michael P. Weber*

Working-Class America: Essays on Labor, Community, and American Society *Edited by Michael H. Frisch and Daniel J. Walkowitz*

Eugene V. Debs: Citizen and Socialist *Nick Salvatore*

American Labor and Immigration History, 1877–1920s: Recent European Research *Edited by Dirk Hoerder*

Workingmen's Democracy: The Knights of Labor and American Politics *Leon Fink*

The Electrical Workers: A History of Labor at General Electric and Westinghouse, 1923–60 *Ronald W. Schatz*

The Mechanics of Baltimore: Workers and Politics in the Age of Revolution, 1763–1812 *Charles G. Steffen*

The Practice of Solidarity: American Hat Finishers in the Nineteenth Century *David Bensman*

The Labor History Reader *Edited by Daniel J. Leab*

Solidarity and Fragmentation: Working People and Class Consciousness in Detroit, 1875–1900 *Richard Oestreicher*

Counter Cultures: Saleswomen, Managers, and Customers in American Department Stores, 1890–1940 *Susan Porter Benson*

The New England Working Class and the New Labor History *Edited by Herbert G. Gutman and Donald H. Bell*

Labor Leaders in America *Edited by Melvyn Dubofsky and Warren Van Tine*

Barons of Labor: The San Francisco Building Trades and Union Power in the Progressive Era *Michael Kazin*

Gender at Work: The Dynamics of Job Segregation by Sex during World War II *Ruth Milkman*

Once a Cigar Maker: Men, Women, and Work Culture in American Cigar Factories, 1900–1919 *Patricia A. Cooper*

A Generation of Boomers: The Pattern of Railroad Labor Conflict in Nineteenth-Century America *Shelton Stromquist*

Work and Community in the Jungle: Chicago's Packinghouse Workers, 1894–1922 *James R. Barrett*

Workers, Managers, and Welfare Capitalism: The Shoeworkers and Tanners of Endicott Johnson, 1890–1950 *Gerald Zahavi*

Men, Women, and Work: Class, Gender, and Protest in the New England Shoe Industry, 1780–1910 *Mary Blewett*

Latin American Migrations to the U.S. Heartland: Changing Cultural Landscapes in
    Middle America   *Edited by Linda Allegro and Andrew Grant Wood*
Man of Fire: Selected Writings   *Ernesto Galarza, ed. Armando Ibarra and Rodolfo D. Torres*
A Contest of Ideas: Capital, Politics, and Labor   *Nelson Lichtenstein*
Making the World Safe for Workers: Labor, the Left, and Wilsonian
    Internationalism   *Elizabeth McKillen*
The Rise of the Chicago Police Department: Class and Conflict, 1850–1894
    Sam Mitrani
Workers in Hard Times: A Long View of Economic Crises   *Edited by Leon Fink,
    Joseph A. McCartin, and Joan Sangster*
Redeeming Time: Protestantism and Chicago's Eight-Hour Movement,
    1866–1912   *William A. Mirola*
Struggle for the Soul of the Postwar South: White Evangelical Protestants and
    Operation Dixie   *Elizabeth Fones-Wolf and Ken Fones-Wolf*
Free Labor: The Civil War and the Making of an American Working Class
    Mark A. Lause
Death and Dying in the Working Class, 1865–1920   *Michael K. Rosenow*
Immigrants against the State: Yiddish and Italian Anarchism in America
    Kenyon Zimmer
Fighting for Total Person Unionism: Harold Gibbons, Ernest Calloway, and Working-
    Class Citizenship   *Robert Bussel*
Smokestacks in the Hills: Rural-Industrial Workers in West Virginia   *Louis Martin*
Disaster Citizenship: Survivors, Solidarity, and Power in the Progressive Era
    Jacob A. C. Remes
The Pew and the Picket Line: Christianity and the American Working Class
    Edited by Christopher D. Cantwell, Heath W. Carter, and Janine Giordano Drake
Conservative Counterrevolution: Challenging Liberalism in 1950s Milwaukee
    Tula A. Connell
Manhood on the Line: Working-Class Masculinities in the American Heartland
    Steve Meyer
On Gender, Labor, and Inequality   *Ruth Milkman*
The Making of Working-Class Religion   *Matthew Pehl*
Civic Labors: Scholar Activism and Working-Class Studies   *Edited by Dennis Deslippe,
    Eric Fure-Slocum, and John W. McKerley*
Victor Arnautoff and the Politics of Art   *Robert W. Cherny*
Against Labor: How U.S. Employers Organized to Defeat Union Activism
    Edited by Rosemary Feurer and Chad Pearson
Teacher Strike! Public Education and the Making of a New American Political
    Order   *Jon Shelton*
Hillbilly Hellraisers: Federal Power and Populist Defiance in the Ozarks   *J. Blake Perkins*
Sewing the Fabric of Statehood: Garment Unions, American Labor, and the
    Establishment of the State of Israel   *Adam Howard*
Labor and Justice across the America   *Edited by Leon Fink and Juan Manuel Palacio*

Frontiers of Labor: Comparative Histories of the United States and Australia
Edited by Greg Patmore and Shelton Stromquist

Women Have Always Worked: A Concise History, Second Edition   *Alice Kessler-Harris*

Remembering Lattimer: Labor, Migration, and Race in Pennsylvania Anthracite
Country   *Paul A. Shackel*

Disruption in Detroit: Autoworkers and the Elusive Postwar Boom   *Daniel J. Clark*

To Live Here, You Have to Fight: How Women Led Appalachian Movements for
Social Justice   *Jessica Wilkerson*

Dockworker Power: Race and Activism in Durban and the San Francisco Bay
Area   *Peter Cole*

Labor's Mind: A History of Working-Class Intellectual Life   *Tobias Higbie*

The World in a City: Multiethnic Radicalism in Early Twentieth-Century
Los Angeles   *David M. Struthers*

Death to Fascism: Louis Adamic's Fight for Democracy   *John P. Enyeart*

Upon the Altar of Work: Child Labor and the Rise of a New American
Sectionalism   *Betsy Wood*

Workers against the City: The Fight for Free Speech in *Hague v. CIO*   *Donald W. Rogers*

Union Renegades: Miners, Capitalism, and Organizing in the Gilded Age
Dana M. Caldemeyer

The University of Illinois Press
is a founding member of the
Association of University Presses.

─────────────────────────

University of Illinois Press
1325 South Oak Street
Champaign, IL 61820-6903
www.press.uillinois.edu